LSAT*

Logic Games Workout

The Staff of The Princeton Review

PrincetonReview.com

Random House, Inc. New York

The Independent Education Consultants Association recognizes The Princeton Review as a valuable resource for high school and college students applying to college and graduate school.

The Princeton Review, Inc.
2315 Broadway
New York, NY 10024
E-mail: editorialsupport@review.com

ISBN: 978-0-375-42931-6
ISSN: 1946-3081

Editor: Andrew Brody
Production Editor: M. Tighe Wall
Production Coordinator: Kim Howie

Printed in the United States.

10 9 8 7 6 5 4 3 2 1

2009 Edition

Acknowledgments

This book is very much a collaborative effort. In addition to our full-time Princeton Review staff, we'd like to thank the following people for the contributions they made to this book: Patrick Tyrrell, Karen Hoover, Melissa Scram, Patrick Choi, Vincent Drybala, David Stoll, Michael Chalaron, and Aleksandra R. Zolley. Special thanks to Mindy Eve Myers for her contributions and expertise.

Table of Contents

...So Much More Online!

More Lessons...

- Step-by-step guide to solving difficult Games and Argument problems
- Tutorials that put our strategies into action
- Interactive, click-through learning
- Overview of the question types you will find on the LSAT

More Practice...

- Sample Reading Comprehension passages and problems
- Many kinds of Arguments
- Full-length practice tests

More Scores...

- Automatic scoring for online tests
- Instant scoring for your book tests
- Optional essay scoring with our LiveGrader℠ service
- Performance analysis to tell you which topics you need to review

More Good Stuff...

- Read the vocabulary "Word du Jour" and review its definition with examples
- Plan your review sessions with study plans based on your schedule—4 weeks, 8 weeks, 12 weeks
- Sign up for e-mail tips and tricks
- Chat with other LSAT students

...then College!

- Detailed profiles for hundreds of law schools help you find the school that is right for you
- Information about financial aid and scholarships
- Dozens of Top 10 ranking lists including Quality of Professors, Diverse Student Population, Best for International Law and tons more

princetonreview.com/cracking

Getting The Most Out of Your Princeton Review Materials

princetonreview.com/cracking

1 Register

Go to PrincetonReview.com/cracking. You'll see a Welcome page where you should register your book using the serial number. What's a serial number, you ask? Flip to the back of your book and you'll see a bunch of letters and numbers printed on the inside back cover. Type this into the window, dashes included. Next you will see a Sign Up/Sign In page where you will type in your e-mail address (username) and choose a password. Now you're good to go!

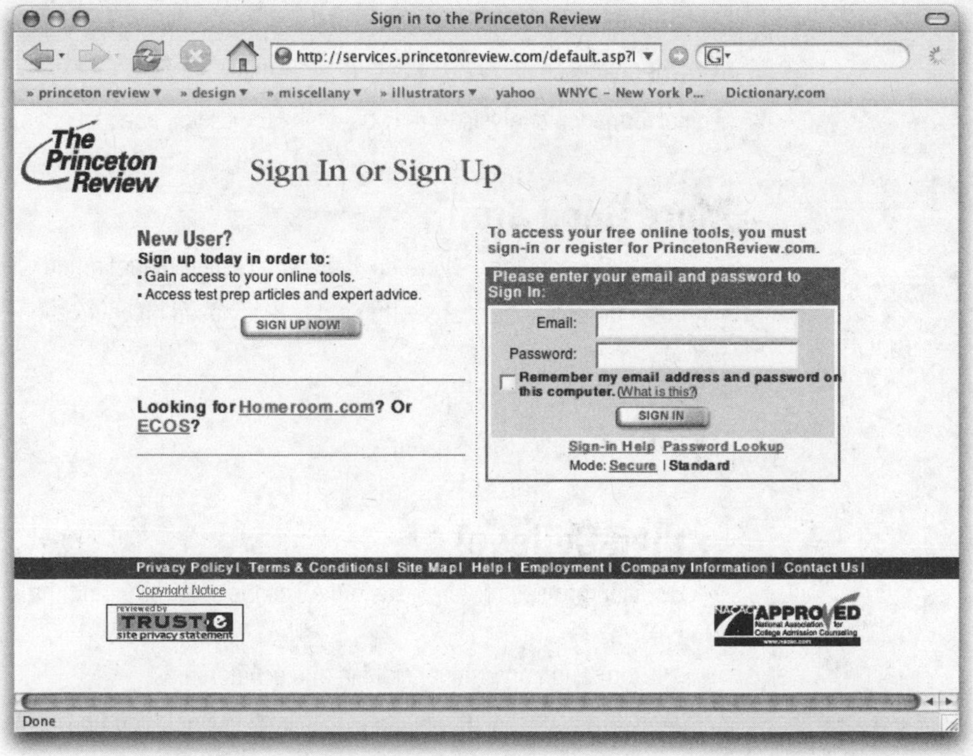

Sign in to the Princeton Review

http://services.princetonreview.com/default.asp?l

» princeton review » design » miscellany » illustrators yahoo WNYC – New York P... Dictionary.com

The Princeton Review

Sign In or Sign Up

New User?
Sign up today in order to:
• Gain access to your online tools.
• Access test prep articles and expert advice.

SIGN UP NOW!

Looking for Homeroom.com? Or ECOS?

To access your free online tools, you must sign-in or register for PrincetonReview.com.

Please enter your email and password to Sign In:

Email:

Password:

Remember my email address and password on this computer. (What is this?)

SIGN IN

Sign-in Help Password Lookup

Mode: Secure | Standard

Privacy Policy | Terms & Conditions | Site Map | Help | Employment | Company Information | Contact Us |

Copyright Notice

reviewed by TRUSTe site privacy statement

NACAC APPROVED National Association for College Admission Counseling

Done

2 Check Out Your Student Tools

Once you are logged in and registered, click on "Your Student Tools." From there, you can access practice tests, online course demos, class information (for current students), important dates and more. Check out the "Advice Library" and "What's New" for additional information. But first, look under "Your Course Tools" and click on the name of your book. Be sure to enable pop-ups! The window that will pop-up when you click on your book is called the dashboard and it will lead you to tons of helpful online components.

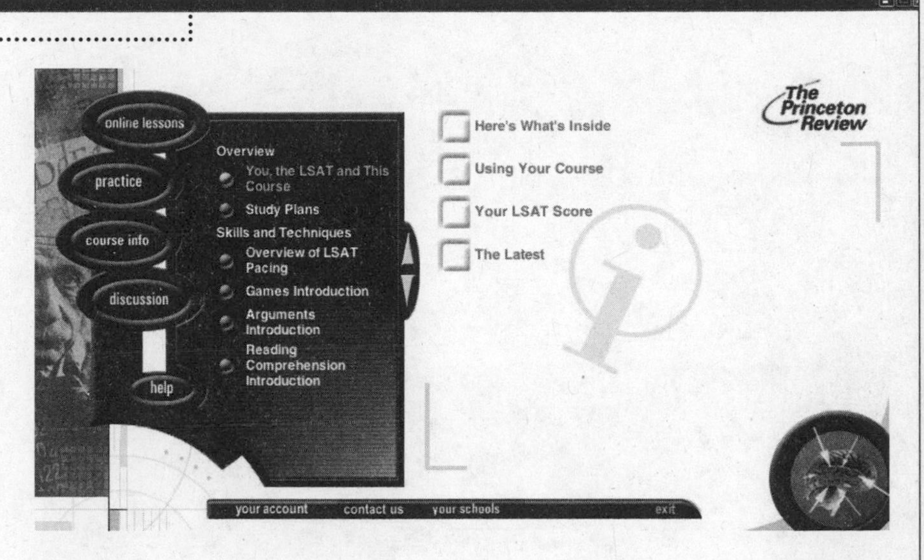

3 Make Use of the Dashboard

The dashboard has 5 buttons displayed vertically. Click on each of these buttons to explore your options. There's a lot of fantastic online content, including drills, problem-solving strategies worked out in examples, a full practice test with automatic grading, a discussion area, and more.

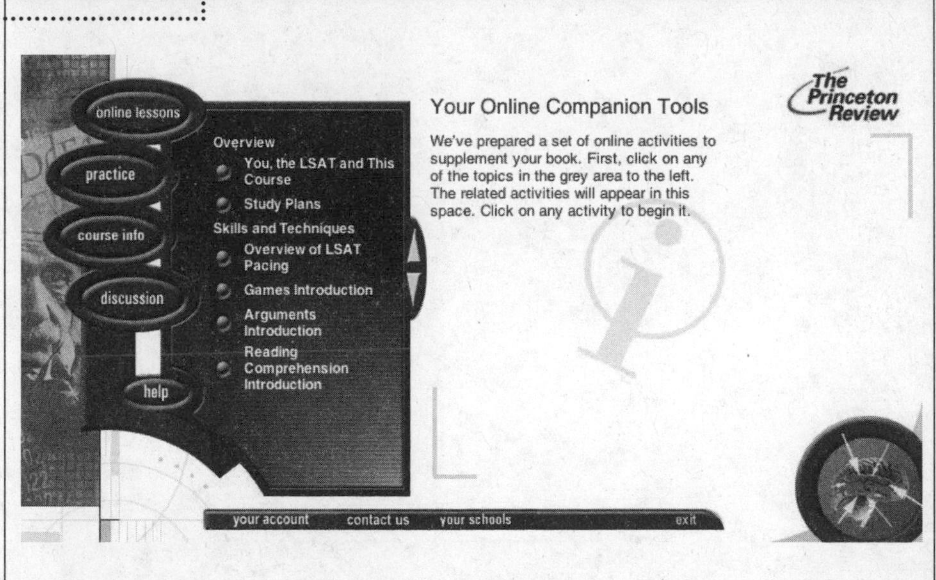

Find the law school that is right for you with our ranking lists. See which school has the most red-tape and lines, the worst library, the best parties, and many more categories. Sign up for email tips about the LSAT and check out the vocabulary "Word du Jour" for a new word each day. Our website is your resource for tons of practice exercises and law school information.

If you have questions about registering or accessing your Student Tools, contact **techsupport@review.com**

The Princeton Review has worked with tens of thousands of people preparing for the LSAT, and we've found that providing instruction and practice in several formats is the best way to help our students reach their goals. This book represents one part of a comprehensive approach to LSAT preparation.

This book contains fifty games that test the same skills as those tested on the Analytical Reasoning section of the Law School Admission Test (LSAT). It is designed as a supplement for people who need to bolster their scores on this section of the LSAT, the section we like to call the Games section. Although The Princeton Review always recommends practicing on actual, released LSAT exams that can be ordered from www.lsac.org, this book is a resource for people who want to pay extra attention to their performance on the Games section. It also makes an excellent companion to our *Cracking the LSAT* book.

In each chapter, we'll introduce you to a new task and walk you through a sample game. You will then be able to practice that skill on several games of a similar type. We've also included several timed sections so you can test your skills against the clock. Explanations take you step-by-step through the most efficient way to solve each game. The most valuable instruction in this book comes in these explanations; with games, the best way to learn is by doing.

Future lawyers of America, good luck!

Andrew Brody
National Content Director, LSAT Programs

5 QUICK TIPS TO INCREASE YOUR LSAT GAMES SCORE

1. **Choose wisely.** Learn the ingredients that test writers combine to make games more or less challenging, and work games in order of difficulty.
2. **Use your pencil.** Write out diagrams, symbolize rules, and work questions on paper, not in your head.
3. **Follow the rules.** Even when games are difficult, paying careful attention to the exact wording of the rules will either guide you to the right answer or help you eliminate wrong answers.
4. **Reorder questions.** To maximize your speed and accuracy, start with Grab-a-rule (full list) questions, then work Specific ("if") questions, move on to General ("which") questions, then finish with Complex (rule-changing) questions.
5. **Keep moving.** Do not let yourself get bogged down by a challenging question or game. If you are spinning your wheels, move away from the question or game, and come back to it later if you have the chance.

What Types of Games are on the LSAT?

Ordering and Grouping are the two major game tasks. Not surprisingly, these terms are used to describe games where you put things in order or put things into groups. We'll break it down even further in the next few chapters in order to create strategies for the most common game tasks. Though we'll cover it in more detail later, here's a basic overview of the different game tasks we will discuss:

Order Games Straightforward Order games (which we will sometimes refer to as 1-D Order games) ask you to put elements in order in a single row.

Group Games Group games ask you to place elements into groups. Sometimes you know exactly how many groups the elements can be assigned to (fixed assignments), and sometimes you are not told how many groups the elements can be assigned to (variable assignments).

2-D Order Games These are games that ask you to put elements in order, but require more than one row in a diagram, usually because you must combine an ordering aspect of the game with a grouping aspect.

In-Out Games These are a subset of Group games where you only have two groups and all of the elements must be in one group or the other. Games where you must select a few elements from a list fit this category.

Distribution Games Distribution games are not a task unto themselves; rather, distribution is a term we use to talk about games with rules that allow you to deduce possible distributions before working the questions.

BASICS

What Is a Game?

"Games" is The Princeton Review's name for the Analytical Reasoning section of the LSAT. This section of the exam tests your ability to organize and understand various arrangements of relationships among elements. You will always see four games per section, and each game will be accompanied by five to seven questions. You can expect to see 22–24 questions in a Games section, which makes this section worth just less than one-fourth of your total score.

I'm Having Trouble with Games. Is This Unusual?

Don't worry if you feel uncomfortable with this section right now. The skills required to do games well are skills you can learn. Once you have grasped the basics, it's simply a matter of learning how to handle variations. The Princeton Review's approach will give you strategies for working all the variations you might encounter on the LSAT.

What Types of Games are on the LSAT?

Ordering and Grouping are the two major game tasks. Not surprisingly, these terms are used to describe games where you put things in order or put things into groups. We'll break it down even further in the next few chapters in order to create strategies for the most common game tasks. Though we'll cover it in more detail later, here's a basic overview of the different game tasks we will discuss:

Order Games

Straightforward Order games (which we will sometimes refer to as 1-D Order games) ask you to put elements in order in a single row.

Group Games

Group games ask you to place elements into groups. Sometimes you know exactly how many groups the elements can be assigned to (fixed assignments), and sometimes you are not told how many groups the elements can be assigned to (variable assignments).

2-D Order Games

These are games that ask you to put elements in order, but require more than one row in a diagram, usually because you must combine an ordering aspect of the game with a grouping aspect.

In–Out Games

These are a subset of Group games where you only have two groups and all of the elements must be in one group or the other. Games where you must select a few elements from a list fit into this category.

Distribution Games

Distribution games are not a task unto themselves; rather, distribution is a term we use to talk about games with rules that allow you to deduce possible distributions before working the questions.

Game Strategy

Developing a systematic approach to LSAT games is essential to achieving your highest potential on this section. We've broken down the steps that you should take on every single game.

HOW TO PREPARE

The game starts with the *setup*. Here you will find the game pieces, hints about what your game board should look like, and rules for how to play the game. Taking the right amount of time to prep the game will save you time when you get to the questions.

Ingredient Scan

Your first job is to get a quick sense of the game. Does it seem familiar or frighteningly unique? Does it seem very difficult or relatively easy? Do this by scanning for the *ingredients of the game*—those features that the test writer's mix-and-match to create a full-fledged game. These are the ingredients:

Task: What are you being asked to do in this game? Often, you are putting items in order, assigning items to groups, or working toward a combination of the two.

Inventory: What are the game pieces—the elements you are being asked to manipulate? These can be people's names, letters, numbers, villages, or anything else the test writers feel like throwing at you. Are all of the elements the same, or do some have special characteristics? Are there groups of elements?

Rules: Do the rules look straightforward and easy to symbolize, or are they complicated or too vague to symbolize?

Questions: How many questions are there? What types of questions are they?

Red Flags: Is there anything about the game that seems unusual or particularly difficult?

Rank: Out of four games in a section, what do you think the difficulty of the game will be on a scale of 1–4, from easiest to most difficult?

The goal of this quick Ingredient Scan is to allow you to make decisions about how best to approach a game, as well as to help you decide if you should approach it at all.

Diagram and Inventory

Although the instructions LSAC provides for the Games section tell you that it may be useful to draw a diagram, the truth is that diagramming is the key to success on this section. To do your best, you must draw a diagram.

Your diagram is a visual representation of the game. Remember that you don't get scratch paper on the LSAT, so use the space below the questions wisely. To conserve space, challenge yourself to write as compactly as you can while retaining legibility. Be sure to choose the area of the page with the most room to write.

Use your understanding of the game task to create a diagram, which serves as your game board. Find the core of the diagram—the fixed arrangement into which you must put the elements. Ask yourself: "What am I doing with these items?" Possible answers include:

- "I am trying to put these items in order."
- "I am ranking these items from highest to lowest."
- "I have to assign these items to different groups."
- "I am determining which items are selected."

Next, write out your inventory (usually just the first letters of the elements from the setup) to the side of the diagram, where you can use it for reference but where it won't interfere with the rest of your diagram.

Symbolize the Rules and Double-Check

The rules are the conditions listed under the setup that describe what can or cannot happen in the game: Think of them as the rules by which you have to play the game. Language-based conditions contain an inherent opportunity for error in translation between the eye, the brain, and the hand. Convert the rules into visual symbols relating to the diagram so that you can more easily see the rules of the game. This reduces the potential errors resulting from misreading or misapplying the rules. Numbering and symbolizing the rules next to the diagram saves time because you don't have to go back and read the clues again each time you answer a question.

Follow the three C's when symbolizing your rules:

- **Be clear.** Your symbols should make sense and accurately represent the information in the rule.
- **Be concise.** Keep your symbols short and simple. Avoid words and algebraic symbols whenever possible.
- **Be consistent.** Your symbols should be consistent with one another and with the format of your diagram. Use symbols as consistently as possible across games types.

Here are some common types of rules, along with The Princeton Review's suggestions for how to symbolize them.

Concrete: James arrives second.

Symbol: Draw this right into your diagram.

Range: Frank's flight departs at some time before Jonas's flight departs.

Symbol: F—J

Fixed Range: There is one flight between Frank's flight and Jonas's flight.

Symbol: F_J

Block: Meave gets off the bus at the stop after the stop at which Sally gets off the bus.

Symbol: SM

AntiBlock: Sally and Meave do not get off the bus at consecutive stops.

Symbol: 

Vertical Block: Sally and Meave get off the bus at the same stop.

Symbol: 

Conditional statement: If Charlie eats a hot dog, then Bianca eats a gyro.

Symbol: $C_h \rightarrow B_g$

Conditional statements should almost always be symbolized with their *contrapositive.* The contrapositive is a logical inference you can derive from a conditional statement from flipping and negating the terms:

$$\sim B_g \rightarrow \sim C_h$$

Don't Forget To Double-Check Your Rules!

There's nothing worse than getting to the last question in a game and realizing you've messed up a rule. Try to generate the wording of the rule from your symbol so you know you've completely understood the meaning.

Deductions

There's more to know about a game than simply what you're given in the setup and the rules, so don't rush headfirst into the questions. By pausing to think about how the game works, you gain additional insights that will make it easier to answer the questions. We call additional information gleaned by studying the diagram and rules *deductions.* Deductions don't just come to you; you have to look for them. A systematic approach will help you make deductions and know when it's time to move on to the questions.

Links: Check the clues to see if there is any overlap of elements or other details that can be linked together to provide more information about the game.

Spatial restrictions: Are any elements limited to only a few spaces? Are any spaces limited to only a few elements? Can the entire game be boiled down to only a few scenarios?

Most restricted: The most restricted element or space is often the driving force of the game and the piece you should keep your eye on as you work the game.

Least restricted: Consider circling the least restricted element; you'll often need your free agent(s) as filler when you get to the "what's left?" part of answering questions.

HOW TO ASSESS, ACT, ANSWER

Question Endings

Always be aware of question endings (*must be true, could be true, must be false, could be false).* Develop the habit of underlining or circling question endings. Must questions require an answer that is undeniably true or false according to the information in your diagram. Eliminate any answers that you cannot definitely prove. *Could* questions sometimes require you to try several answer choices in search of one that meets all the requirements of the game? Answer *could be true* questions by finding the answer that is possible or by eliminating the choices that must be false. Answer *could be false* questions by finding the answer that is possibly false or by eliminating choices that must be true.

Attack questions in this order: Grab-a-Rule, Specific, General, and Complex. Answering the questions in this order yields the greatest accuracy in the least amount of time. Save the questions that require the deepest level of understanding of the game for later, working first those questions that you can answer accurately without knowing everything about the game.

Grab-a-Rule

Many games on the LSAT start with a question that asks which arrangement is possible given the clues in the setup. We call these Grab-a-Rule questions because they test your understanding of the game's conditions. Grab-a-Rule questions ask for a possible acceptable order and include every space in the answer choices.

To answer these questions swiftly, take one rule at a time and eliminate answers that violate that rule. If there is a Grab-a-Rule question, it will always be the first question, and you should always do this one first. Besides being relatively painless, doing this question first serves as another way to double-check your rules: If you have two possibilities left or if you eliminate all your answer choices, you've missed something or do not understand your rules completely.

Specific

Specific questions give you a new piece of information that serves as a jumping-off point for doing work on that question. The questions usually begin with *if* and provide a condition that applies for that question only. Working the Specific questions first is helpful because the additional information in the question gives you a way to enter the game even if you haven't made every possible deduction. In addition, the work you do to answer Specific questions will be useful when you answer General questions.

To answer these questions, start a new line in your diagram and symbolize the new information either in the diagram or off to the side, depending on the type of information. Number the new line in your diagram so you can retrace the work you did for each question number in case you have to refer to or correct any previous work. Because Specific questions provide conditions that apply for that question only, make sure to symbolize any new information away from your original rules so that you don't get them confused later on in the game. After you've symbolized the new information, look for links with your original rules and deductions and size up what you know for sure about the game, filling in as much of the diagram as you can.

General

General questions do not give you any new information to add to your diagram. They often begin with *which* and ask what's true or false about the game in general.

To answer these questions, use your understanding of the game, your deductions, and the answers to previous questions to determine the answers to these questions. Process of Elimination (POE) usually plays a very strong role in answering General questions because you can use previous work and answers to Specific questions to eliminate answers you know are wrong. Avoid simply plugging in answer choices to test their viability unless you are sure that doing so is your only option.

Complex

Complex questions change or remove one of the original rules or involve some other complicated task. Work them after you have worked all of the questions that keep the rules intact. Luckily, questions that change or remove conditions, if they are present at all, are always last in a game, and they are easy to identify.

When you answer Complex questions, make sure you understand what the question asks and how it affects the game. Because complex questions change or remove a condition, you will need to rethink deductions, and you may not be able to use work from previous questions.

A Few Tips

1. As you practice, look for similarities among games. Notice patterns in setups, rules, questions, and answer choices and use those similarities to relate new games to games you've already done.
2. Do your work in pencil so that you can come back to the same game later. You will see new aspects of the game each time you attempt it. Use the blank space on the sides of the pages as notes areas.
3. Don't obsess over time, especially at first. Keep track of how long games are taking you, but don't count down against a clock until you're working a timed section. Increased accuracy should be your initial focus; concern yourself with pacing once you feel comfortable with the many games variations.
4. Work every game three times. Just get through the game the first time. The second time, focus on understanding the structure of the game and all of the deductions. The third time, pretend you are explaining it to a friend who is studying for the LSAT. If you are able to explain the game to someone else, you'll know that you have mastered it. The next time you encounter a similar game, you'll recognize the ingredients and know what to expect.

Ready to begin?

When a setup involves placing items in a sequence or in a relative ranking, you are playing an Order game. Your first instinct might be to keep track of an Order game like this:

__ __ __ __ __ __
1 2 3 4 5 6

That would be a great idea if you only had to answer one question. However, because you're faced with a set of questions, you'll be better off with a diagram that keeps you organized and allows you to apply information you learn in one question to a later question. Order game diagrams look like this:

	1	2	3	4	5	6
ABCDEF						

Learning through an example is the best way to jump right into games. Follow the step-by-step explanations for the game on the next page, then try out the Order games that follow.

A E F C B

C B

SOLAR PANELS

A home improvement contractor has been hired to install solar panels on the roofs of six different houses. He will work on exactly one house at a time, and he must finish installing the panels on one house before he begins installation on any other house. Each house is owned by exactly one of six different families—the Abbotts, the Beardens, the Chases, the Dardens, the Engels, or the Fosters. The contractor must install the solar panels according to the following conditions:

The contractor will install solar panels on the Abbotts' house at some time before he installs them on the Engels' house.

The contractor will install solar panels on the Engels' and Fosters' houses consecutively, though not necessarily in that order.

The contractor will install solar panels on the Chases' house at some time before he installs them on the Beardens' house.

The contractor will install solar panels on the Fosters' house at some time before he installs them on the Chases' house.

1. Which one of the following could be an accurate list of the first three houses for which the contractor installs solar panels, listed in order from first to third?

(A) the Abbotts, the Dardens, the Fosters
(B) the Beardens, the Dardens, the Abbotts
(C) the Dardens, the Chases, the Abbotts
(D) the Dardens, the Fosters, the Abbotts
(E) the Dardens, the Fosters, the Engels

2. If exactly one installation occurs between the Dardens' installation and the Beardens' installation, then for exactly how many houses can the order of the installations be determined?

(A) two
(B) three
(C) four
(D) five
(E) six

3. Which one of the following must be false?

(A) The Abbotts' installation occurs immediately before or immediately after the Dardens' installation.
(B) The Beardens' installation occurs immediately before or immediately after the Dardens' installation.
(C) The Chases' installation occurs immediately before or immediately after the Abbotts' installation.
(D) The Engels' installation occurs immediately before or immediately after the Chases' installation.
(E) The Fosters' installation occurs immediately before or immediately after the Abbotts' installation.

4. The contractor could install solar panels on the Chases' house

(A) first
(B) second
(C) third
(D) fifth
(E) sixth

5. If the Engels' installation occurs immediately before or immediately after the Chases' installation, each of the following could be true EXCEPT:

(A) The Abbotts' house is the second to have solar panels installed.
(B) The Engels' house is the fourth to have solar panels installed.
(C) The Fosters' house is the fourth to have solar panels installed.
(D) The Beardens' house is the fifth to have solar panels installed.
(E) The Dardens' house is the fifth to have solar panels installed.

6. It must be false that the fourth house to have solar panels installed is

(A) the Beardens' house
(B) the Chases' house
(C) the Dardens' house
(D) the Engels' house
(E) the Fosters' house

7. If the Engels' house is the fourth house to have solar panels installed, then for exactly how many of the six houses can the order in which the solar panels are installed be determined?

(A) two
(B) three
(C) four
(D) five
(E) six

ANSWERS TO SOLAR PANELS

1. A
2. C
3. C
4. D
5. C
6. A
7. C

EXPLANATIONS TO SOLAR PANELS

Prepare

Ingredient Scan

Task: Order
Inventory: 6 elements, 6 slots, 1:1 ratio
Rules: Very straightforward Order game rules, mostly range clues
Questions: 7 questions: 3 Specific, 4 General
Red Flags: No major red flags
Rank: 1

Diagram and Inventory

You have six elements: A, B, C, D, E, and F. Create an Order diagram with six columns, 1–6.

Symbolize the Rules and Double-Check

Rule 1: A—E
Rule 2: [EF] *or* [FE]
Rule 3: C—B
Rule 4: F—C

Don't forget to double-check your rules!

Deductions

Links: There are several overlapping elements in these rules, so link them together. Linking together rules 3 and 4 gives you F—C—B. Adding on rule 2 gives you FE/EF—C—B. Adding on rule 1 gives you A—EF/FE—C—B. Because the order of E and F relative to each other does not matter, use arrows to note their interchangeability so that you're not visually tempted to assume one comes before the other.

A — [EF] — C — B

Since five of the six elements all link together, this game looks extremely promising. The only element not limited by that chain is D, your free agent (circle D to remind yourself of this). When you have a chain that involves most/all of the elements, don't worry about noting all the deductions that can be made in your diagram, but determine how limited the extremities are. What can go in slot 1? Only A and D could, so put an A/D placeholder in slot 1. What's the latest A could go? Four elements must come after A in your chain, so the latest A could go is slot 2. You can add to your diagram that A must go in slot 1 or 2. What can go last? Only B or D could go in slot 6, so add a B/D placeholder to slot 6. What's the earliest B could go? Four elements must come before B in your chain, so the earliest B can go is slot 5. You can add to your diagram that B must go in slot 5 or 6.

Spatial restrictions: Everything in your chain is limited to two or three spaces.
Most restricted: A and B
Least restricted: D

Here is your diagram:

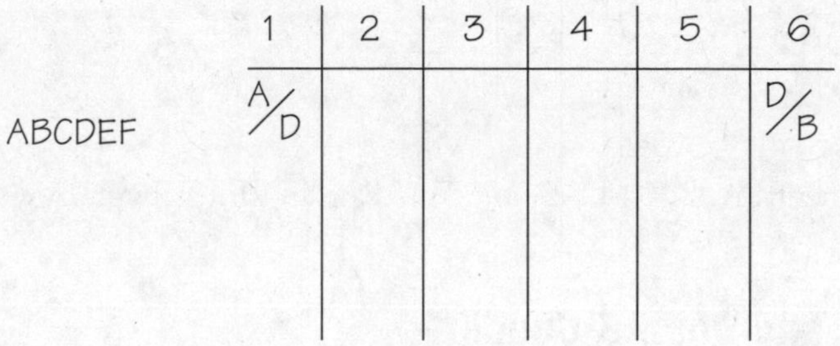

ABCDEF

1	2	3	4	5	6
A/D					D/B

Assess, Act, Answer

Question 1 is almost a Grab-a-Rule but it only shows three of the six elements in place. This doesn't lend itself as much to applying one rule at a time to the answer choices, so come back to it. Even though it might be relatively easy and you might be tempted to do it first, it will not get any more difficult later and might get a whole lot easier.

Question 2 is the first Specific question, so tackle that one.

For question 2, symbolize the condition that you must meet for this question: D_B or B_D. Since B is limited to only slots 5 or 6, it would be impossible to have B_D (even with B in slot 5, as that would mean D comes seventh). So the order of the condition must be D_B. Does it matter if B is in slot 5 or slot 6? If B were in slot 5, that would force D to be in slot 6, since slot 6 only has B/D as its two options. So, B can't be in slot 5 and must go in slot 6. With B in slot 6, D must go in slot 4 according to this D_B condition. Use the chain to fill in the remaining elements. Because D is already used and slot 1 can only be A/D, A must go in slot 1. The EF block must come in slots 2 and 3, although the order of E and F doesn't matter, so write E/F and F/E into slots 2 and 3. Finally, C will have to go in slot 5. The question is basically asking how many slots have elements set in stone. The only flexible slots for this scenario are slots 2 and 3. Slots 1, 4, 5, and 6 are fixed. **Four slots are fixed, so choice (C) is the credited response.**

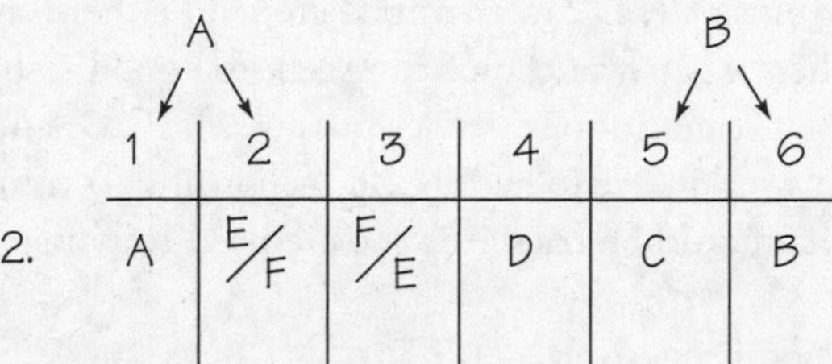

Question 5 is the next Specific question.

For questions 5, symbolize the condition being described: EC or CE. Analyze the feasibility of each option. Can E go after C? Not according to your chain. Thus, it must be EC. Since F is attached to E, it must be FEC. The chain for this question, then, looks like: A—FEC—B. D can fit in the gaps before or after A and before or after B. The question wants something that *must be false* **(impossible),** so judge whether each choice is impossible by looking at this question's chain. Choice (A) says A goes second, which is fine since D can go first. Choice (B) says E goes fourth, which is possible because A, D, and F can be the first three. Choice (C) says F goes in slot 4. That seems impossible, since F is the second part of the chain. If D comes first or second, that would still only let F come as late as third. **Since choice (C) says something is impossible, it is the credited response.**

Question 7 is the final Specific question, so do that one next.

For question 7, place E in slot 4 and look at your chain to determine what follows. E and F are inextricably linked. That means F must go in slot 3 or 5. However, F can't go slot 5 because two more elements, C and B, still have to come after F and wouldn't have room. Thus, F must go in slot 3. C and B must squeeze into the remaining slots, 5 and 6, respectively. That just leaves slots 1 and 2 for elements A and D. Since they would be interchangeable, put A/D and D/A in slots 1 and 2. Again, the question task is asking how many slots have fixed elements. Everything is fixed except slots 1 and 2. **Since four slots are fixed, choice (C) is the credited response.**

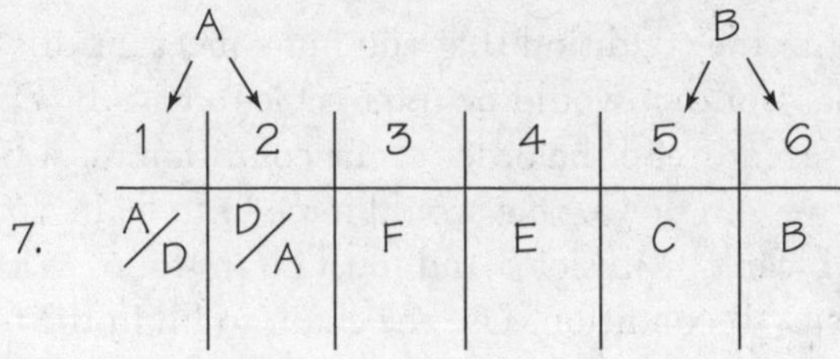

Go back to question 1, the first General question.

You have 5 of the 6 elements chained together and know that D can fall anywhere in the chain. So, although this isn't a Grab-a-Rule proper, it still seems very manageable. Choice (A) seems possible since A is allowed to go in slot 1, D can go anywhere, and either E or F has to be the next member of the chain. Picking the first answer choice can seem too good to be true, but you can quickly sketch out the rest of that scenario to verify it's possible. If A, D, and F occupy slots 1, 2, and 3, then slots 4, 5, and 6 would have to be E, C, B (according to your chain). **Because choice (A) describes something that could be true, it is the credited response.**

The next General question is question 3.

Question 3 asks you to pick an answer that describes something impossible, so eliminate anything that is possible. Choice (A) could be true, as seen in the work from question 7. Choice (B) seems possible since D is a free agent and could go anywhere. Choice (C) is impossible because C and A will never be next to each other. Looking at your chain, the FE block always comes between A and C. **Because choice (C) describes something impossible, it is the credited response.**

Question 4 is the next General question.

Question 4 asks where C could go. From previous work on question 7, you can see that C can go fifth. **Hence, choice (D) is the credited response.**

Question 6 is your final question.

Question 6 asks which element can NEVER be in slot 4. Look at your chain and your diagram. Neither A nor B could ever be in slot 4 since they are both limited to the first two or the last two slots. Scan the answer choices for A or B. **This makes choice (A) the credited response.**

MOTHER'S DAY BOUQUETS

A florist is selling bouquets of roses on Mother's Day. He has six bouquets, one in each of the following colors: orange, pink, red, violet, white, and yellow. Each bouquet is sold one at a time, in accordance with the following conditions:

The pink bouquet is the first, third, or fifth bouquet sold.

At least two bouquets are sold after the white bouquet is sold but before the violet bouquet is sold.

Exactly one bouquet is sold after the orange bouquet is sold but before the yellow bouquet is sold.

1. Which one of the following could be an accurate list of the bouquets sold in order from first to last?
   (A) orange, white, yellow, violet, pink, red
   (B) pink, white, red, violet, orange, yellow
   (C) yellow, white, orange, pink, red, violet
   (D) violet, yellow, red, orange, pink, white
   (E) red, white, pink, orange, violet, yellow

2. If the florist sells the red bouquet fifth, which one of the following must be true?
   (A) The violet bouquet is sold sixth.
   (B) The pink bouquet is sold third.
   (C) The yellow bouquet is sold second.
   (D) The orange bouquet is sold first.
   (E) The white bouquet is sold first.

3. If the yellow bouquet is sold immediately after the white bouquet, which one of the following could be the second bouquet sold?
   (A) red
   (B) pink
   (C) orange
   (D) violet
   (E) yellow

4. Each of the following bouquets could be sold immediately after the pink bouquet EXCEPT
   (A) orange
   (B) red
   (C) violet
   (D) white
   (E) yellow

5. If the white bouquet is sold second, then which one of the following must be false?
   (A) The red bouquet is sold first.
   (B) The pink bouquet is sold third.
   (C) The red bouquet is sold fifth.
   (D) The yellow bouquet is sold fifth.
   (E) The violet bouquet is sold sixth.

6. If the pink bouquet is sold immediately before the yellow bouquet, which one of the following could be the fourth bouquet sold?
   (A) pink
   (B) red
   (C) violet
   (D) white
   (E) yellow

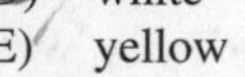

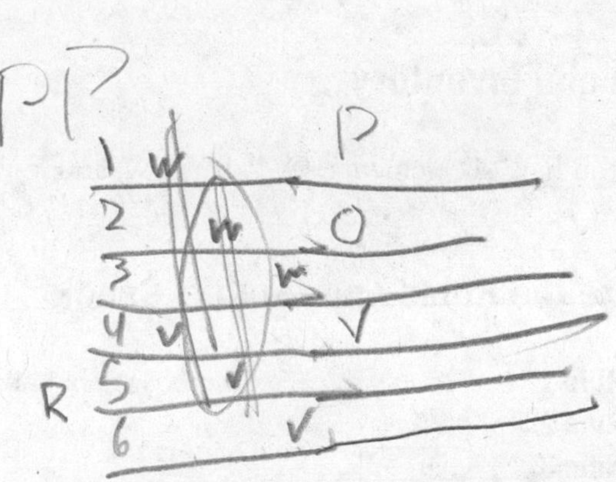

ANSWERS TO MOTHER'S DAY BOUQUETS

1. E
2. A
3. C
4. B
5. C
6. E

EXPLANATIONS TO MOTHER'S DAY BOUQUETS

Prepare

Ingredient Scan

Task: 1D Order
Inventory: 6 elements, 6 slots, 1:1 ratio
Rules: The second rule, which describes "at least two spaces" coming in between two elements, looks a little tricky to symbolize.
Questions: 6 questions: 1 Grab-a-Rule, 4 Specific, 1 General
Red Flags: None. This is a very straightforward Order game.
Rank: 1

Diagram and Inventory

You have six elements: O, P, R, V, W, and Y. Create a diagram with six columns, labeled 1–6.

Symbolize the Rules and Double-Check

Rule 1: P = 1, 3, or 5. Symbolize this above your diagram.
Rule 2: W _ _+ V
Rule 3: [O _ Y]

Rule 2 is the most difficult to symbolize. You can use the convention of a plus sign "+" to notate "at least." Because the spacing of rule 2 is flexible, do not turn it into a block. Because the spacing of rule 3 is fixed; draw a box around it.

Don't forget to double-check your rules!

Deductions

Links: None of the rules contain overlapping elements, so there are no links.
Spatial restrictions: W, V, and P each have 3 options. As always, if the rules give you any block of elements that go together, begin by asking yourself how many different ways the chunk could be placed. In this case, rule 2 deals with at least four of the six available slots. Since the number of spaces between W and V can be two or more, there are a handful of different ways W and V could be placed. If there were only two or three ways it might be worth writing a scenario for each, but since there are more than three it's best to move on. Consider the limitations of W and V individually. The latest W could go is slot 3. The earliest V could go is slot 4. Represent on your diagram that W must go in slots 1, 2, or 3 and V must go in slots 4, 5, or 6. What about the other chunk, the O_Y block? Exclude the slots that O and Y can never go. O must have two elements come after it, so O can't be in slots 5 or 6. Conversely, Y has two elements before it, so Y can't be in 1 or 2.
Most restricted: The interaction of the two chunks will be the key spacing issue for each question.
Least restricted: R is in none of the rules, so it is a free agent. Circle it.

Here is your diagram:

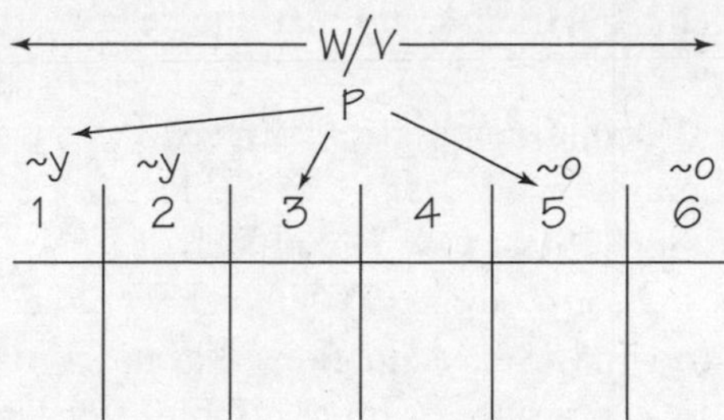

Assess, Act, Answer

Question 1 is a Grab-a-Rule, so do it first.

For question 1, take one rule at a time, picture how it would look broken or what you need to check to see if it's valid, and check all the answer choices for that rule only. Rinse and repeat with the other rules. Rule 1 eliminates choice (C). Rule 2 eliminates choices (A), (B), and (D). **Because only choice (E) remains, it is the credited response.**

Question 2 is your first Specific question, so do it next.

For question 2, place R in slot 5. Are there any rules that relate to R or to slot 5? R is a free agent, but you do know from rule 1 that P must go in slots 1, 3, or 5, so now only slots 1 and 3 remain. Draw two scenarios, one with P in slot 1 (and R in slot 5) and the other with P in slot 3 (and R in slot 5). Now consider your blocks of elements. In the scenario with P in slot 1, W could still go in slot 2 or 3. V, however, must go in slot 6. Slot 5 is already taken by R, and slot 4 would require that W be in slot 1, which is already taken by P. So V must go in slot 6. With only slots 2, 3, and 4 open, you have no options for the O_Y block except to place O in slot 2 and Y in slot 4. That leaves W in slot 3. Now flesh out the scenario in which P is in slot 3. W could still be in slot 1 or

2. V could still be in slot 4 or 6. What about the O_Y block? O and Y would either have to be in slots 2 and 4, or they would have to be in slots 4 and 6. However, if you place them in slots 4 and 6, that would only leave slots 1 and 2 open for W and V, which would break the rule. So, O and Y must go in slots 2 and 4. That forces W into slot 1 and V into slot 6. Since the question asks what *must be true* and you have two possible scenarios, scan vertically to see which slots have the same element in both scenarios. Slot 2 must be O, slot 4 must be Y, and slot 6 must be V. The answer choice will have to deal with O, Y, or V. **Choice (A) is the credited response.**

W/V

P

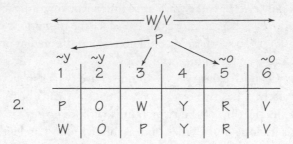

	~y	~y			~O	~O
	1	2	3	4	5	6
2.	P	O	W	Y	R	V
	W	O	P	Y	R	V

Question 3 is another Specific question, so do that one next.

For question 3, symbolize the condition it gives you next to your row for question 3: a WY block. What else do you know about W or Y? Y is in a fixed block with O, so you can add O to your condition to get an OWY block. Since OWY is a block of three elements, determine where it can fit. W can only go in slots 1, 2, or 3, so the OWY block would either have to be in slots 1–3 or 2–4. Make a row for each scenario and make deductions. For the scenario in which OWY is in slots 1–3, you know that P must go in slot 5, since its other options, slot 1 and slot 3, are already filled. With only slots 4 and 6 open, V must go in slot 6 to be far enough away from W. Free agent R lands in slot 4. For the scenario in which OWY is in slots 2–4, P could still be in slot 1 or 5. V, however, must go in slot 6 in order to be far enough away from W. Since P and R would be interchangeable in slots 1 and 5, write in P/R and R/P into those slots. The question asks what element could be second. In one scenario you have W in slot 2, in the other you have O in slot 2. W or O must be the answer. **Choice (C) is the credited response.**

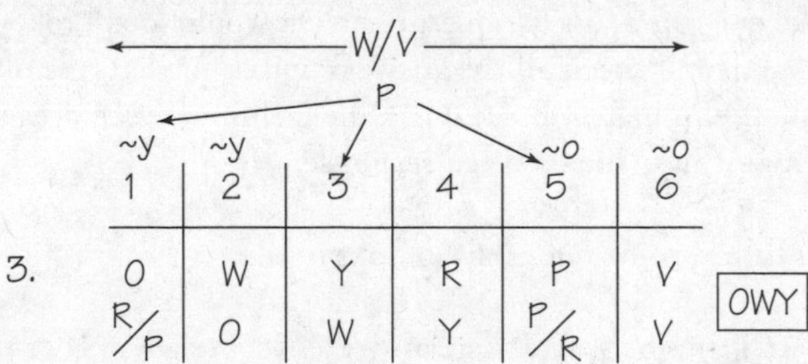

Question 5 is the next Specific question, so do that one next.

For question 5, place W in slot 2. The question asks for something that *must be false.* Check any scenarios from previous questions with W in slot 2 and eliminate any answer choice that applies to those. The Grab-a-Rule scenario from question 1 eliminates choices (A) and (B). The work from the first scenario of question 3 eliminates choice (E). All that remain are choices (C) and (D). Check to see if choice (C) is possible by placing R in slot 5. Can the other rules be accommodated? Start with the O_Y block since its shape is fixed. O and Y could either go in slots 1 and 3, which would make it impossible for P to go in slots 1, 3, or 5, or O and Y could go in slots 4 and 6, which would leave no way for V to be in slots 4, 5, or 6. **Because this choice describes something impossible, choice (C) is the credited response.**

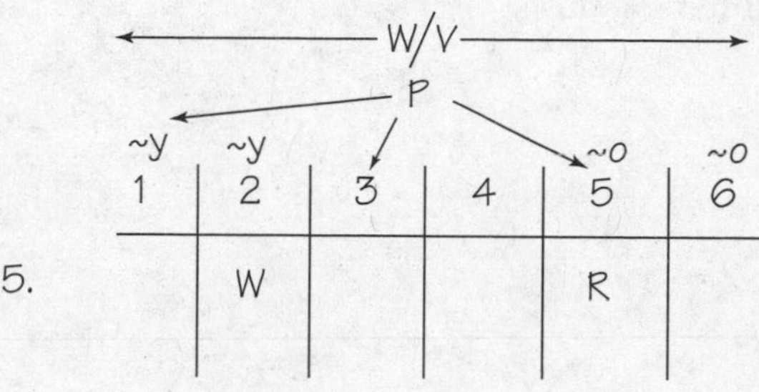

Question 6 is the next Specific question, so do that one next.

For question 6, symbolize the condition next to your new row: a PY block. What other rules apply to P or Y? Y is in a fixed block with O, so add O to the condition to get OPY. P must go in slots 1, 3, or 5. Since an OPY block prevents P from going in slot 1, try a scenario in which P is in slot 3 and a scenario in which P is in slot 5. For the first scenario, OPY goes into slots 2–4, which forces W into slot 1. R and V are left for slots 5 and 6 and are interchangeable there, so write in R/V and V/R. For the second scenario in which OPY goes into slots 4–6, there is no valid slot left in which to place V. Thus, cross out your work for this scenario since it is impossible (and you should never leave bad work on your diagram). Because the question asks which element could go fourth and there is only one scenario to choose from, the answer should be Y. **Choice (E) is the credited response.**

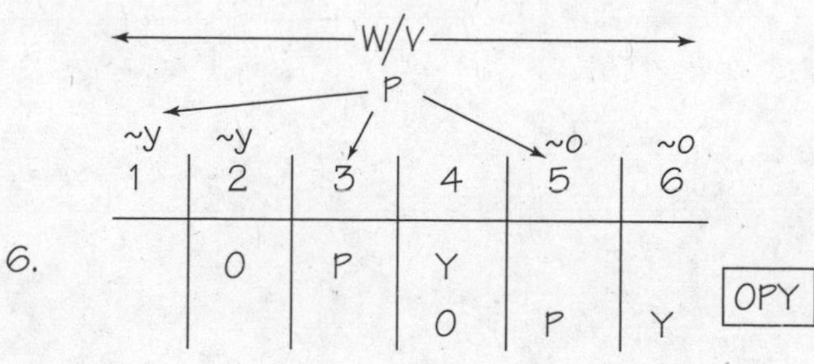

Go back to question 4, which is a General question.

Question 4 asks which element cannot come immediately to the right of P. Use your previous work to find things that *did* come immediately to the right of P and eliminate those answer choices. So far, Y, V, and O have come right after P so eliminate choices (A), (C), and (E). The remaining two answer choices are R and W, so go ahead and plug those in. R is a free agent, while W is forced to be in the first three slots, so it will be quicker to test W. Because the question demands that W come immediately after P, you're looking at a PW block. P can only go in slots 1, 3, or 5 so the only valid PW block would have to come in slots 1 and 2. Place P in slot 1 and W in slot 2 and see if the rest of the scenario seems feasible. Is there room for the O_Y block? Sure, you can place O and Y in slots 3–5 or slots 4–6. Either way, V has a slot open in the final three and R can go anywhere. Since the choice (D) scenario is possible, eliminate it. **Because choice (B) is all that remains, it is the credited response.**

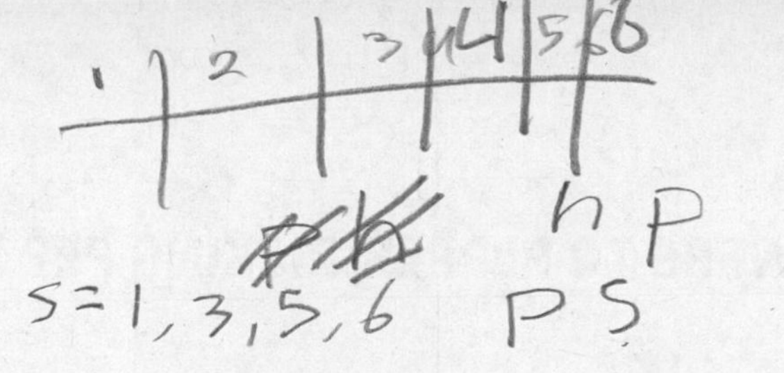

PEPPER-PICKING PEP RALLY

Pete picked several pairs of peppers and has been asked to present at a pepper-picking pep rally. The rally will last six consecutive days with Pete presenting exactly one pepper per day. Pete picked two each of the following types of peppers: banana, habanera, lemon, pequin, scotch bonnet and wax. He must present the peppers according to the following conditions:

A habanera pepper is not presented unless a pequin pepper is presented on the following day.
A pequin pepper is not presented unless a scotch bonnet pepper is presented on the following day.
Neither day 2 nor day 4 is a day on which a scotch bonnet pepper is presented.

1. Which of the following could be an order for the presentation of the peppers from day 1 to day 6?
   (A) banana, habanera, pequin, wax, scotch bonnet, lemon
   (B) wax, banana, scotch bonnet, lemon, banana, wax
   (C) lemon, banana, scotch bonnet, habanera, scotch bonnet, pequin
   (D) scotch bonnet, wax, lemon, pequin, banana, wax
   (E) banana, lemon, pequin, scotch bonnet, banana, lemon

2. If two pequin peppers are presented, which one of the following CANNOT be true?
   (A) A lemon pepper is presented on day 6.
   (B) A scotch bonnet pepper is presented on day 5.
   (C) A habanera pepper is presented on day 1.
   (D) A wax pepper is presented on day 4.
   (E) A banana pepper is presented on day 3.

3. If the two pequin peppers are presented on days 2 and 5, then the pepper presented on day 1 CANNOT be
   (A) banana
   (B) habanera
   (C) scotch bonnet
   (D) lemon
   (E) wax

4. Which of the following is a complete and accurate list of the days, any one of which could be a day on which a pequin pepper is presented?
   (A) day 1, day 3
   (B) day 2, day 4
   (C) day 1, day 3, day 5
   (D) day 2, day 4, day 5
   (E) day 2, day 5, day 6

5. If a habanera pepper is presented at some time after a scotch bonnet pepper, then a scotch bonnet pepper must be presented on
   (A) day 1 or else day 3
   (B) day 3 or else day 5
   (C) day 1
   (D) day 3
   (E) day 5

6. If neither banana peppers nor pequin peppers are presented during the pep rally, which one of the following must be true?
   (A) Either a lemon pepper or a scotch bonnet pepper is presented on day 3.
   (B) Either a lemon pepper or a wax pepper is presented on day 2.
   (C) A scotch bonnet pepper is presented on day 1.
   (D) A scotch bonnet pepper is presented on day 5.
   (E) A wax pepper is presented on day 4.

7. If two banana peppers are presented on days 3 and day 5, which of the following peppers could be presented on day 1 and day 6, respectively?
   (A) a habanera and a lemon pepper
   (B) a scotch bonnet pepper and a wax pepper
   (C) a banana pepper and a wax pepper
   (D) a scotch bonnet and a habanera pepper
   (E) a scotch bonnet pepper and a pequin pepper

ANSWERS TO PEPPER-PICKING PEP RALLY

1. B
2. E
3. C
4. D
5. A
6. B
7. B

EXPLANATIONS TO PEPPER-PICKING PEP RALLY

Prepare

Ingredient Scan

Task: 1D Order
Inventory: 12 elements, 2 each of 6 different types, for 6 slots; not all of the 6 types must be used each time
Rules: A couple of conditional clues linked to element order
Questions: 7 total: 1 Grab-a-Rule, 5 Specific, 1 General
Red Flags: Not a 1:1 game; two of each element type may be harder to keep track of when dealing with order
Rank: 3

Diagram and Inventory

The setup describes an Order game in which twelve peppers of six different types—b, h, l, p, s, and w—are assigned to six days. Only one pepper is assigned per day, and not every type must be used over the six days.

Symbolize the Rules and Double-Check

Rule 1: 

h → [hp]   ~[hp] → ~h

Rule 2: p → [ps]   ~[ps] → ~p

Rule 3: s≠2/4. Put this in your diagram.

When you symbolize the conditionals in rules 1 and 2, be sure to include the sequence element in your clue—this way you won't need to keep looking back to recall whether an element was supposed to precede or follow another one.

Don't forget to double-check your rules!

Deductions

Links: You can combine rules 1 and 2 to form a bigger block of elements.

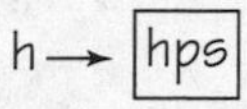

h → [hps]

Spatial restrictions: From rule 3 you know that s cannot go on day 2 or day 4. Since rule 2 demands that p be followed the next day by s, this means p cannot be on either day 1 or day 3, as s is not available to follow it. In addition, p cannot be on day 6, again because s could not come after it. Along the same lines, rule 1 says that h must always be followed by p. Therefore, h cannot be on day 2, day 5, or day 6, as it is not possible to have p follow the next day.
Most restricted: Pepper types p and h are each limited to only 3 possible days; if h is selected, it sets off a very specific sequence of elements.
Least restricted: Pepper types b, l, and w are not discussed in any of the rules.

Here is your diagram:

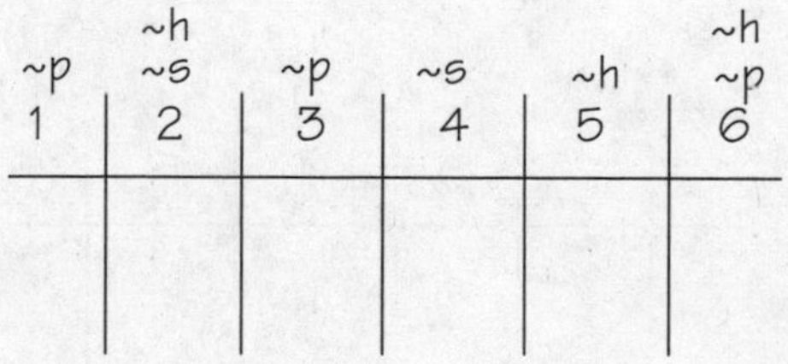

~p	~h ~s	~p	~s	~h	~h ~p
1	2	3	4	5	6

Assess, Act, Answer

Question 1 is a Grab-a-Rule, so start there.

For question 1, use the rules to eliminate answer choices. Rule 1 eliminates choice (C), rule 2 eliminates choice (A) and choice (D), and rule 3 eliminates choice (E). **The only choice left, and therefore the credited response, is choice (B).**

Now move on to the Specific questions, beginning with question 2.

Question 2 requires you to use both p's; from your deductions, you know they can only go on days 2, 4, or 5. Because p needs to be followed by s (rule 2), putting p on days 4 and 5 is not possible. This leaves two potential scenarios—days 2 and 4 or days 2 and 5. Put each in your diagram, making sure that s is on the following day each time.

Here is your diagram:

	~p 1	~h ~s 2	~p 3	~s 4	~h 5	~h ~p 6
2.		p	s	p	s	
		p	s		p	s

The question asks for something that essentially must be false, so compare the answer choices to your two scenarios. Because p is on day 2 and s is therefore on day 3 in both cases, choice (E) is not possible and must be false. There is no need to try out the other choices. **Choice (E) is the credited response.**

The next Specific question is question 3.

For question 3, place p in days 2 and 5 on your diagram. You now know that s must be on days 3 and 6 (rule 2).

Here is your diagram:

	~p 1	~h ~s 2	~p 3	~s 4	~h 5	~h ~p 6
3.		p	s		p	s

The question asks which pepper cannot be on day 1. You have already used up both p and s, so they are not possibilities. **Choice (C) is the credited response.**

The next Specific question is question 5.

Question 5 stipulates that one of the h's must come after one of the s's. Since having h requires the hps block (from your earlier deductions), this means you will use both s peppers. Figure out where the block can go first. From your deductions, you know that h cannot go on day 2, and since it must be preceded by s for this question you can't put h on day 1 either. That leaves either days 3, 4, and 5 or days 4, 5, and 6. Try each scenario on your diagram. If the block is placed on days 3, 4, and 5, then s must go on day 1 because it cannot go on day 2 (rule 3). If the block is placed on days 4, 5, and 6, then s could go on either day 1 or day 3.

Here is your diagram:

	~p 1	~h ~s 2	~p 3	~s 4	~h 5	~h ~p 6
5.	s		h	p	s	
				h	p	s

The question asks which day s must be presented; the credited response must be true based on both of the scenarios in your diagram. Since s must show up on either day 1 or day 3, choice (A) is your answer. **Choice (A) is the credited response.**

The next Specific question is question 6.

For question 6, if p is not presented, then h cannot be presented either (rule 1), so that leaves you with only l, s, and w for the six days. From rule 3 you know that s cannot be on days 2 or 4, so those days must have either l or w instead.

Here is your diagram:

	~p 1	~h ~s 2	~p 3	~s 4	~h 5	~h ~p 6
6.		l/w		l/w		

The question asks for something that *must be true,* so compare your answer choices to the diagram. While choice (A), choice (C), choice (D), and choice (E) all could be true, the only choice that must be true is choice (B). **Choice (B) is the credited response.**

The final Specific question is question 7.

For question 7, place b on days 3 and 5. Since b is never mentioned in the rules, you don't know much about what else must go into the diagram. Use your deductions to eliminate answer choices.

Here is your diagram:

	~p	~h ~s	~p	~s	~h	~h ~p
	1	2	3	4	5	6
7.			b		b	

The question asks which peppers can be on day 6 and day 1. From your deductions, you know that neither p nor h can be on day 6; cross out choice (D) and choice (E). You have also used up both b's, and you cannot have a third one; eliminate choice (C). There are two choices left. For choice (A), putting h on day 1 would require p to go on day 2 and s to go on day 3 (deduction from rules 1 and 2 combined). Since b is on day 3, this possibility doesn't work. Eliminate choice (A) and you're left with choice (B), which you don't need to try. Choice (B) is the credited response.

Move on to the General question—question 4.

Question 4 asks for all the possible days on which p could be presented. From both question 2 and your deductions, you know that only days 2, 4, and 5 are possible. **Choice (D) is the credited response.**

SKYDIVERS

Eight skydivers—Bjorn, Dextra, Huxley, Jethro, Kenneth, Neka, Skye, and Victoria—are jumping out of an airplane. Each skydiver jumps only once and every skydiver jumps out of the airplane one at a time. The order must conform to the following conditions:

Skye does not jump last.
Victoria jumps after both Jethro and Neka have jumped.
The first person to jump is either Bjorn or Dextra.
Huxley jumps before Jethro, with exactly one person jumping in between them.
Kenneth jumps before Neka, with exactly two people jumping in between them.

1. Which one of the following could be an acceptable order in which the skydivers jump of the airplane?
   (A) Dextra, Kenneth, Skye, Huxley, Neka, Bjorn, Jethro, Victoria
   (B) Dextra, Skye, Kenneth, Huxley, Neka, Jethro, Bjorn, Victoria
   (C) Bjorn, Kenneth, Skye, Huxley, Neka, Jethro, Victoria, Dextra
   (D) Bjorn, Huxley, Kenneth, Jethro, Dextra, Neka, Victoria, Skye
   (E) Bjorn, Skye, Dextra, Kenneth, Victoria, Huxley, Neka, Jethro

2. If Victoria jumps before Bjorn, then the second skydiver to jump could be which one of the following?
   (A) Skye
   (B) Jethro
   (C) Neka
   (D) Huxley
   (E) Dextra

3. Which of the following must be true?
   (A) The earliest that Neka can jump is fifth.
   (B) The earliest that Jethro can jump is fifth.
   (C) The earliest that Kenneth can jump is third.
   (D) The earliest that Skye can jump is third.
   (E) The earliest that Victoria can jump is eighth.

4. Huxley can jump in all of the following positions, EXCEPT:
   (A) sixth
   (B) fifth
   (C) fourth
   (D) third
   (E) second

5. Which of the following could be true?
   (A) Dextra jumps fifth and Victoria jumps eighth.
   (B) Skye jumps seventh and Neka jumps eighth.
   (C) Bjorn jumps first and Skye jumps eighth.
   (D) Jethro jumps third and Neka jumps seventh.
   (E) Kenneth jumps second and Huxley jumps third.

6. If Skye jumps before Jethro, then the earliest that Jethro could jump is
   (A) second
   (B) third
   (C) fourth
   (D) fifth
   (E) sixth

ANSWERS TO SKYDIVERS

1. C
2. D
3. A
4. A
5. A
6. D

EXPLANATIONS TO SKYDIVERS

Prepare

Ingredient Scan

Task:	D Order game
Inventory:	8 elements total for 8 slots, 1:1 ratio
Rules:	Mostly straightforward and easy to symbolize
Questions:	6 total: 1 Grab-a-Rule, 2 Specific, 3 General
Red Flags:	Two blocks that overlap with each other
Rank:	1

Diagram and Inventory

The setup describes a 1:1 Order game in which you must determine the order in which 8 skydivers—b, d, h, j, k, n, s, and v—jump out of an airplane.

Symbolize the Rules and Double-Check

Rule 1: s≠8. Put in your diagram.

Rule 2: j—v; n—v

Rule 3: 1=b/d. Put in your diagram.

Rule 4: [h _ j]

Rule 5: [k _ _ n]

Don't forget to double-check your rules!

Deductions

Links: Combining rule 2 with rules 4 and 5 gives you more information about v.

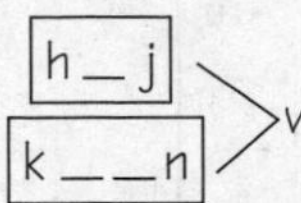

Because v must be preceded by h, j, k, and n, and because the two blocks can only overlap enough to take up 5 spaces at minimum, v cannot be in slots 2 through 6. This limits v to either slot 7 or slot 8.

Spatial restrictions: From rule 2, neither j nor n can go last, and v cannot be in slots 2 or 3, since slot 1 is already restricted by rule 3. Rule 4 tells you that h cannot be seventh or eighth and that j cannot be second or third. Similarly, from rule 5, k cannot be in slots 6, 7, or 8, and n cannot be in slots 2, 3, or 4.

Most restricted: v is limited to only two possible slots, and the two blocks will help determine which of the two slots v ends up in.

Least restricted: b, d, and s have the fewest limitations on where they can go in the line-up.

Here is your diagram:

	1	2	3	4	5	6	7	8
		~n ~j ~v	~n ~j ~v	~v ~n	~v	~v ~k	~k ~h	~k ~j ~n ~s ~h
bdhjknsv	b/d							

Assess, Act, Answer

Question 1 is a Grab-a-Rule, so begin there.

For question 1, use the rules to eliminate answer choices. Rule 1 eliminates choice (D), rule 2 eliminates choice (E), rule 4 eliminates choice (A), and rule 5 eliminates choice (B). **The only choice left, and therefore the credited response, is choice (C).**

Now move to the Specific questions. The first Specific question is question 2.

Question 2 stipulates that v must jump before b. This means that d will have to be in slot 1 and v will have to go in slot 7 with b in slot 8. This leaves only 5 slots for the two blocks; they must overlap, leaving two possible scenarios.

Here is your diagram:

	1	2	3	4	5	6	7	8
		~n ~j ~v	~n ~j ~v	~v ~n	~v	~v ~k	~k ~h	~k ~j ~n ~s ~h
2.	d	h k	k s	j h	s n	n j	v	b

The question asks who could be in slot 2. Eliminate any answer choice that conflicts with either of the two possible cases, which leaves only choice (D). **Choice (D) is the credited response.**

The other Specific question of the game is question 6.

Question 6 requires s to jump before j. This means that in addition to all the elements that must come before v, you now have one more, s, since j also comes some time before v. This means v is definitely in slot 8. You also know from your previous deductions that j cannot jump either second or third, so eliminate choice (A) and choice (B). In order to have j jump as early as possible, put the block involving h and j before the block involving k and n.

Here is your diagram:

	1	2	3	4	5	6	7	8
		~n ~j ~v	~n ~j ~v	~v ~n	~v	~v ~k	~k ~h	~k ~j ~n ~s ~h
6.	b/d	s	h	k	j	d/b	n	v

Based on your diagram, if s jumps some time before j, the earliest j can jump is slot 5. **Choice (D) is the credited response.**

Move on to the General questions. The first General question is question 3.

Question 3 asks for something that must be true. Use your deductions and past work to eliminate answer choices that aren't always true. From your work on question 2, eliminate choice (B), choice (C), and choice (E). Your work on question 6 allows you to cross out choice (D) as well, leaving only choice (A), which is supported by the deductions you made earlier. **Choice (A) is the credited response.**

The next General question is question 4.

Question 4 asks for which slot h cannot be in, meaning there will be four choices that are possible for h. Use your deductions and past work to eliminate what you can. In question 2 you saw that h could be in either slot 2 or slot 4; eliminate choice (C) and choice (E). In question 6 h was in slot 3, so eliminate choice (D). You have two choices left, so try choice (B). If h is in slot 5, then j must be in slot 7 (rule 4) and v in slot 8. In order to fit the other block into the diagram, k would have to go in slot 3 and n in slot 6. This seems to be an acceptable scenario.

Here is your diagram:

		~n ~j ~v	~n ~j ~v	~v ~n	~v	~v ~k	~k ~h	~k ~j ~n ~s ~h
	1	2	3	4	5	6	7	8
4. (B)	b/d		k		h	n	j	v

Since choice (B) is possible, you can eliminate it, leaving choice (A) as the answer. There is no need to test it out. **Choice (A) is the credited response.**

The final General question is question 5.

Question 5 asks for what could be true. Again, use your deductions and past work to eliminate answer choices. From your deductions, you know that n cannot be in slot 8; eliminate choice (B). Eliminate choice (C) based on rule 1 and choice (D) from your deduction that j cannot be third. You have two choices left, so try choice (A). If d is in slot 5 and v is in slot 8, then slot 1 must be b. The only way to fit the two blocks is to put h in slot 2, j in slot 4, k in slot 3, and n in slot 6, leaving s in slot 7. This seems to be an acceptable scenario.

Here is your diagram:

		~n ~j ~v	~n ~j ~v	~v ~n	~v	~v ~k	~k ~h	~k ~j ~n ~s ~h
	1	2	3	4	5	6	7	8
5. (A)	b	h	k	j	d	n	s	v

Since choice (A) is possible, it must be the answer; there is no need to check choice (E). **Choice (A) is the credited response.**

BLOG RATER

A website ranks the popularity of six political blogs: Bipartisan, Centrist, Doublespeak, Flip-Flop, Gravitas, and Hubris. Popularity ratings are decided by the number of websites that link to each blog, and the blogs are ranked from most popular (first) to least popular (sixth). No blogs are tied. The blogs are ranked according to the following conditions:

Bipartisan is more popular than either Centrist or Doublespeak, but not both.

Hubris is less popular than Doublespeak.

If Centrist is less popular than Doublespeak, then neither Flip-Flop nor Hubris is more popular than Gravitas.

If Centrist is more popular than Doublespeak, then Flip-Flop is more popular than both Gravitas and Hubris.

1. Which of the following could be an accurate ranking of the blogs, from most popular to least popular?
   (A) Centrist, Bipartisan, Doublespeak, Hubris, Flip-Flop, Gravitas
   (B) Flip-Flop, Doublespeak, Bipartisan, Gravitas, Centrist, Hubris
   (C) Gravitas, Flip-Flop, Hubris, Doublespeak, Bipartisan, Centrist
   (D) Doublespeak, Gravitas, Bipartisan, Flip-Flop, Centrist, Hubris
   (E) Flip-Flop, Gravitas, Centrist, Doublespeak, Hubris, Bipartisan

2. Each of the following could be the most popular blog EXCEPT
   (A) Doublespeak
   (B) Bipartisan
   (C) Flip-Flop
   (D) Centrist
   (E) Gravitas

3. If Bipartisan is less popular than Hubris, then which one of the following could be true?
   (A) Bipartisan is more popular than Gravitas.
   (B) Bipartisan is more popular than Doublespeak.
   (C) Centrist is more popular than Flip-Flop.
   (D) Centrist is more popular than Doublespeak.
   (E) Centrist is more popular than Hubris.

4. If Centrist is the second-most popular blog, then each of the following must be false EXCEPT:
   (A) Hubris is more popular than Bipartisan.
   (B) Gravitas is more popular than Bipartisan.
   (C) Doublespeak is more popular than Bipartisan.
   (D) Doublespeak is more popular than Centrist.
   (E) Gravitas is more popular than Flip-Flop.

5. Each of the following could be true EXCEPT:
   (A) Centrist is the most popular blog.
   (B) Flip-Flop is the most popular blog.
   (C) Gravitas is the second most popular blog.
   (D) Hubris is the least popular blog.
   (E) Hubris is the second most popular blog.

6. If Doublespeak is less popular than Gravitas and more popular than Flip-Flop, then which one of the following could be true?
   (A) Centrist is more popular than Bipartisan.
   (B) Bipartisan is more popular than Doublespeak.
   (C) Centrist is more popular than Doublespeak.
   (D) Hubris is more popular than Gravitas.
   (E) Flip-Flop is more popular than Hubris.

ANSWERS TO BLOG RATER

1. D
2. B
3. C
4. B
5. E
6. E

EXPLANATIONS TO BLOG RATER

Prepare

Ingredient Scan

Task: 1D Order
Inventory: 6 elements, 6 slots, 1:1 ratio
Rules: Range clues and some odd conditional statements
Questions: 6 total: 1 Grab-a-Rule, 3 Specific, 2 General
Red Flags: Conditional rules that involve range relationships, are confusing to symbolize
Rank: 3/4

Diagram and Inventory

The setup describes an Order game in which you have to rank the popularity of 6 blogs from 1 (most popular) to 6 (least popular).

Symbolize the Rules and Double-Check

Rule 1: D—B—C or C—B—D
Rule 2: D—H
Rule 3: D—C→G—F and G—H; H—G or F—G→C—D
Rule 4: C—D→F—G and F—H; G—F or H—F→D—C

Don't forget to double-check your rules!

Deductions

Links: In a ranking game such as this one, attempt to figure out the relationships among as many elements as possible. Rule 1 can be linked with rule 2. Rule 3 applies when the order is C—B—D, and Rule 4 applies when the order is D—B—C. Note that because B is always less popular than C or D, it cannot be ranked first, and because it is always more popular than C or D, it cannot be ranked last. From rule 2, you also know that D can never be ranked last, and H can never be ranked first. Combining rules 2, 3, and 4, you can also determine that when D is first, D and G are both ranked higher than H, and that when C is first, C and F are both ranked higher than H, so H is never ranked first or second. By combining all 4 clues, you can find that there are only two possible scenarios:

```
D–B–C            C–B–D–H
 >H       or         /
G<F              F–G
```

Most restricted: Because the two scenarios hinge on whether D is ranked higher than C or C higher than D, these elements are the most restricted.

Here is your diagram:

BCDFGH	1	2	3	4	5	6
	~B ~H	~H				~B ~D

Assess, Act, Answer

Question 1 is a Grab-a-Rule question, so start there.

For question 1, use the rules to eliminate answer choices. Rule 1 eliminates choice (E), rule 2 eliminates choice (C), rule 3 eliminates choice (B), and rule 4 eliminates choice (A). **The only choice left, and therefore the credited response, is choice (D).**

Question 3 is the first Specific question, so answer that one next.

For question 3, because H is already less popular than D, the only way for it to be more popular than B is in the D—B—C scenario. Here is your diagram:

```
D–H–B–C
 /
G–F
```

You are looking for something that *could be true.* The only situation that could be true choice (C). **Choice (C) is the credited response.**

Question 4 is the next Specific question.

Question 4 places C in the second slot, so you need the scenario in which the order is C—B—D. The only element that can be first is F. Here is your diagram:

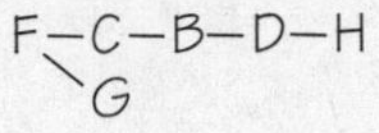

```
F—C—B—D—H
 \G
```

You are asked for something that *must be false EXCEPT,* which means you are looking for the answer that could be true. The only choice that could be true in this scenario is choice (B). **Choice (B) is the credited response.**

Question 6 is the last Specific question, so answer it next.

Question 6 puts D ahead of F, but after G. The only scenario in which this can work is when the order is D—B—C. Here is your diagram:

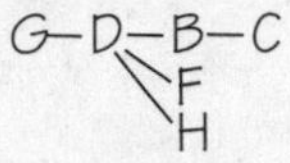

```
G—D—B—C
   \F
    \H
```

Since the question asks for something that *could be true,* use the diagram to determine what is flexible. The only answer that could be true is choice (E). **Choice (E) is the credited response.**

Question 2 is the first General question, so answer that one next.

Question 2 asks for what cannot be the most popular blog. According to your deductions, B and H cannot be in the first position. **B is in choice (B), so choice (B) is the credited response.**

Question 5 is the final General question.

Question 5 asks for something that *could be true EXCEPT,* which really means something that *must be false.* Based on the initial deductions, the only answer choice that must be false is choice (E). **Choice (E) is the credited response.**

THE GREAT BANK BAILOUT

In October, eight large financial institutions—Aijah House, Barnet Group, Frankie & Sons, Goldin Ketch, Jordan LLC, Lehana Sisters, Merlin Inc, and Stella Moran—will be bailed out by the government. Each institution is bailed out exactly once, and no two institutions are bailed out at the same time. The bailouts proceed consistent with the following conditions:

Aijah House is bailed out before Jordan LLC.
Goldin Ketch is bailed out before Frankie & Sons.
Barnet Group is bailed out after both Goldin Ketch and Stella Moran.
Merlin Inc is bailed out after Barnet Group but before Jordan LLC.
Barnet Group is bailed out after Lehana Sisters.

1. Which one of the following could be the order, from first to last, in which the financial institutions are bailed out?

(A) Stella Moran, Frankie & Sons, Goldin Ketch, Aijah House, Lehana Sisters, Barnet Group, Merlin Inc, Jordan LLC
(B) Stella Moran, Aijah House, Goldin Ketch, Lehana Sisters, Jordan LLC, Barnet Group, Merlin Inc, Frankie & Sons
(C) Goldin Ketch, Frankie & Sons, Lehana Sisters, Aijah House, Stella Moran, Barnet Group, Merlin Inc, Jordan LLC
(D) Aijah House, Goldin Ketch, Frankie & Sons, Stella Moran, Barnet Group, Merlin Inc, Lehana Sisters, Jordan LLC
(E) Lehana Sisters, Goldin Ketch, Stella Moran, Barnet Group, Merlin Inc, Frankie & Sons, Jordan LLC, Aijah House

2. If Goldin Ketch is the fourth institution bailed out, then each of the following must be false EXCEPT

(A) Lehana Sisters is the third institution bailed out.
(B) Frankie & Sons is the second institution bailed out.
(C) Aijah House is the fifth institution bailed out.
(D) Merlin Inc is the fifth institution bailed out.
(E) Stella Moran is the sixth institution bailed out.

3. Each of the following could be false EXCEPT

(A) At least one institution is bailed out before Stella Moran is bailed out.
(B) No more than one institution is bailed out after Jordan LLC is bailed out.
(C) At least two institutions are bailed out before Aijah House is bailed out.
(D) No more than three institutions are bailed out after Barnet Group is bailed out.
(E) No more than three institutions are bailed out before Lehana Sisters is bailed out.

4. If Aijah House is the first institution bailed out and Frankie & Sons is the third institution bailed out, then which one of the following could be false?

(A) Goldin Ketch is the second institution bailed out.
(B) Lehana Sisters is the fourth institution bailed out.
(C) Barnet Group is the sixth institution bailed out.
(D) Merlin Inc is the seventh institution bailed out.
(E) Jordan LLC is the eighth institution bailed out.

5. The fifth institution bailed out CANNOT be

(A) Barnet Group
(B) Frankie & Sons
(C) Lehana Sisters
(D) Goldin Ketch
(E) Merlin Inc

6. If Jordan LLC is the seventh institution bailed out, then the second institution bailed out CANNOT be

(A) Aijah House
(B) Goldin Ketch
(C) Lehana Sisters
(D) Stella Moran
(E) Frankie & Sons

7. If Frankie & Sons is the second institution bailed out, then which one of the following must be false?

(A) Aijah House is the third institution bailed out.
(B) Stella Moran is the fifth institution bailed out.
(C) Barnet Group is the fourth institution bailed out.
(D) Merlin Inc is the sixth institution bailed out.
(E) Aijah House is the seventh institution bailed out.

ANSWERS TO THE GREAT BANK BAILOUT

1. C
2. A
3. B
4. B
5. D
6. E
7. C

EXPLANATIONS TO THE GREAT BANK BAILOUT

Prepare

Ingredient Scan

Task: 1D Order
Inventory: 8 elements, 8 slots, 1:1 ratio
Rules: All straightforward range rules
Questions: 7 total: 1 Grab-a-Rule, 4 Specific, 2 General
Red Flags: None
Rank: 2

Diagram and Inventory

The setup describes eight institutions—A, B, F, G, J, L, M, and S—that are going to be bailed out in a particular order. This is a straightforward Order game with 1–8 forming the core of the diagram.

Symbolize the Rules and Double-Check

Rule 1: A—J

Rule 2: G—F

Rule 3: G > B < S (G and S each before B)

Rule 4: B—M—J

Rule 5: L—B

The key to an Order game with all range rules is to connect the order together into a composite. This can be messy, and may take more than one try to get everything to line up, but it is worth the effort when you can answer the questions more quickly and accurately as a result.

Here is what the final connected composite rule looks like:

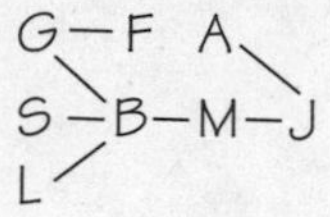

```
G—F  A
  \    \
S —B—M—J
  /
L
```

Don't forget to double-check your rules!

Deductions

Spatial restrictions: When you have a visual composite of the spatial limitations of the elements, focus on the extremities of the diagram instead of writing out the restrictions of every element. In this particular game, J is restricted to slots 7 or 8, and the only two elements that can go in slot 8 are J or F.
Most restricted: B has elements that must come before it and after it, meaning that if you know where B fits in the diagram you should be able to figure out where most everything else can go as well.
Least restricted: F and A are each only tied to one other element.

Here is your diagram:

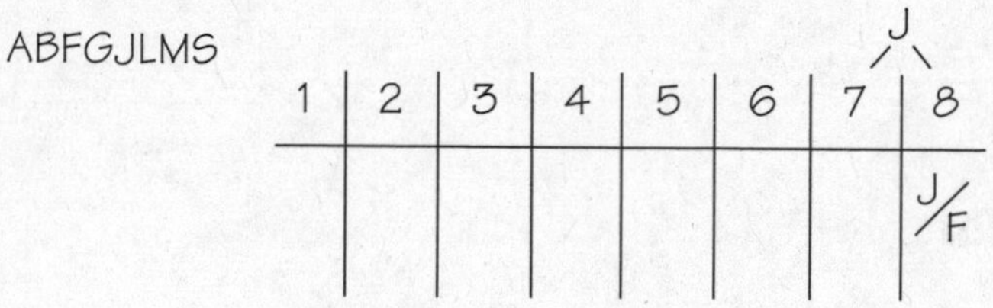

ABFGJLMS

1	2	3	4	5	6	7	8
							J/F

(J above slots 7 and 8)

Assess, Act, Answer

Question 1 is a Grab-a-Rule question.

For question 1, start there and use the rules to eliminate answer choices. Rule 1 eliminates choice (E), rule 2 eliminates choice (A), rule 4 eliminates choice (B), and rule 5 eliminates choice (D). **The only choice left, and therefore the credited response, is choice (C).**

Question 2 is a Specific question, so answer that one next.

For question 2, place G in slot 4. Look at the linked rules to see what you know. F, B, M, and J must all come after G, and it just so happens there are only four slots after G in this setup. That means A, S, and L all must come before G.

Here is your diagram:

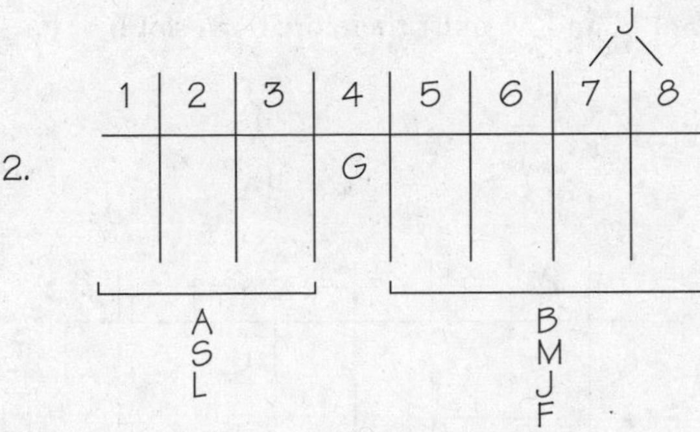

The question asks for something that *could be true.* The only possibility among the choices that could be true is that L is in slot 3. **Therefore, choice (A) is the credited response.**

Move on to question 4, the next Specific question.

For question 4, place A in slot 1 and F in slot 3. J must be in slot 8 (from the deductions) and G must be in slot 2 (rule 2). Since S and L must both come before B and M (rules 3 and 4), M is in slot 7 and B is in slot 6. S and L are interchangeable in slots 4 and 5.

Here is your diagram:

	1	2	3	4	5	6	7	8
4.	A	G	F	S/L	L/S	B	M	J

Because you are looking for something that *could be false,* eliminate anything that must be true. The only possibility here that does not have to be true is that L is in slot 4. **This means choice (B) is the credited response.**

The next Specific question is question 6.

Question 6 stipulates that J is in slot 7. From the deductions you know that if J is not in slot 8 then F is in slot 8. The question asks for something that cannot be in slot 2. Since you know that F is in slot 8, it is certainly not in slot 2. **Choice (E) is the credited response.**

The final Specific question is question 7.

Question 7 stipulates that F is now in slot 2. That means G is in slot 1 (rule 2) and J is in slot 8 (deductions). From the rules, you know that S and L must come before B which comes before M. A can go anywhere, so you can't nail any of these elements down to one slot. You can determine, though, that because S and L both have to come before B, B cannot be in any slot earlier than slot 5. B must be in slot 5 or 6, and M must therefore be in slot 6 or 7.

Here is your diagram:

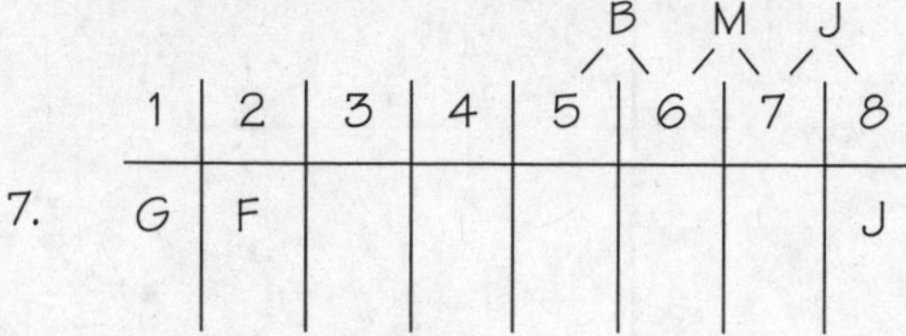

You are looking for something that cannot be true. The only possibility that cannot be true is that B is in slot 4. **Therefore, choice (C) is the credited response.**

Now that the Specific questions are complete, attack the General questions, starting with question 3.

Question 3 asks for something that *must be true.* From the deductions, J must be in slot 7 or 8, which means that no more than one institution will be bailed out after J. **This makes choice (B) the credited response.**

Move on to question 5, the final General question.

Question 5 asks for institutions that cannot be in slot 5. From the diagram you know that G and J cannot be assigned to slot 5. **Choice (D) is the credited response.**

PAGEANT INTERVIEWS

Exactly seven contestants—Faustine, Galena, Holly, Ikata, Jinx, Kiana, and Louise—have reached the interview round of the All-State Beauty Pageant. Each contestant will be interviewed once, in order, according to the following conditions:

Ikata is interviewed either first or last.
Either Galena or Jinx must be interviewed fourth.
Holly is the contestant interviewed immediately before Louise
Galena is interviewed at some point before Kiana
Jinx is not interviewed immediately before or immediately after Kiana

1. Which of the following could be an accurate list of the order in which the contestants are interviewed, from first to last?

(A) Holly, Louise, Kiana, Galena, Faustine, Jinx, Ikata
(B) Ikata, Faustine, Galena, Jinx, Kiana, Holly, Louise
(C) Ikata, Holly, Louise, Galena, Jinx, Faustine, Kiana
(D) Ikata, Holly, Galena, Jinx, Faustine, Kiana, Louise
(E) Galena, Holly, Louise, Jinx, Ikata, Kiana, Faustine

2. If Galena is interviewed immediately after Louise, then which of the following could be true?

(A) Holly is interviewed fifth.
(B) Faustine is interviewed second.
(C) Galena is interviewed last.
(D) Jinx is interviewed first.
(E) Galena is interviewed second.

3. Which contestant CANNOT be interviewed first?

(A) Faustine
(B) Jinx
(C) Galena
(D) Kiana
(E) Holly

4. If the sixth contestant to be interviewed is Holly, then which contestant must be interviewed first?

(A) Louise
(B) Ikata
(C) Jinx
(D) Galena
(E) Faustine

5. If Faustine is interviewed second, then which candidate could be interviewed third?

(A) Jinx
(B) Holly
(C) Ikata
(D) Louise
(E) Kiana

6. Each of the following must be false, EXCEPT:

(A) Holly is interviewed third.
(B) Louise is interviewed fifth.
(C) Kiana is interviewed third.
(D) Galena is interviewed first.
(E) Galena is interviewed seventh.

ANSWERS TO PAGEANT INTERVIEWS

1. C
2. D
3. D
4. B
5. A
6. D

EXPLANATIONS TO PAGEANT INTERVIEWS

Prepare

Ingredient Scan

Task: 1D Order
Inventory: 7 elements for 7 spaces, 1:1 ratio
Rules: Straightforward range clues
Questions: 6 total: 1 Grab-a-Rule, 3 Specific, 2 General
Red Flags: None
Rank: 1

Diagram and Inventory

The setup describes an Order game in which you must place seven contestants to be interviewed—F, G, H, I, J, K, and L—in order from first to last, one person at a time.

Symbolize the Rules and Double-Check

Rule 1: I=1/7

Rule 2: 4=G/K

Rule 3: HL

Rule 4: G—K

Rule 5: ~~JK~~ ~~KJ~~

Don't forget to double-check your rules!

Deductions

Links: Combining rule 2 with rule 5, if J=4, then K cannot be third or fifth.
Spatial restrictions: From rule 1, I cannot be in slots 2–6. From rule 3, H cannot be last and L cannot be first. Also, because slot 4 is restricted to G or J by rule 2, H cannot be third and L cannot be fifth. From rule 4, you know that G cannot be last and K cannot be first.
Most restricted: Slot 4 has only two options, G and J, each of which is linked to other elements.
Least restricted: F is never mentioned in the rules.

Here is your diagram:

	~L ~K	~I	~H ~I		~L ~I	~I	~H ~G
FGHIJKL	1	2	3	4	5	6	7
				G/J			

Assess, Act, Answer

Question 1 is a Grab-a-Rule question.

For question 1, use the rules to eliminate answer choices. Rule 1 eliminates choice (E), rule 3 eliminates choice (D), rule 4 eliminates choice (A), and rule 5 eliminates choice (B). **The only choice left, and therefore the credited response, is choice (C).**

Question 2 is a Specific question, so answer it next.

Question 2 tells you that G comes immediately after L, which means the block formed from rule 3 is now a bit larger. Combined with rule 4, you now have this:

[HLG]—K

Since the block involves G, link it with rule 2 to determine who is in slot 4. Either G can be there, which sets the block in slots 2–4, or else J is in slot 4, and the block fits into slots 1 –3. In this latter scenario, you can further determine that I is in slot 7 (rule 1) and K is in slot 6 (rule 5 and prior deductions), leaving F in slot 5.

Here is your diagram:

	~L ~K	~I	~H ~I		~L ~I	~I	~H ~G
	1	2	3	4	5	6	7
2.		H	L	G			
	H	L	G	J	F	K	I

The question asks for what could be true. Since you have only two possible scenarios, eliminate anything that contradicts what you have in your diagram. Choices (A), (B), (C), and (E) all contradict the possibilities noted. While choice (D) isn't actually on your diagram, it is possible in the first scenario, and so it must be the right answer. **Choice (D) is the credited response.**

The next Specific question is question 4.

For question 4, place H in slot 6. This means L is in slot 7 (rule 3) and I is in slot 1 (rule 1).

The question asks who must be interviewed first, so you already have your answer. **Choice (B) is the credited response.**

The final Specific question is question 5.

For question 5, place F in slot 2. Since F is an unrestricted element, use what you know from your deductions about slot 3 to eliminate choices. Eliminate choice (B) and choice (C) in this manner. From rule 3, eliminate choice (D); if H is not in slot 2, L cannot be in slot 3. That leaves only two choices remaining. Try choice (A) and put J in slot 3. That means G will be in slot 4, so K must be in one of slots 5, 6, or 7 (rule 4). You also have to leave room for H and L in those slots, because there is no other place to put the block. They will have to occupy either slots 5 and 6 or slots 6 and 7. This means I must go into slot 1.

Here is your diagram:

	~L ~K	~I	~H ~I		~L ~I	~I	~H ~G
	1	2	3	4	5	6	7
5.	I	F	J	G	K	H	L
					H	L	K

Since this scenario appears to work, you know that J can indeed be third and that this must be the answer. There is no need to try choice (E). **Choice (A) is the credited response.**

Now move on to the General questions. The first General question is question 3.

Question 3 asks who cannot be in slot 1. Use your deductions to help you eliminate answer choices. You know that L and K cannot be in slot 1, and K is one of the answer choices. **Choice (D) is the credited response.**

The final General question is question 6.

Question 6 asks you to find four choices that must be false and eliminate them; the credited response will be something that could be true. Use your deductions and past work to help you eliminate choices. From your earlier deductions, eliminate choice (A), choice (B), and choice (E), as they are all indeed not true. This leaves two choices; try one. Start with choice (C). If you put K in slot 3, then J cannot be in slot 4, as that would violate rule 5. But then G also cannot go in slot 4, because it is supposed to come before K (rule 4). Choice (C) therefore isn't possible and must be false. Eliminate it and choose choice (D); there is no need to try it out. **Choice (D) is the credited response.**

LOUNGE CRAWL

Mitch is celebrating his twenty-first birthday and makes exactly one stop at each of the following six lounges—Kramer's, Onyx, Pandora, Roxanne's, Tenzin, and Zaina's—though not necessarily in that order. The order must conform to the following conditions:

Either Zaina's is visited later than Roxanne's or it is visited earlier than Pandora, but not both.

Mitch visits Onyx later than Kramer's but earlier than Roxanne's.

If Mitch visits Zaina's later than Kramer's, then he visits Pandora later than Tenzin.

Onyx is visited later than Pandora.

1. Which one of the following could be the order in which the lounges are visited, from first to last?

(A) Zaina's, Kramer's, Pandora, Onyx, Tenzin, Roxanne's
(B) Tenzin, Pandora, Kramer's, Onyx, Zaina's, Roxanne's
(C) Pandora, Kramer's, Tenzin, Onyx, Roxanne's, Zaina's
(D) Zaina's, Kramer's, Roxanne's, Pandora, Onyx, Tenzin
(E) Zaina's, Kramer's, Onyx, Roxanne's, Pandora, Tenzin

2. If the fourth lounge visited is Kramer's, then which of the following must be true?

(A) Zaina's is visited first.
(B) Pandora is visited second.
(C) Pandora is visited third.
(D) Tenzin is visited second.
(E) Onyx is visited fifth.

3. If Tenzin is visited later than Roxanne's, then which one of the following could be true?

(A) Kramer's is visited first.
(B) Pandora is visited third.
(C) Onyx is visited third.
(D) Tenzin is visited fifth.
(E) Zaina's is visited second.

4. Which one of the following CANNOT be true?

(A) Kramer's is visited first.
(B) Onyx is visited fifth.
(C) Pandora is visited third.
(D) Tenzin is visited second.
(E) Zaina's is visited fourth.

5. If Zaina's and Tenzin are visited first and third, respectively, then which one of the following must be true?

(A) Kramer's is visited second.
(B) Pandora is visited second.
(C) Roxanne's is visited fifth.
(D) Roxanne's is visited last.
(E) Pandora is visited fourth.

6. Which one of the following must be true?

(A) Kramer's is visited earlier than Tenzin.
(B) Onyx is visited earlier than Tenzin.
(C) Tenzin is visited earlier than Onyx.
(D) Pandora is visited earlier than Roxanne's.
(E) Zaina's is visited earlier than Pandora.

ANSWERS TO LOUNGE CRAWL

1. A
2. E
3. B
4. E
5. D
6. D

EXPLANATIONS TO LOUNGE CRAWL

Prepare

Ingredient Scan

Task: 1D Order
Inventory: 6 elements, 6 slots, 1:1 ratio
Rules: Some of the rules look tricky to symbolize
Questions: 6 total: 1 Grab-a-Rule, 3 Specific, 2 General
Red Flags: Rules 1 and 3 are vague and difficult to symbolize
Rank: 2

Diagram and Inventory

The setup describes an Order game. The six elements are K, O, P, R, T, and Z. Create a diagram with six columns numbered 1–6 as the core.

Symbolize the Rules and Double-Check

Rule 1: Z—P, Z—R (Z before both P and R) or R—Z, P—Z (R and P both before Z)

Rule 2: K—O—R

Rule 3: K—Z→T—P; P—T → Z—K

Rule 4: P—O

The third rule is a rare conditional ordering rule. Both the left and right halves of the conditional look like normal ordering rules. When you make the contrapositive, there's no point in writing the negation of T—P as ~T—P when that means the same thing as P—T. The first rule gives you two conditions that are mutually exclusive. In symbolizing each condition, you also need to make sure the other condition isn't happening. When Z is earlier than P, you must ensure that Z is not also later than R. If Z isn't later than R, it's earlier than R. So one scenario has Z earlier than P and R. By applying the same thought process to "Z is later than R and can't be earlier than P," you get a scenario in which Z must be later than R and P.

Don't forget to double-check your rules!

Deductions

Links: The second and fourth rules both involve O, so link them together accordingly.

```
K\
  >O—R
P/
```

This helps you see that R has three things that must come before it, so the earliest R can go is slot 4. The third rule is conditional, so it should only be used for a deduction if you know the left half applies. The first rule says that one of two scenarios will always apply. It would probably be worth testing each of these scenarios. (Whenever there are three or fewer master scenarios to your game, it's worth sketching them out to see if you can deduce anything else.) One scenario is that Z comes before P and R. The other scenario is that Z is after P and R. P and R are already in your linked chain of rules 2 and 4. Draw two copies of that chain and add where Z would fit in for each of its two scenarios.

```
   K\            K\
     >O—R   or     >O—R—Z
   P/            P/
 Z/
```

One of those two chains is the backbone of every single scenario in the game. Do they let you know that the conditional rule applies? In the second scenario, in which Z is after P and R, you can see that K comes before Z. According to rule 3, this means T must come before P. Add T to that chain where it belongs.

```
   K\
     >O—R—Z
   P/
 T/
```

The contrapositive of rule 3 is impossible to determine because T is not included in either of your master scenarios. Considering that one of these chains has 5 of the 6 elements and the other chain has all 6 elements, you are sitting pretty and do not need to worry about writing in all the slots each element cannot go in.

Spatial restrictions: The two big chains restrict almost everything.
Most restricted: Z is always going to be near the front or near the back. R has to be in the back half. O is always stuck in the middle.
Least restricted: T and K are relatively flexible.

Here is your diagram:

KOPRTZ	1	2	3	4	5	6

Assess, Act, Answer

The first question is a Grab-a-Rule so begin there.

For question 1, use the rules to eliminate answer choices. Rule 1 eliminates choice (B). Rule 2 eliminates choice (D). Rule 3 eliminates choice (C). Rule 4 eliminates choice (E). **Because choice (A) is all that remains, it is the credited response.**

Question 2 is Specific, so do that one next.

For question 2, place K in slot 4 and look for something that *must be true.* Because K is closer to the back, look at what must come after K in both of your master chains. Three things come after K in the six-piece chain, so that one can't be used. In the five-piece chain, two things come after K, so slots 5 and 6 must be O and R. All that's left is Z, P, and T to fill slots 1, 2, and 3. It seems like there is still some flexibility there. Z must come before P, so you can rule out P in slot 1 and Z in slot 3. Because the question asks for something that *must be true,* check the answers for O in slot 5 or R in slot 6. **Choice (E) is the credited response.**

	1	2	3	4	5	6	
2.	Z/T		P/T	K	O	R	Z–PT

Question 3 is Specific, so do that one next.

Question 3 offers you a condition, so symbolize it: R—T. Neither of your master chains applies: The six-piece chain doesn't allow you to put R before T, so you only need to work on the five-piece chain. R before T means that T will be the new endpoint of the chain. Because T must be in slot 6, work backward. R must be in slot 5, and O must be in slot 4. Next, there is uncertainty. Slot

3 could be K or P so enter a K/P. Look at rule 3 to see if the conditional tells you anything. You know for sure that P will come before T (since T is last), so according to rule 3, Z must be before K. That means that Z will have to be first because it has to come before K and P. Slot 2 could be K or P so enter a P/K. Because the question asks for something that *could be true,* the answer normally derives from the yet to be determined possibilities, not the fixed elements. Scan for answers relating to K or P coming second or third. **Choice (B) is the credited response.**

	1	2	3	4	5	6
3.	Z	K/P	P/K	O	R	T

Question 5 is the next Specific question, so do that one next.

For question 5, place Z in slot 1 and T in slot 3. Look at your two master chains and determine if both are applicable. With Z in slot 1, only the five-piece chain is applicable. K, P, O, and R have to fit in the four remaining slots. The end of the chain is more limited than the beginning of the chain, so work backwards. R has to come last so place it in slot 6. O must come before R in slot 5. K and P are left for slots 2 and 4 and their order doesn't seem to matter. Since the question is *must be true,* see if anything you already figured out is the answer. Scan the choices for R in slot 6 or O in slot 5. **Choice (D) says that R must be slot 6, so it is the credited response.**

	1	2	3	4	5	6
5.	Z		T		O	R

Go back to your first General question, question 4.

Question 4 asks for something that is impossible. You can eliminate anything that is possible, so check your previous work to see if any answer choices have already been covered. Otherwise, check your master chains to see if something looks impossible. Choice (A) asks if K can go in slot 1. So far it hasn't, but according to the master scenarios it looks possible. Don't eliminate, but keep moving for now. Choice (B) is possible according to the work for question 5. Eliminate it. Choice (C) is possible according to the work for questions 2 and 3. Eliminate it. Choice (D) is possible from your work for question 2. Eliminate it. Choice (E) should be correct because it is all that's left and it does seem impossible for Z to be in slot 4. In your five-piece chain, three things must come after Z, so it could not be as late as slot 4. In your six-piece chain, Z must be last. **Because choice (E) is impossible, it is the credited response.**

Question 6 is your final General question, so do it next.

Question 6 asks for something that *must be true* (something unavoidable). To eliminate each answer choice, attempt to avoid whatever scenario it describes. Choice (A) says that K must come before T. The work for question 5 allows the possibility that T would come before K. Eliminate choice (A). Choice (B) says that O must come before T. Again, question 5 contradicts this with a scenario in which T comes before O. Eliminate choice (B). Choice (C) says that T must come before O. Your work for questions 2 and 3 contradict this, so eliminate choice (C). Choice (D) says that P must come before R. So far, all the scenarios you've attempted have reflected this. Look at your master chains to see if there's reason to believe P must always come before R. Indeed, in both chains, P must come before R. **Choice (D) is the credited response.**

In the last chapter, you practiced games that asked you to put elements in order. Besides ordering, the other major task you will encounter in the Games section is grouping. A Group setup asks you to sort elements into two or more groups and does not refer to order. When a game refers to grouping and not order, the groups form the core of your diagram. Look for information in the setup or rules about how many elements may be placed in each group.

Blocks and antiblocks usually play an important role in Group games, so you should keep an eye out for these rule types. Also, in the games that follow, you'll often use *placeholders* when you know that one of only a few elements can belong to a particular space.

Many Group games have *fixed assignments*. In these games, you know exactly how many times each element can be used in a game (usually exactly once). With these games, it's fairly easy to use the group names as the core of the diagram. Those diagrams look something like this:

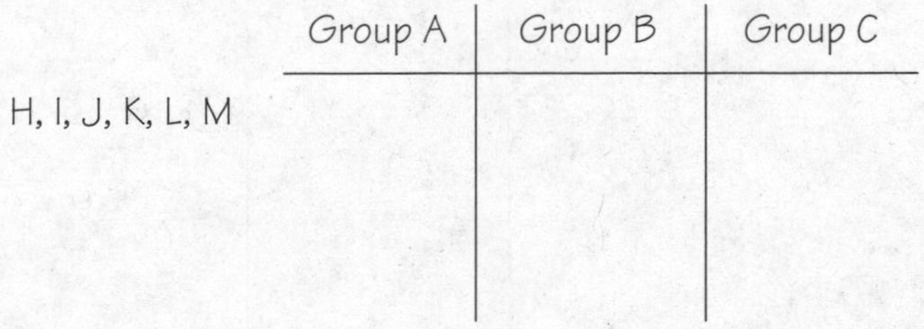

H, I, J, K, L, M

Group A	Group B	Group C

Other Group games have *variable assignments*. With these games, you usually know that elements must be used at least once, but you don't know exactly how many times they can be assigned. In these games, it can be a confusing task figuring out which list is supposed to be the group names and which list is supposed to be the element names. In Group games with variable assignments, it is often (but not always) easiest to use the list with the larger number of elements as the core of your diagram. If you have any question about the best way to set up the diagram, scan the language of the rules and create a diagram that allows you to easily symbolize those rules. Here is an example:

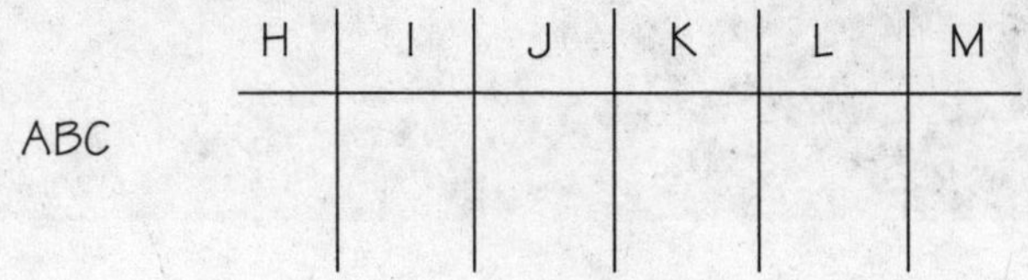

ABC

H	I	J	K	L	M

MIXED NUTS

A mixed nut packaging plant processes six varieties of nuts—almonds, brazil nuts, cashews, macadamia nuts, pecans, and walnuts—each of which is included in at least one mixture. There are three mixtures produced at this plant, and exactly one variety of nut is included in all three mixtures. The following conditions apply:

Each mixture consists of exactly three varieties of nuts.
Pecans are not used in the same mixture as walnuts.
If almonds are used in a mixture, then macadamia nuts are not.

1. Which of the following could be true?
   (A) Walnuts are in every mixture that brazil nuts are in and every mixture that cashews are in.
   (B) Brazil nuts arc in cvcry mixture that cashews are in and cashews are in every mixture that brazil nuts are in.
   (C) Cashews are in every mixture that macadamia nuts are in and every mixture that brazil nuts are in.
   (D) Walnuts are in all three mixtures.
   (E) Almonds are in all three mixtures.

2. If macadamia nuts are in every mixture that contains brazil nuts, then which of the following must be true?
   (A) Pecans are in a mixture with cashews.
   (B) Pecans are in a mixture with almonds.
   (C) Almonds are in a mixture with brazil nuts.
   (D) Brazil nuts are in a mixture with pecans.
   (E) Macadamia nuts are in a mixture with almonds.

3. Which of the following must be true?
   (A) All three mixtures contain almonds.
   (B) All three mixtures contain brazil nuts.
   (C) Brazil nuts are in a mixture with cashews.
   (D) Pecans are in a mixture with macadamia nuts.
   (E) Cashews are in a mixture with almonds.

4. If cashews are in every mixture that pecans are in and every mixture that walnuts are in, then which of the following must be true?
   (A) Brazil nuts are in every mixture containing macadamia nuts.
   (B) Almonds are in all mixtures containing pecans and all mixtures containing walnuts.
   (C) Walnuts are in exactly one mixture.
   (D) Brazil nuts are in exactly one mixture.
   (E) Cashews are in exactly three mixtures.

5. If macadamia nuts are in every mixture that brazil nuts are in, then which of the following could be true?
   (A) Pecans are in a mixture with brazil nuts.
   (B) Walnuts are in a mixture with brazil nuts.
   (C) Brazil nuts are in more than one mixture.
   (D) Macadamia nuts are in more than one mixture.
   (E) Pecans are in more than one mixture.

6. Which one of the following must be true?
   (A) No mixture contains brazil nuts, macadamia nuts, and pecans.
   (B) No mixture contains pecans, almonds, and cashews.
   (C) Either almonds or cashews are in exactly one mixture.
   (D) Either brazil nuts or macadamia nuts are in exactly one mixture.
   (E) There is some variety of nut in exactly two of the mixtures.

ANSWERS TO MIXED NUTS

1. C
2. A
3. C
4. E
5. D
6. E

EXPLANATIONS TO MIXED NUTS

Prepare

Ingredient Scan

Task: Group game with fixed assignments; assign nuts to each of 3 mixtures
Inventory: 6 elements
Rules: Typical group game rules with a simple conditional statement
Questions: 6 questions: 3 Specific, 3 General
Red Flags: There are 6 elements to be assigned to 9 spaces; repeatable elements are a red flag. Questions are worded as conditional statements, not just hypotheticals
Rank: 2/3

Diagram and Inventory

The elements are the six nuts: A, B, C, M, P, and W. The three mixtures are not identified in any way, so just make three columns numbered 1–3. The numbers here are standing in for groups; the actual order is irrelevant. All the elements must appear at least once. One important part of the setup is that one element must appear in all three groups. You should make some sort of note about one element needing to be the "All" element and keep track of any elements that cannot be the "All."

Symbolize the Rules and Double-Check

Rule 1: Three spaces per group. Draw on your diagram.

Rule 2: [P/W] (P and W in a box, struck through)

Rule 3: A⟶~M; M⟶~A

Don't forget to double-check your rules!

Deductions

Links: There are no overlapping elements in these rules, so there are no links.
Rule 2 tells you that P and W can never be in the same group. That means that neither P nor W can be the "All" element, since that would force P and W to be together at some point. Similarly, the conditional rule 3 tells you that A and M could never be together in the same group. It follows that neither A nor M could be the All without excluding the other from all three groups. Make a note: All ≠ P, W, A, M. That's a pretty extensive list when there are only 6 elements in the game. Who *can* be the All? Only C and B remain.
Spatial restrictions: The All, C or B, takes up three of the nine spaces. Among the remaining six spaces, at least one goes to C or B (whichever one wasn't the All three, and four spaces go towards allocating P, W, A, and M so that the antiblocks are not in the same group. That leaves one remaining spot in which any of the five could potentially be used again.
Most restricted: The driving force of this game will be figuring out the All, C or B.
Least restricted: C or B. Whichever one is not the All 3 could go in two groups without any antiblocks to worry about.

Here is your diagram:

	1			2			3		
ABCMPW	C/B	B/C	P/W	C/B	W/P	A/M	C/B	M/A	

Assess, Act, Answer

There is no Grab-a-Rule on this game because the first question does not show all six elements. Move on to your first Specific question.

Question 2 is your first Specific question, so do that one first.

Question 2 gives you a conditional rule: B→M. This means B cannot be the All element, because that would force M to also happen 3 times, which is not possible. Now you know for sure that C is the All. You've figured out something that must be true, so check to see if any answer choices deal with C. Choice (A) says that P will be with C. **Since C is the All, everything will be with C, so that makes choice (A) the credited response.**

Your next Specific question is question 4, so do that one next.

Question 4 gives you two conditionals: P→C and W→C. Unlike question 2, this doesn't preclude

C from being the All because it's the independent half (the right half) of these conditionals. It also doesn't necessarily guarantee C is the All, because one of the other elements can go twice. Try a scenario with C as the All and a scenario with B as the All. The scenario with B as the All is more restricted, so begin with that. You must put a PC block in one group, and a WC block in another. That fills up the first two groups. A and M must go with B in the final group which violates rule 3. Cross out that scenario to clearly mark it as a broken scenario. Since C must be the All, and the question asks for what *must be true,* check your answers for anything about C that must be true. **Choice (E) identifies C as the All, so it is the credited response.**

	1	2	3
4.	CD B/C	CW	C
	~~BPC~~	~~BWC~~	~~BAM~~

Question 5 is the next Specific question, so do it next.

For question 5, you should symbolize the new information conditionally: B→M. Does affect B's ability to be the All? Yes, because if B were in all three groups, then M would also have to be. That means, once again, that C is the All. Fill in a C for each group. At least one group must have a B, so place a B (and the M that comes with it according to this problem) into the first group. In the remaining two groups, P and W must be split up, so put a P/W placeholder in one group and a W/P placeholder in the other. One space remains in each of two groups. A still must go somewhere, so fill in one space as an A. What elements are eligible for the remaining space? That group currently has C and W/P, so all of those three cannot be eligible. B can't be used because, for this question, that requires putting M in the group as well. That leaves A and M as the only two possibilities for that final space, so put an A/M placeholder in the final space. The question asks for something possible (*could be true*). Choices (A) and (B) are not possibilities according to your diagram. B is locked in a group with C and M. Choice (C) is also not possible since B is only happening once. **Choice (D) is possible, so it is the credited response.**

	1	2	3
5.	CBM	CA P/W	C W/P A/M

Go back to your first General question, question 1.

Question 1 asks for something possible. Use your previous work to see if any of the answer choices describe a scenario you've already explored or relate to a scenario that could be easily adapted to fit the answer choice. Choice (A) says that anywhere you see B or C, you'll see W. That can't be possible because either B or C is going to be the All and W isn't allowed to be in all three groups.

Eliminate it. Choice (B) says B and C are always together. For the same reason, that is impossible. That would make them both the All. Eliminate it. Choice (C) says that anywhere you find M or B there will be a C. That is possible according to your previous work from questions 4 and 5. **Because choice (C) is possible, it is the credited response.**

Your next General question is question 3.

Question 3 asks for something that *must be true.* Your goal on *must be true* questions is to try to prove something can be avoided so that you can eliminate the answer. Choice (A) is impossible because A can't be the All. Eliminate it. Choice (B) is possible but not unavoidable. Your work for questions 4 and 5 proves that choice (B) does not have to be true. Eliminate it. Choice (C) says that in some group B and C must be together. That seems hard to avoid. Since either B or C will always be the All, and whichever is not will still have to appear at least once, they cannot avoid being together in at least one group. **Because choice (C) says something is unavoidable, it is the credited response.**

Question 6 is your final question.

Question 6 also asks for something unavoidable. Again, your task is to try to prove a counterexample to every answer choice so that you can eliminate it. Choice (A) says it's impossible for a group to consist of B, M, and P. You haven't yet seen this, but could you make it happen? If B were the All, would there be any harm in putting M and P in the same group? There shouldn't be. Eliminate it. Choice (B) says you can never get a group to consist of C, P, and A. Your work for question 5 shows this is possible. Eliminate it. Choice (C) says that either A or C must happen exactly once. To avoid this, you need to find a scenario where they both happen more than once. Again, the work for question 5 shows that it's possible that C would go three times and A would go twice. Eliminate it. Choice (D) says either B or M must go exactly once. You haven't seen this yet, but B is interchangeable in this game with C, and M is interchangeable in this game with A. So, essentially, this is the exact same statement as choice (C) and would be invalidated by a scenario in which B is the All and M happens twice. Eliminate it. Choice (E) says that one element must go exactly twice each time. From your deductions, you know this must be true. The All claims three of the nine spaces. The other five elements claim five of the remaining six spaces. That means one of those five must repeat to fill up the final space. **Because choice (E) describes an unavoidable fact, it is the credited response.**

SIX BLIND MICE

In a large house, each of six blind mice—Agatha, Boris, Edward, Helen, Jovita, and Karl—will be caught by one of three cats—Mozart, Norbert, and Olga. Each cat will catch exactly two of the mice in accordance with the following conditions:

If Agatha is caught by Olga, then Edward is caught by Mozart.

If Olga does not catch Boris, then Norbert catches Karl.

Helen cannot be caught by Mozart.

Agatha is not caught by the same cat as Boris; nor is Edward caught by the same cat as Jovita; nor is Helen caught by the same cat as Karl.

1. Which one of the following could be an accurate matching of the cats to the mice they catch?

   (A) Mozart: Boris, Jovita; Norbert: Edward, Karl; Olga: Agatha, Helen
   (B) Mozart: Boris, Karl; Norbert: Agatha, Jovita; Olga: Edward, Helen
   (C) Mozart: Edward, Jovita; Norbert: Agatha, Helen; Olga: Boris, Karl
   (D) Mozart: Edward, Karl; Norbert: Agatha, Jovita; Olga: Boris, Helen
   (E) Mozart: Agatha, Helen; Norbert: Boris, Edward; Olga: Jovita, Karl

2. If Olga catches Edward and Helen, then which one of the following must be true?

   (A) Agatha is caught by the same cat as Karl.
   (B) Jovita is caught by Mozart.
   (C) Boris is caught by the same cat as Jovita.
   (D) Agatha is caught by Norbert.
   (E) Boris is caught by Mozart.

3. If Karl is caught by Olga, which one of the following must be true?

   (A) Edward is caught by Norbert
   (B) Edward is caught by Mozart
   (C) Jovita is caught by Mozart
   (D) Helen is caught by Mozart
   (E) Agatha is caught by Mozart

4. If Mozart catches Agatha and Karl, then it must be false that Olga catches each of the following pairs of mice EXCEPT:

   (A) Boris and Helen
   (B) Edward and Jovita
   (C) Boris and Jovita
   (D) Edward and Helen
   (E) Jovita and Helen

5. Norbert CANNOT catch which of the following pairs of mice?

   (A) Boris and Helen
   (B) Agatha and Edward
   (C) Agatha and Karl
   (D) Edward and Helen
   (E) Jovita and Karl

6. Mozart CANNOT catch which one of the following pairs of mice?

   (A) Agatha and Edward
   (B) Agatha and Jovita
   (C) Boris and Jovita
   (D) Jovita and Helen
   (E) Jovita and Karl

ANSWERS TO SIX BLIND MICE

1. D
2. B
3. E
4. C
5. A
6. D

EXPLANATIONS TO SIX BLIND MICE

Prepare

Ingredient Scan

Task: Group game with fixed assignments; assign 2 mice to each of 3 cats
Inventory: 6 elements for 6 spaces, 1:1 correspondence
Rules: Normal group rules, a few antiblocks and a couple conditional statements
Questions: 6 total: 1 Grab-a-Rule, 3 Specific, 2 General
Red Flags: Conditional rules could make the game more complicated
Rank: 2/3

Diagram and Inventory

The setup describes a Group game in which 3 cats catch 2 mice each.

Symbolize the Rules and Double-Check

Rule 1: $A_O \rightarrow E_M$: $\sim E_M \rightarrow \sim A_O$

Rule 2: $\sim B_O \rightarrow K_N$; $\sim K_N \rightarrow B_O$

Rule 3: H in O or N. Write this directly on your diagram.

Rule 4: [A/B] [E/J] [H/K] (each pair boxed and struck through)

Don't forget to double-check your rules!

Deductions

Links: Rule 1 combines with the antiblocks in rule 4 to give you: $A_O \rightarrow E_M$ and $-B_O$ and $-J_M$; J_M or B_O or $-E_M \rightarrow -A_O$.
Rule 2 combines with rules 3 and 4 to give you: $-B_O$ or $A_O \rightarrow K_N$ and H_O; $-K_N$ or $H_N \rightarrow B_O$ and $-A_O$.
Spatial restrictions: Each cat catches exactly two mice, so each group has two spaces.
Most restricted: H, A, and B have the most restrictions.
Least restricted: J is only restricted by one antiblock

Here is your diagram:

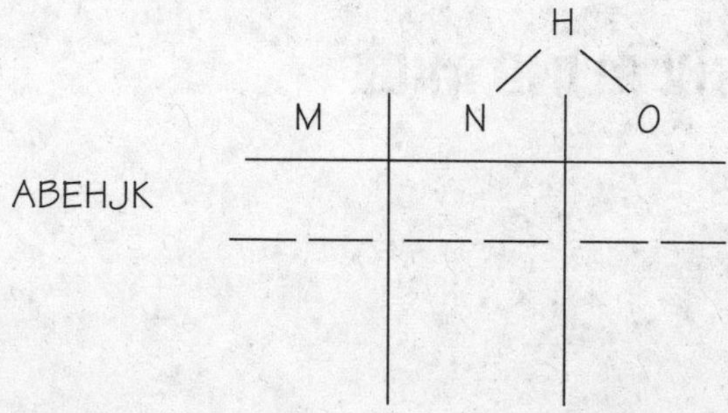

Assess, Act, Answer

Question 1 is a Grab-a-Rule question, so start there.

For question 1, use the rules to eliminate answer choices. Rule 1 eliminates choice (A), rule 2 eliminates choice (B), rule 3 eliminates choice (E), and rule 4 eliminates choice (C). **The only choice left, and therefore the credited response, is choice (D).**

Question 2 is a Specific question, so answer it next.

For question 2, place E and H in your diagram in group O. Because B is not in group O, K is in N. Also, because A and B cannot be together, one must be in group M and the other in group N. That leaves J, which must now go into group M.

Here is your diagram:

H
M N O
2. A/B J | K B/A | E H

The question asks for something that *must be true.* According to the diagram, J must be in M. **Choice (B) is the credited response.**

Question 3 is the next Specific question.

For question 3, place K in group O. From rule 2, if K is not in group N, then B is in group O. From rule 3, H must now be in group N. From rule 4, you know that because E and J cannot be together, one must be in group M and the other in group N. That leaves only one space in group M for A.

Here is your diagram:

H (N or O)

	M		N		O	
3.	E/J	A	J/E	H	K	B

Again you need something that *must be true.* From the diagram, A must be in group M. **Choice (E) is the credited response.**

Question 4 is the next Specific question.

Question 4 stipulates that A and K are in group M. From rule 2, if K is not in group N, then B is in group O and H is in group N (rule 3). E and J are interchangeable in the two remaining spaces.

Here is your diagram:

H (N or O)

	M		N		O	
4.	A	K	H	E/J	B	J/E

The question asks which pair of mice can be in group O. From the diagram, you know that it must be either B and E or B and J. **Choice (C) is the credited response.**

Since there are no more Specific questions, move on to question 5, the first General question.

Question 5 asks which pair of mice cannot be in group N. In question 2, K and A could be in group N, so eliminate choice (C). The work from question 3 eliminates choice (D). Try out the remaining choices, starting with choice (A). Place B and H in group N; rule 2 says that if B is not in group O, then K is in group N and H is in group O. Since you are looking for something that cannot be in group N and have just found it, there is no need to try out the remaining choices. **Choice (A) must be the credited response.**

Question 6 is the final General question.

Question 6 is similar to question 5, but this time you are looking for a pair of mice that cannot go into group M. Eliminate choices (A) and (B) based on the work from question 3, and eliminate choice (C) based on the work from question 2. Rule 3 tells us that H must be in group N or group O, not in group M. **Choice (D) breaks rule 3 and is therefore the credited response.**

COALITION OF CONSERVATIONISTS

The coalition of conservationists has three lobbying groups: Antlers Dominion, Bear Arms, and Creature Comfort. Each group will lobby to put exactly two of the following five animals—emus, fur seals, quolls, Tasmanian devils, and wombats—on the endangered species list. Each of these animals will be lobbied for by at least one group in the coalition in accordance with the following condition.

Bear Arms will not lobby for any animal that Creature Comfort lobbies for.

Antlers Dominion will lobby for quolls if, but only if, Bear Arms does so as well.

None of the groups will lobby for both wombats and emus.

If Bear Arms lobbies for fur seals, then both Antlers Dominion and Creature Comfort will lobby for Tasmanian devils.

1. Which one of the following could be an accurate list, for each of the lobbying groups, of the animals they will lobby for?
   (A) Antlers Dominion: quolls, fur seals; Bear Arms: emus, Tasmanian devils; Creature Comfort: quolls, wombats
   (B) Antlers Dominion: emus, wombats; Bear Arms: emus, Tasmanian devils; Creature Comfort: fur seals, quolls
   (C) Antlers Dominion: fur seals, wombats; Bear Arms: emus, Tasmanian devils; Creature Comfort: emus, quolls
   (D) Antlers Dominion: emus, fur seals; Bear Arms: emus, Tasmanian devils; Creature Comfort: quolls, wombats
   (E) Antlers Dominion: emus, Tasmanian devils; Bear Arms: emus, fur seals; Creature Comfort: quolls, wombats

2. If Tasmanian devils and wombats are both lobbied for by Creature Comfort, then which one of the following must be true?
   (A) Bear Arms lobbies for fur seals.
   (B) Bear Arms lobbies for emus
   (C) Antlers Dominion lobbies for emus.
   (D) Antlers Dominion lobbies for Tasmanian devils.
   (E) Antlers Dominion lobbies for wombats.

3. Which one of the following pairs of animals CANNOT be lobbied for by Bear Arms?
   (A) fur seals and Tasmanian devils
   (B) fur seals and wombats
   (C) quolls and wombats
   (D) emus and fur seals
   (E) emus and quolls

4. If both quolls and Tasmanian devils are lobbied for by Antlers Dominion, then which one of the following could be true?
   (A) Creature Comfort lobbies for Tasmanian devils.
   (B) Creature Comfort lobbies for quolls.
   (C) Bear Arms lobbies for fur seals.
   (D) Bear Arms lobbies for emus.
   (E) Bear Arms lobbies for Tasmanian devils.

5. If fur seals is lobbied for by two groups, which of the following could be false?
   (A) Antlers Dominion lobbies for fur seals.
   (B) Bear Arms lobbies for Tasmanian devils.
   (C) Bear Arms lobbies for wombats.
   (D) Creature Comfort lobbies for fur seals.
   (E) Creature Comfort lobbies for quolls.

6. It CANNOT be the case that both Antlers Dominion and Creature Comfort lobby for which one of the following animals?
   (A) wombats
   (B) Tasmanian devils
   (C) fur seals
   (D) emus
   (E) quolls

ANSWERS TO COALITION OF CONSERVATIONISTS

1. D
2. B
3. A
4. D
5. C
6. E

EXPLANATIONS TO COALITION OF CONSERVATIONISTS

Prepare

Ingredient Scan

Task: Group game with fixed assignments; assign 2 animals to each of 3 lobbying groups
Inventory: 5 elements total for 6 spaces, one element goes twice
Rules: A few difficult conditional rules
Questions: 6 total: 1 Grab-a-Rule, 3 Specific, 2 General
Red Flags: Not a 1:1 game
Rank: 2/3

Diagram and Inventory

The setup describes a Group game in which we must place five animals—e, f, q, t, and w—into 3 groups—A, B, and C. The setup tells you they must go in two at a time.

Symbolize the Rules and Double-Check

Rule 1: $B \neq C$

Rule 2: $A_q \leftrightarrow B_q$; $\sim B_q \leftrightarrow \sim A_q$

Rule 3: [WE with slash through it]

Rule 4: $B_f \rightarrow A_t$ and C_t; $\sim A_t$ or $\sim C_t \rightarrow \sim B_f$

Notice how the rules are relatively straightforward and easy to symbolize, but rule 2 has a little twist. The "if, but only if" phrasing means that either both A and B will have q, or they both will not have q.

Don't forget to double-check your rules!

Deductions

Links: Rules 2 and 4 both have the potential to create repeated elements (q for rule 2 and t for rule 4), so they might come into conflict.
Spatial restrictions: With only six slots for five elements, there can only ever be one repeated element at time.
Most restricted: With three rules involving B, it seems to be the most restricted aspect of the game.
Least restricted: e and w are relatively unrestricted, and they are interchangeable

Here is your diagram:

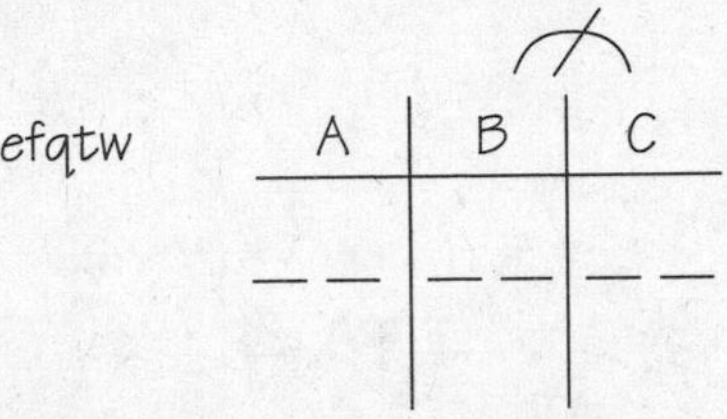

Assess, Act, Answer

Question 1 is a Grab-a-Rule question, so start there.

For question 1, use the rules to eliminate answer choices. Rule 1 eliminates choice (C), rule 2 eliminates choice (A), rule 3 eliminates choice (B), and rule 4 eliminates choice (E). **The only choice left, and therefore the credited response, is choice (D).**

Question 2 is a Specific question, so answer that one next.

For question 2, place t and w in group C. The other three elements—e, f, and q—have to be spread out between groups A and B, but you know from rule 2 that if q is in either A or B, it has to be in both, so place q in both groups A and B. That leaves you with f and e to split up between groups A and B. Rule 4 tells you that if f goes in B, then groups A and C must contain t; however, there won't be any room left in A for t, so place f in group A and e in group B.

Here is your diagram:

	A	B	C
2.	q f	q e	t w

The question asks for something that must be true, and the only possibility that must be true of the given choices is that group B must contain e. **Therefore, choice (B) is the credited response.**

Move on to question 4, the next Specific question.

For question 4, place q and t in group A. Because of rule 2, you have to place q in group B whenever q is in group A, so place q in group B. With q in two groups already, no other elements can be repeated, so you cannot place f in group B or else you'll set off rule 4; f must go into group C. The remaining two elements, w and e, must be split between groups B and C.

Here is your diagram:

	A	B	C
4.	q t	q w/e	f e/w

You're looking for something that could be true. The only choice not contradicted by the diagram is choice (D). **Choice (D) is the credited response.**

The final Specific question is question 5.

Question 5 stipulates that f is a repeated element. Only one element can be repeated, so you must use f twice without setting off the two rules that lead to repeat elements—rule 2 and rule 4. That means q must go in group C, and the two f's must go in groups A and C. Group C is full and, from rule 3, you have to split up w and e between groups A and B. The only spot left for t is in group B.

Here is your diagram:

	A	B	C
5.	f w/e	e/w t	q f

The question asks for something that could be false, so eliminate anything that your diagram shows must be true. **The only answer choice that does not have to be true is choice (C), the credited response.**

Now that the Specific questions are complete, attack the General questions, starting with question 3.

Question 3 asks for a pair of animals that cannot be together in group B. Eliminate choices (B) and (D) because you saw these combinations in the diagram for question 5. Eliminate choice (E) because you saw this combination in question 2. You will have to try out choices (A) and (C), so start with choice (A). Place f and t in group B. With f in group B, you also have to place f in groups A and C, because of rule 4. Now you have a problem—three f's—which means you have found a pair of animals that cannot be together in group B. Don't leave bad work unmarked in your diagram.

Here's how your diagram should look:

	A	B	C
3.	f _	f t	f _

No need to even try out choice (B) at this point. **Choice (A) is the credited response.**

The final question is question 6, a General question.

Question 6 asks what element groups A and C are not allowed to both contain at the same time. The only answer choice that you can eliminate right off the bat is choice (C), because you saw this possibility in question 5. You can pass over w in choice (A) and e in choice (D) as well because they are interchangeable elements; they both have the exact same restrictions so there's no way that one choice could be right and the other wrong. That leaves you with choices (B) and (E), so try them out. Place t in groups A and C. In order not to create another repeated element, you have to place q in group C (rule 2). Because of rule 3, split up w and e between groups A and B, leaving group B the only place left for f.

Here's the diagram:

	A	B	C
6.	t w/e	e/w f	t q

Because t can be in both groups A and C at the same time, choice (B) is not the credited response. **The only choice left is choice (E), the credited response.**

BY DESIGN

An interior designer chooses from exactly six types of items—artwork, bookshelves, candles, lamps, mirrors, and side tables—to decorate a house. Each type of item is used in one or more of exactly three rooms: a den, a foyer, and a parlor. The following must obtain:

Fewer items are used to decorate the parlor than the foyer.

Lamps are used to decorate the den and exactly one other room.

Candles are used to decorate more rooms than are mirrors.

Neither artwork nor bookshelves is used to decorate any room the side tables are.

A side table and exactly two other items are used to decorate the den.

Mirrors are not used to decorate any room that lamps are.

1. Which of the following could be a complete and accurate list of each of the rooms that are decorated with lamps?

(A) den
(B) parlor
(C) den, foyer
(D) parlor, foyer
(E) parlor, den, and foyer

2. If the side table is used to decorate two of the rooms, which of the following CANNOT be true?

(A) Artwork is used to decorate the foyer.
(B) Candles are used to decorate the foyer.
(C) Exactly two rooms are decorated with three items each.
(D) Exactly one room is decorated with four items.
(E) Exactly three of the rooms are decorated with three items each.

3. If there are exactly two items used to decorate the parlor, then which of the following could be a complete and accurate list of the items used to decorate the foyer?

(A) bookshelves, lamps
(B) candles, mirrors
(C) artwork, bookshelves, candles
(D) artwork, bookshelves, candles, mirrors
(E) artwork, bookshelves, candles, lamps, mirrors

4. Which of the following must be true?

(A) Mirrors are used to decorate the foyer.
(B) Lamps are used to decorate the foyer.
(C) Candles are used to decorate the den.
(D) Side tables are used to decorate exactly one room.
(E) Candles are used to decorate exactly two rooms.

5. If the number of candles used to decorate the rooms is the same as the number of side tables used to decorate the rooms, then which of the following is a pair of items that must be used to decorate the same room as each other?

(A) artwork and bookshelves
(B) artwork and lamps
(C) bookshelves and mirrors
(D) candles and mirrors
(E) candles and side tables

ANSWERS TO BY DESIGN

1. C
2. E
3. D
4. C
5. A

EXPLANATIONS TO BY DESIGN

Prepare

Ingredient Scan

Task: Group game with variable assignment of elements; assign at least 1 but up to 3 rooms to each of 6 groups.
Inventory: 3 elements total for an unspecified number of spaces within each of 6 groups
Rules: Easy rules (fixed elements) mixed with challenging rules (numerical/distributive) rules
Questions: 5 total: 3 Specific, 2 General
Red Flags: Elements can be reused an unspecified number of times, number of spaces in each group isn't fixed
Rank: 4

Diagram and Inventory

The setup describes a Group game in which we must put 6 types of items—A, B, C, L, M, and S—into 3 different rooms—p, d, and f. Each type of item must be placed in at least one room, but also may be placed in more than one room.

Symbolize the Rules and Double-Check

Rule 1: P<F
Rule 2: L=d; L=2 slots. Put this information in your diagram.
Rule 3: C>M
Rule 4: C>M
Rule 5: ddd; S=d. Put this in your diagram.
Rule 6: M≠L

Don't forget to double-check your rules!

Deductions

Links: Because the d's have all been placed, you'll need to keep track of how p's and f's are distributed in order to stay within the confines of rule 1, rule 4, and rule 6.
Spatial restrictions: Begin with what you already have in your diagram, which is that both groups L and S contain d (rules 2 and 5, respectively). From rule 6, you know that group M cannot contain d, and from rule 4 you know that neither group A nor group B can contain d. This means the third d (rule 5) must go in group C. You have several rules dealing with the number of elements per group, so examine those next. Since group L must have 2 spaces (rule 2) and cannot share elements with group M (rule 6), you know for certain that group M has exactly one space. From rule 3, you now know that group C must have at least 2 spaces, though it could also have three. In addition, you know from rule 4 that group S cannot share elements with either group A or group B. This means that each of these groups can have a maximum of 2 spaces each and a minimum of 1 space each, as per the setup. Note all this distribution information in your diagram.
Most restricted: Groups A and B are closely tied to group S; if group S has two elements, then groups A and B have only one apiece.
Least restricted: Group C is the least restricted, as it already contains d and can have either p or f or both.

Here is your diagram:

1/2 ~d A	1/2 ~d B	2/3 C	L	≠ ~d M	1/2 S
_	_	d _	d _	_	d

Assess, Act, Answer

Since there is no Grab-a-Rule question, begin with the Specific questions. Question 2 is the first Specific question, so start with that one.

For question 2, group S must have two spaces, so this means groups A and B each have one (rule 4 and earlier deductions). Since you need to have more f's than p's (rule 1), put f in groups A and B and p in group S. You also know that either p or f will be in group L and group M; since you'll only have one of each, it doesn't matter which one goes in which group. Finally, either f or f and p, but not just p, can be added to group C; adding only p would violate rule 1. The question asks for something that must be false. The only choice that contradicts your diagram is choice (E). **Choice (E) is the credited response.**

2.

1/2 ~d A	1/2 ~d B	2/3 C	L	≠ ~d M	1/2 S
f	f	d f(p)	d f/p	p/f	d p

The next Specific question is question 3, so move on to that one.

Question 3 tells you that you can only have 2 p's, and from rule 6 and your deductions you know that one of those p's must go in either group L or group M, though it doesn't matter which one specifically. This means that in order to accommodate rule 4, you must place the other p in group S and f's in groups A, B, and C. The question asks you to identify which choice contains a complete list of all the groups that could contain f at the same time. The only one that matches what you have in your diagram is choice (D). Note that choice (E) violates rule 6; you can have f in either group L or group M, but not both at once. **Choice (D) is the credited response.**

3.

1/2 ~d A	1/2 ~d B	2/3 C	L	≠ ~d M	1/2 S
f	f	d f	d p/f	f/p	dp

The final Specific question is question 5, so do that one next. For question 5, the number of spaces in groups C and S must be the same; from your earlier deductions, this means you must have exactly 2 spaces in both groups. Therefore groups A and B will each have only one space (rule 4 and prior deductions). Because you must have more f's than p's (rule 1), and because you already have one p and one f in groups L and M, place f in groups A, B, and p in group S. To prevent the number of p's and f's from being equal, place f in group C as well. The question asks which choice contains items that must be in the same room as each other. The only choice that must be true according to your diagram is choice (A). **Choice (A) is the credited response.**

5.

1/2 ~d A	1/2 ~d B	2/3 C	L	≠ ~d M	1/2 S
f	f	d f	d p/f	f/p	d p

Now move on to the General questions. The first General question is question 1.

Question 1 asks for a possible list of elements found in group L. From your deductions you know that group L must contain d and has only two spaces. Only answer choice (C) fits both these criteria. **Choice (C) is the credited response.**

Move on to the final General question, which is question 4.

Question 4 asks for something that must be true. Use your deductions to eliminate answer choices. While all the other choices are possibilities that could be true, only choice (C) must be true in every instance. **Choice (C) is the credited response.**

A-HUNTING WE WILL GO

In one week, an elected official goes hunting with exactly one representative from each of 6 industries—agriculture, banking, construction, oil, steel, and tobacco. The elected official goes hunting with exactly two representatives on Monday, two on Tuesday and two on Wednesday, in accordance with the following conditions:

The construction representative goes hunting on the same day as the steel representative.

The tobacco representative does not go hunting on the same day as the oil representative.

If the agriculture representative goes hunting on Monday, then the tobacco representative goes hunting on Tuesday.

If the banking representative goes hunting on Wednesday, then the oil representative goes hunting on Tuesday.

1. Which one of the following could be a complete and accurate matching of representatives to the day they go hunting with the elected official?

(A) Monday: the tobacco representative, the construction representative
Tuesday: the oil representative, the steel representative
Wednesday: the agriculture representative, the banking representative

(B) Monday: the agriculture representative, the banking representative
Tuesday: the tobacco representative, the oil representative
Wednesday: the construction representative, the steel representative

(C) Monday: the tobacco representative, the agriculture representative
Tuesday: the construction representative, the steel representative
Wednesday: the oil representative, the banking representative

(D) Monday: the construction representative, the steel representative
Tuesday: the oil representative, the agriculture representative
Wednesday: the tobacco representative, the banking representative

(E) Monday: the construction representative, the steel representative
Tuesday: the tobacco representative, the agriculture representative
Wednesday: the oil representative, the banking representative

2. Which one of the following must be true?

(A) The agriculture representative does not go hunting on the same day as the tobacco representative.
(B) The banking representative does not go hunting on the same day as the oil representative.
(C) The agriculture representative does not go hunting on the same day as the banking representative.
(D) The tobacco representative does not go hunting on the same day as the banking representative.
(E) The agriculture representative does not go hunting on the same day as the oil representative.

3. If the tobacco representative goes hunting on the same day as the agriculture representative, then which of the following must be true?

(A) The oil representative goes hunting on Monday.
(B) The agriculture representative goes hunting on Tuesday.
(C) The construction representative goes hunting on Monday.
(D) The banking representative does not go hunting on Wednesday.
(E) The steel representative does not go hunting on Wednesday.

4. If the banking representative goes hunting the day after the oil representative, then which of the following CANNOT be true?

(A) The oil representative goes hunting on Monday.
(B) The agriculture representative goes hunting on Monday.
(C) The steel representative goes hunting on Tuesday.
(D) The tobacco representative goes hunting on Tuesday.
(E) The steel representative goes hunting on Wednesday.

5. If the steel representative goes hunting the day after the tobacco representative, then which one of the following CANNOT go hunting on Tuesday?

(A) the steel representative
(B) the oil representative
(C) the construction representative
(D) the banking representative
(E) the agriculture representative

ANSWERS TO A-HUNTING WE WILL GO

1. D
2. C
3. D
4. C
5. B

EXPLANATIONS TO A-HUNTING WE WILL GO

Prepare

Ingredient Scan

Task: Group game with fixed assignments, assign 2 people to each of 3 days
Inventory: 6 elements, 6 spaces, 1:1 ratio
Rules: Typical for a group game. There are a few elements that must go together, a few elements that can't go together, and a couple conditionals.
Questions: 6 questions: 1 Grab-a-Rule, 4 Specific, 1 General
Red Flags: The conditional rules may be awkward to symbolize or use
Rank: 2

Diagram and Inventory

Make three columns: Mon, Tues, and Wed. Put two spaces in each column as placeholders. The elements are A, B, C, O, T, and S.

Symbolize the Rules and Double-Check

Rule 1: [CS]

Rule 2: [T/O] (T and O crossed out: not together)

Rule 3: $A_M \rightarrow T_T$ $\sim T_T \rightarrow \sim A_M$

Rule 4: $B_W \rightarrow O_T$ $\sim O_T \rightarrow \sim B_W$

In this game you could rewrite the contrapositive to rule 3 without the negation, as $T_{M \text{ or }} T_W \rightarrow A_{T \text{ or }} A_W$. The same logic applies to rule 4's contrapositive.

Don't forget to double-check your rules!

Deductions

Links: O and T are not allowed to be together, and they are each involved in their own conditional rules. That lends itself to deductions down the line whenever either conditional rule applies.
Spatial restrictions: Rule 1 is a CS block. In any game that has a block or chunk of some sort, consider how many different places it could go. In this game, the CS block could go Monday, Tuesday, or Wednesday. You can write three master scenarios, one for each CS position, to see if any other deductions are applicable. For each scenario, once CS fills up one day, there are only two days left. Since rule 2 forces you to split up T and O, you should put a T/O placeholder into one of the open days and an O/T placeholder in the other. By the same token, you may realize that A and B will always be split up into the remaining two spaces. This means that A and B will never be in a group together. You can add an AB antiblock to your rules. Do either of the conditional rules apply? Looking at them as written, it is impossible to apply without knowing the whereabouts of A or B. However, using the contrapositives, you can apply them. The contrapositive to rule 3 says "if T is not on Tuesday" (in other words, if T is on Monday or Wednesday). In scenario 2, in which the CS block fills Tuesday, you know this condition holds. That means A can't go on Monday, which only leaves A to Wednesday. The final letter, B, must go in the remaining spot in Monday. The contrapositive to rule 4 says "if O is not on Tuesday." It would also apply to scenario 2 in which the CS block fills Tuesday. It ends up telling you what you already know: B can't go on Wednesday and must go on Monday.
Most restricted: The CS block will always occupy one day. The TO antiblock will have to be split up between the remaining two groups, and B and A will probably be frequently determined by the conditionals.
Least restricted: All of the elements could potentially be on any of the three days, but they're all inextricably tied to each other.

Here is your diagram:

ABCOTS

	Mon		Tues		Wed	
i.	C	S	T/O		O/T	
ii.	T/O	B	C	S	O/T	A
iii.	T/O		O/T		C	S

Assess, Act, Answer

Question 1 is a Grab-a-Rule so do that one first.

For question 1, use the rules to eliminate answer choices. Rule 1 eliminates choice (A). Rule 2 eliminates choice (B). Rule 3 eliminates choice (C). Rule 4 eliminates choice (E). **Because choice (D) is all that remains, it is the credited response.**

Question 3 is the first Specific question, so do that one next.

Question 3 forces you to use a TA block. Coupled with the CS block you already have, that means that the other day will be filled by OB. How do those blocks relate to rules 3 and 4 since rule 3 deals with A and T, and rule 4 deals with O and B? Rule 3 would divide up the TA block if it ever went on Monday, so it must be true that TA never goes on Monday. Since the question asks what *must be true*, check the answers to see if anything says T or A can't go on Monday. No luck. Moving on, rule 4 would divide up the OB block if it ever went on Wednesday, so OB cannot go on Wednesday. Do any answers talk about O or B not being able to go on Wednesday? **Yes, choice (D) says that, so it is the credited response.**

Had this initial observation eluded you, you could also try placing the TA block into each of the original three CS scenarios. You would make three rows for question 4, one for each placement of CS (Monday, Tuesday, and Wednesday). For each scenario, you would use the conditionals to determine where the OB and TA blocks should go.

	Mon	Tues	Wed	
4.	CS	BO	TA	TA
	BO	TA	CS	
	BO	CS	TA	

Once you had fleshed out the three possibilities, you would have found that only choice (D) applied to all three.

Question 4 is the next Specific question, so do that one next.

Question 4 states that O must come the day before B. How many different ways could this happen? O on Monday and B on Tuesday, or O on Tuesday and B on Wednesday. Make two rows for question 5, one with each scenario. In the first one, CS will have to be in Wednesday. In the second scenario CS will have to be in Monday. In the first scenario, A and T are left and are interchangeable in the remaining two spaces, so put an A/T placeholder in one and a T/A placeholder in the other. In the second scenario, B and O remain and are interchangeable, so add B/O and O/B placeholders to the remaining spaces.

	Mon	Tues	Wed
6.	BT	CS	OA
	CS A/B	T B/A	CS

The answer asks for something impossible, so eliminate any answer choices that are possible. **Only choice (C) describes something impossible, so it is the credited response.**

Question 5 is the next Specific question, so do that one next.

Question 5 is similar to question 5, forcing two possible scenarios: T on Monday/S on Tuesday and T on Tuesday/S on Wednesday. Draw a row for each scenario. S is part of the CS block so fill that in for each scenario. O cannot go with T, so put O on whatever day remains open for each scenario. Check the conditionals to determine where A and B can go for each scenario. For the first scenario, if A goes on Monday, rule 3 will be broken because T can't go on Tuesday in this scenario. That means A must go on Wednesday, and B must go in Monday. For the second scenario, neither conditional rule presents any issues, so B and A are interchangeable on Monday and Tuesday. Put in B/A and A/B placeholders. The question asks for an element that cannot go on Tuesday. Look at who can go on Tuesday and eliminate those choices. C, S, T, B, and A are all shown as possibilities for Tuesday. That means only O cannot go on Tuesday. **Choice (B) is the credited response.**

	Mon	Tues	Wed
5.	BT	CS	OA
	CS A/B	T B/A	CS

Question 2, the General question, is the only question remaining.

Question 2 asks for something that *must be true,* so any choice that you can prove is avoidable should be eliminated. Choice (A) says that A can never go with T. The work for question 4 proves A and T can go together, so eliminate choice (A). Question 4 eliminates choice (B) as well, since it shows that B and O can go together. Choice (C) says that A can never go with B. This seems to be true according to all your previous work. Also, by looking at your three master scenarios, you see that CS always fills a day, rule 2 requires that O and T be split up into the remaining two days, and therefore, there is never room for A and B to be together. **Since choice (C) is unavoidable, it is the credited response.**

DANCE TEACHERS

The five dance teachers at Northcliff Studio—Indra, Jean, Klara, Marcy, and Porter—each teach one or more of the following classes: bachata, capoeira, dilan, and the electric slide. The teachers do not teach any other classes. The assignment of teachers to classes adheres to the following conditions:

Porter and Jean have no classes in common.
Only two teachers teach capoeira.
Marcy teaches more classes than Klara teachers.
Klara teaches only dilan and the electric slide.
Indra teaches more classes than anyone at the studio.
Marcy teaches capoeira.

1. If only one of the five teachers teaches bachata, then which one of the following could be true?
   (A) Klara and Jean teach exactly two of the same types of dance.
   (B) Marcy and Jean teach exactly two of the same types of dance.
   (C) Klara and Marcy teach exactly two of the same types of dance.
   (D) Indra and Porter teach exactly two of the same types of dance.
   (E) Jean and Indra teach exactly two of the same types of dance.

2. Which one of the following must be true?
   (A) Klara and Jean teach exactly the same number of dances.
   (B) Jean and Porter teach exactly the same number of dances.
   (C) Marcy teaches at least one more type of dance than Porter.
   (D) Porter teaches at least one more type of dance than Klara.
   (E) Indra teaches exactly two more types of dance than Marcy.

3. If bachata is taught by both Jean and Marcy, then which of the following could be true?
   (A) Klara and Jean have two types of dance classes in common.
   (B) Marcy and Porter have two types of dance classes in common.
   (C) Marcy and Klara have no dance classes in common.
   (D) Klara and Porter have no dance classes in common.
   (E) Marcy and Porter have no dance classes in common.

4. If Jean and exactly two other teachers teach dilan, then which one of the following must be true?
   (A) Marcy and Porter teach no types of dance in common.
   (B) Marcy and Jean teach at least one type of dance class in common.
   (C) Marcy and Porter teach at least one type of one dance class in common.
   (D) Klara and Porter teach at least one type of dance class in common.
   (E) Klara and Jean teach at least two types of dance classes in common.

5. Which of the following could be true?
   (A) Marcy teaches bachata and dilan but not capoeira or electric slide.
   (B) Indra teaches bachata, dilan and capoeira, but not electric slide.
   (C) Klara teaches capoeira but not electric slide or dilan.
   (D) Porter teaches bachata and electric slide but neither dilan nor capoeira.
   (E) Jean teaches bachata, dilan, and electric slide but not capoeira.

6. Which one of the following could be true?
   (A) Only Marcy, Klara, and Jean teach the electric slide.
   (B) Only Marcy and Jean teach capoeira.
   (C) Only Klara and Indra teach dilan.
   (D) Marcy, Indra, and Porter all teach capoeira.
   (E) Marcy, Jean, and Porter all teach bachata.

ANSWERS TO DANCE TEACHERS

1. C
2. C
3. E
4. C
5. D
6. C

EXPLANATIONS TO DANCE TEACHERS

Prepare

Ingredient Scan

Task: Group game with variable assignments; assign at least 1 but up to 4 classes to each of 5 dance teachers
Inventory: 4 elements total for an unspecified number of spaces within each of 5 groups
Rules: Easy rules (fixed elements) mixed with challenging rules (numerical/distributive) rules
Questions: 6 total: 3 Specific, 3 General
Red Flags: Elements can be reused an unspecified number of times, number of spaces in each group isn't fixed
Rank: 2/3

Diagram and Inventory

The setup describes a Group game in which you must distribute four types of dance classes—b, c, d, and e—into 5 groups—I, J, K, M, and P. There is no fixed number of spaces given for each group.

Symbolize the Rules and Double-Check

Rule 1: P≠J
Rule 2: *exactly two c's*
Rule 3: M>K
Rule 4: K=*d*, *e only*. Put directly into your diagram.
Rule 5: *I greatest number of classes*
Rule 6: M=*c*. Put directly into your diagram.

Don't forget to double-check your rules!

Deductions

Links: Since groups J and P cannot share elements and since neither can have c in it, anything that limits the number of times b, d, or e can be used creates a possibility for conflict.
Spatial restrictions: Start with group K, which can only have d and e (rule 4). This means it can't have b and c. Because rule 3 states that M must teach more than K, this means group M can have three or four spaces. However, because rule 5 says I must teach the greatest number of classes, group I must have four spaces and group M must have three. Group I is now filled with b, c, d, and e, so you're done with it. Group M now has c (rule 6) and two more spaces. This means c is no longer an option; you only had two to use (rule 2) and they are in groups I and M. Write ~c above groups J and P.
Groups J and P cannot have the same type of elements, but each must have at least one element.
Most restricted: Group M must have exactly two more elements added to it.
Least restricted: b is unrestricted and is never mentioned in the rules.

Here is your diagram:

bcde

I	~c J	~b ~c K	M	~c P
bcde		de	c_ _	

Assess, Act, Answer

Question 1 is a Specific question, so begin there.

Question 1 tells you that b is only used once, and from your deductions you know that b must be in group I. This means that group M must have both d and e, while groups J and P each have one of either d or e.

	I	~c J	~b ~c K	M	~c P
1.	bcde	d/e	de	cde	e/d

The question asks for what could be true; the only choice not contradicted by the diagram is choice (C). **Choice (C) is the credited response.**

The next Specific question is question 3.

For question 3, place b in both group M and group J. This means the final space in group M will be either d or e. For group P, either d or e, or possibly both, are options. Group J has b for certain, but could also contain either d or e, depending on what is placed into group P. Since you don't know exactly where else d and e may show up, you can't place them on the diagram beyond groups M and P, but it is useful to know your options in order to eliminate answer choices.

Here is your diagram:

		~c	~b ~c		~c
	I	J	K	M	P
3.	bcde	b	de	cb d/e	d/e

The question asks for something that *could be true.* The only choice that could be true based on your diagram is choice (E). **Choice (E) is the credited response.**

The final Specific question is question 4.

For question 4, place d into group J. This means that the remaining two spaces in group M will be taken by b and e. Group P must have at least one of b or e, since all groups must have at least one element. It is also possible to place b into group J along with d, though only d is certain.

Here is your diagram:

		~c	~b ~c		~c
	I	J	K	M	P
4.	bcde	d	de	cbe	(~d)

The question asks for something that *must be true.* Based on your diagram, only choice (C) must be true in all cases; group P must contain at least one of b or e, both of which are in group M. **Choice (C) is the credited response.**

Now move on to the General questions. Start with question 2.

Question 2 asks what must be true in all instances. Use your deductions as well as past work to eliminate choices. You already know from your deductions that group I has four elements while group M has three. Eliminate choice (E). If you look back at your work from question 1, you'll see that both choice (A) and choice (D) can be eliminated because they were not true in that case. Choice (B) is eliminated by your work for both questions 3 and 4; in each case, it was possible for both group K and group P to each have two elements. That leaves choice (C) as the only remaining answer. **Choice (C) is the credited response.**

The next General question is question 5.

Question 5 asks for something that *could be true*. Go through the answer choices, using your deductions and past work to eliminate whatever you can. Choice (A) can be ruled out because it violates rule 6. Choice (B) can be eliminated based on your deduction that group I contains all four elements. Choice (C) is out because it violates rule 4. Choice (D) is actually supported by the work you did for question 4, so this looks like your answer. Since you know choice (D) is possible, there's no need to check choice (E). **Choice (D) is the credited response.**

The final General question is question 6.

Question 6 also asks for something that *could be true*, so your approach should be the same as that for question 5—using deductions and past work to eliminate answer choices. Your deductions eliminate choice (A) and choice (B), since group I must contain all four elements. Choice (D) violates rule 2 and choice (E) violates rule 1. **The only choice left, and therefore the credited response, is choice (C).**

Sometimes a setup asks you to put elements in order, but a basic Order diagram isn't sufficient to represent all of the aspects of the game. Here are a few situations where you might need to adjust your diagram:

- if you have to put elements in order and into groups
- if you have to represent a spatial relationship beyond a linear relationship
- if you can place more than one element in each slot

In these cases, you will need another level to your diagram. We call games with these features two-dimensional, or 2-D, games because we have to represent the game in two dimensions by adding rows or tiers. You will have to make some adjustments in order to visually represent all the information, but the basic approach remains the same.

Here are a few examples of 2-D Order game diagrams:

	M	T	W	R	F
ABCDE					
X/Y					

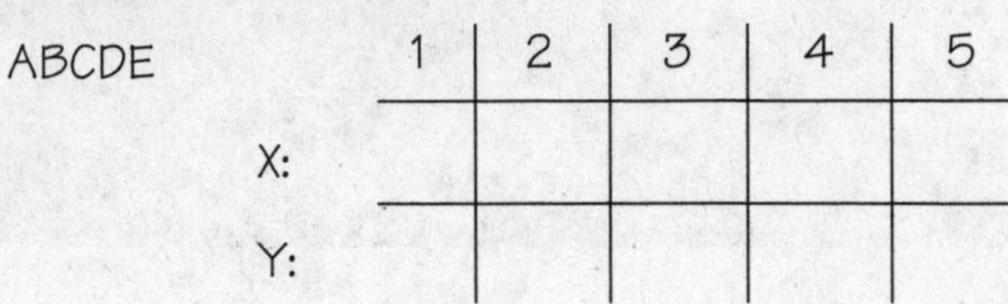

HIJ					
	1	3	5	7	9
	2	4	6	8	10

One feature you'll notice right away is that it is not as easy to simply build another row into your diagram. You will find that sometimes you'll have to rewrite your main diagram several times, so continue to think about the best ways to use your space. Remember, though, as you've seen already, you learn from previous work, so don't even think about erasing work from your diagrams.

STILL LIFE

A painter is planning to create three different still-life paintings. He will paint only one still life at a time, and he must complete each painting before beginning a new one. He will select one of three tablecloth colors—sapphire, umber, and vermilion—for the background. Each painting will contain exactly two of six fruits—durian, fig, guava, jackfruit, kumquat, and lychee—to be placed on the tablecloth. Each tablecloth and each fruit must be used in exactly one painting. The painter must adhere to the following conditions:

The kumquat must be selected with the umber tablecloth.
The lychee is selected for the second still life.
The durian and the jackfruit are not chosen for the same painting.
The still life containing the jackfruit is painted earlier than the still life containing the fig.
The umber tablecloth is used in an earlier painting than is the vermilion tablecloth.

1. Which one of the following could be an accurate list of the fruits selected for each of the three paintings?
   (A) first painting: jackfruit and kumquat
   second painting: guava and lychee
   third painting: durian and fig
   (B) first painting: durian and jackfruit
   second painting: kumquat and lychee
   third painting: fig and guava
   (C) first painting: fig and kumquat
   second painting: jackfruit and lychee
   third painting: durian and guava
   (D) first painting: guava and jackfruit
   second painting: fig and lychee
   third painting: durian and kumquat
   (E) first painting: durian and guava
   second painting: jackfruit and kumquat
   third painting: fig and lychee

2. If the jackfruit is chosen with the vermilion tablecloth, which of the following could be true?
   (A) The jackfruit is painted first.
   (B) The guava is painted first.
   (C) The durian is painted second.
   (D) The fig is painted second.
   (E) The kumquat is painted second.

3. If the guava is selected for the second painting, which one of the following could be true?
   (A) The durian is selected with the umber tablecloth.
   (B) The lychee is selected with the umber tablecloth.
   (C) The guava is selected with the umber tablecloth.
   (D) The jackfruit is selected with the vermilion tablecloth.
   (E) The fig is selected with the sapphire tablecloth.

4. The kumquat could be paired with any one of the following fruits EXCEPT:
   (A) durian
   (B) fig
   (C) guava
   (D) jackfruit
   (E) lychee

5. If the durian is chosen for a still life painted earlier than the one containing the vermilion tablecloth, then which of the following statements could be true?
   (A) The sapphire tablecloth is painted first.
   (B) The guava is painted first.
   (C) The jackfruit is painted first.
   (D) The umber tablecloth is painted second.
   (E) The fig is painted second.

6. If the jackfruit and the lychee are chosen for the same still life, then for how many fruits can it be determined exactly for which paintings they will be selected?
   (A) two
   (B) three
   (C) four
   (D) five
   (E) six

ANSWERS TO STILL LIFE

1. A
2. B
3. E
4. B
5. C
6. C

EXPLANATIONS TO STILL LIFE

Prepare

Ingredient Scan

Task: 2-D Order game, combining order and groups; assign one tablecloth and two fruits to three different paintings created one after the other
Inventory: Three tablecloths and six fruits
Rules: Block and range clues with vertical and horizontal relationships
Questions: 6 total: 1 Grab-a-Rule, 4 Specific, 1 General
Red Flags: Proper setup of the diagram is crucial to working this game efficiently
Rank: 2/3

Diagram and Inventory

The setup describes an Order game in which you must assign fruits and tablecloths to paintings. The setup specifically states that each painting is assigned two fruits and one tablecloth. The best way to represent this is in a two-tiered diagram with one tier for fruit and one tier for tablecloths.

Symbolize the Rules and Double-Check

Rule 1: [K over U, boxed]

Rule 2: Enter this information directly into the diagram.

Rule 3: [DJ boxed, struck through]

Rule 4: J—F

Rule 5: U—V

Don't forget to double-check your rules!

Deductions

Links: Rules 1 and 5 can and should be combined to make a single rule:

[K/U] – V

This now means that K cannot go with painting 3.
Spatial restrictions: With range clues, keep track of where elements cannot go. Neither F nor V can go with painting 1, and neither J nor U can go with painting 3.
Most restricted: J and K are both quite restricted.
Least restricted: G and S have no restrictions at all.

Here is your diagram:

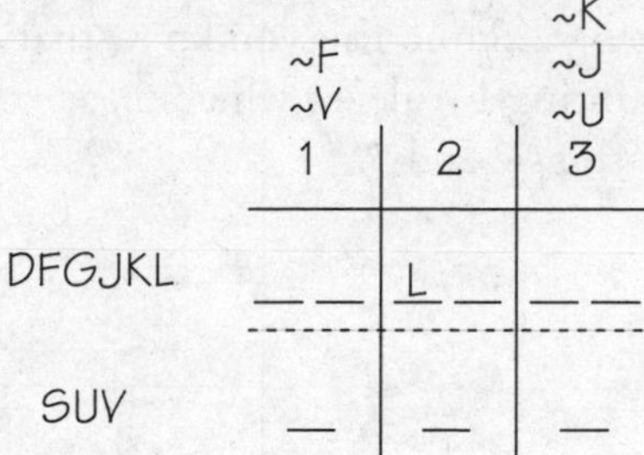

Assess, Act, Answer

Question 1 is a Grab-a-Rule question, so start there.

For question 1 use the rules to eliminate answer choices. Rule 2 eliminates choice (E), rule 3 eliminates choice (B), rule 4 eliminates choice (C), and rules 1 and 5 eliminate choice (D). **The only choice left, and therefore the credited response, is choice (A).**

Question 2 is a Specific question, so answer that one next.

For question 2, J has to be with V. Because V cannot be in painting 1, now J cannot be there either. You also already know that J cannot be in painting 3, so that means that J, and therefore V, must be in painting 2. According to rule 5, U is now in painting 1, and so is K (rule 1). The only tablecloth left is S, so put that in painting 3. The remaining fruit is interchangeable.

Here is your diagram:

	~F ~V 1	2	~K ~J ~U 3
2.	K _	L J	_ _
	U	V	S

The question asks for something that *could be true.* The only possibility that could be true out of these choices is that G could be in painting 1. **Choice (B) is the credited response.**

Move on to question 3, the next Specific question.

Question 3 places G in painting 2. From this you know that K and U must be in painting 1 (rules 1 and 5). J must also be in painting 1 (rule 4,) which means that D and F are in painting 3. S and V are interchangeable in paintings 2 and 3.

Here is your diagram:

	~F ~V 1	2	~K ~J ~U 3
3.	K J	L G	E D
	U	S/V	V/S

The question asks for what can be true. The only possibility that can be true based on the diagram is that F can be with S. **Choice (E) is the credited response.**

The next Specific question is question 5.

For question 5, you are given the rule that D—V. Remember to keep your pencil moving. If you're not sure where to start, pick something! If you try K and U in painting 2, then V is in painting 3 (rule 5) and J is in painting 1 (rule 4). D cannot be in painting 3 if it is to be in an earlier painting than V, so the only place for it is painting 1, but that doesn't work because of rule 3. What have you learned? That K and U must be in painting 1. Since neither J nor D can be in painting 3, they become interchangeable in paintings 1 and 2, and that leaves F and G for painting 3.

Here is your diagram:

	~F ~V 1	2	~K ~J ~U 3
5.	D/J K	L J/D	F G
	U	S/V	V/S

The question asks for something that *could be true*. You can see from the diagram that J could be in painting 1. **This makes choice (C) the credited response.**

Question 6 is the final Specific question.

For question 6 place J in painting 2 with L. From this you know that F must be in painting 3 (rule 4) and that K and U must be in painting 1 (rules 1 and 5). G and D are interchangeable, as are S and V.

Here is your diagram:

	~F ~V 1	2	~K ~J ~U 3
6.	K D/G	L U	F G/D
	—	—	—

The question asks how many fruits can be placed for certain. You know K, L, J, and F. **That means choice (C) is the credited response.**

Now that the Specific questions are complete, attack question 4 since it is a General question.

Question 4 asks what K cannot be paired with. Eliminate choice (A) because you saw K with D in questions 2 and 5. Eliminate choice (C) since K could be paired with G in question 2, and eliminate choice (D) because K was paired with J in questions 1 and 3. You are left with choices (B) and (E) to try. Start with choice (B). According to the original diagram, F cannot be in painting 1, and K cannot be in painting 3. Since L is already in painting 2, there is no painting for K and F to be in together. Since this does not work, there is no need to try choice (E). **Choice (B) is the credited response.**

WALRUS TRAINING

Mr. Mustard works at Rigby's Aquarium every day, Monday through Friday. He trains six walruses: Anna, Bill, Kite, Lucy, Rocky, and Sadie. Three of them—Anna, Kite, and Rocky—are veteran performers. Two walruses are trained each day, and each of them is trained at least once during the week according to the following:

At least one veteran performer is trained each day.

Sadie is not trained on any day before the first day that Rocky is trained that week.

Lucy is trained both Tuesday and Wednesday.

Any day on which Bill is trained is the first day during that week that some other walrus is trained.

Of the days Kite is trained during the week, at least two are consecutive.

1. Which one of the following could be an accurate training schedule for the walruses?
   (A) Monday: Anna, Bill; Tuesday: Anna, Lucy; Wednesday: Kite, Lucy; Thursday: Kite, Sadie; Friday: Bill, Rocky
   (B) Monday: Rocky, Sadie; Tuesday: Lucy, Rocky; Wednesday: Kite, Lucy; Thursday: Anna, Bill; Friday: Kite, Rocky
   (C) Monday: Anna, Bill; Tuesday: Kite, Lucy; Wednesday: Kite, Rocky; Thursday: Bill, Rocky; Friday: Anna, Sadie
   (D) Monday: Anna, Bill; Tuesday: Kite, Lucy; Wednesday: Kite, Lucy; Thursday: Bill, Rocky; Friday: Rocky, Sadie
   (E) Monday: Rocky, Sadie; Tuesday: Lucy, Rocky; Wednesday Kite, Lucy; Thursday: Bill, Kite; Friday: Anna, Sadie

2. Which of the following could be true?
   (A) Lucy and Bill are trained on Tuesday.
   (B) Bill is trained on Monday, Wednesday, and Friday.
   (C) Kite is trained on Wednesday with Lucy and on Thursday with Bill.
   (D) Kite is trained on Wednesday and Friday only.
   (E) Sadie is trained on Monday, and Rocky is trained on Tuesday.

3. If Bill and Rocky are trained on Thursday, one of the walruses trained on Friday must be
   (A) Rocky
   (B) Sadie
   (C) Bill
   (D) Kite
   (E) Anna

4. Each of the following could be the pair of walruses trained on Monday EXCEPT:
   (A) Bill and Rocky
   (B) Kite and Lucy
   (C) Anna and Kite
   (D) Anna and Sadie
   (E) Rocky and Sadie

5. If exactly one veteran performer is trained each day, which of the following would determine exactly when each of the remaining walruses is trained?
   (A) Anna and Bill are trained on Monday.
   (B) Rocky and Sadie are trained on Friday.
   (C) Anna is trained on Monday and Thursday.
   (D) Kite is trained Monday and Thursday.
   (E) Kite is trained Monday and Friday.

6. Each of the following could be true EXCEPT:
   (A) Bill and Rocky are trained on Friday.
   (B) Rocky is trained on Monday and on Friday.
   (C) Anna and Bill are trained on Thursday.
   (D) Sadie is trained on Monday and Friday.
   (E) Anna is trained on Monday and Tuesday.

ANSWERS TO WALRUS TRAINING

1. D
2. E
3. B
4. D
5. C
6. A

EXPLANATIONS TO WALRUS TRAINING

Prepare

Ingredient Scan

Task: 2-D Order game; assign 2 per day, Monday through Friday

Inventory: 6 elements for a total of 10 slots, two element types; every element must be used at least once

Rules: A couple of tricky ordering rules that hinge on the first time an element shows up

Questions: 6 total: 1 Grab-a-Rule, 1 Specific, 3 General, 1 Complex

Red Flags: Not a 1:1 ratio. Elements can be used multiple times, which makes the ordering rules more complicated to work with.

Rank: 4

Diagram and Inventory

The setup describes a two-tiered Order game in which six walruses—a, b, k, l, r, and s—must be trained over five days, Monday through Friday, two per day. Three of the walruses are veterans—A, K, and R. Each walrus must be trained at least once but can be trained on multiple days as well.

Symbolize the Rules and Double-Check

Rule 1: 1+ veteran per day. Put in your diagram.

Rule 2: $R_1 \ldots s_1$ or $\boxed{\begin{matrix} R_1 \\ s_1 \end{matrix}}$

Rule 3: l=Tues, Wed. Put in your diagram.

Rule 4: $\boxed{\begin{matrix} —_1 \\ b \end{matrix}}$

Rule 5: $\boxed{KK^+}$

Note the use of subscripts to stipulate an element's first usage. Also, to distinguish those who are veterans, use capital letters for veterans and lowercase for non-veterans. Finally, notice that the blocks are set up the same way as the diagram; vertical blocks indicate same-day relationships while horizontal blocks indicate order relationships across days.

Don't forget to double-check your rules!

Deductions

Links: There aren't many links to be drawn among the rules, but you'll need to watch out for the sequencing aspect of rules 2 and 4.
Spatial restrictions: From rule 1, you know that neither b nor s is trained on Tuesday or Wednesday, since l is already there (rule 3).
Most restricted: b can only be with an element when that element first shows up during the week. Furthermore, b must be trained alongside a veteran.
Least restricted: A is never mentioned in the rules.

Here is your diagram:

veterans: AKR
non-veterans: bls

	M	T (~b ~s)	W (~b ~s)	Th	F
v:	___	___	___	___	___
	___	l	l	___	___

Assess, Act, Answer

Question 1 is a Grab-a-Rule, so start there.

For question 1, use the rules to eliminate answer choices. Rule 2 eliminates choice (A), rule 3 eliminates choice (C), rule 4 eliminates choice (E), and rule 5 eliminates choice (B). **The only choice left, and therefore the credited response, is choice (D).**

Move on to the Specific question, which is question 3.

For question 3, place b and R on Thursday. You can deduce from rule 4 that this must be R's first appearance during the week, which means s will have to follow it (rule 2), since all elements must show up at least once. This means s is on Friday.

Here is your diagram:

	M	~b ~s T	~b ~s W	Th	F
3. v:	__	__	__	R	__
	__	l	l	b	s

The question is asking for who must be trained on Friday, which you now know must be s. **Choice (B) is the credited response.**

Now turn to the General questions. The first General question is question 2.

Question 2 asks for something that *could be true.* Use the rules and any deductions or past work you have available. Rule 1 eliminates choice (A), rule 3 in conjunction with rule 1 eliminates choice (B), rule 4 eliminates choice (C), and rule 5 eliminates choice (D). **Therefore, choice (E) must be the credited response.**

The next General question is question 4.

Question 4 asks for a pair of walruses that cannot be together on Monday. Because Monday is the first day of the week, b should be fine with whichever veteran it is paired with. Eliminate choice (A), as you want a pair that's not possible. From rule 2, you can eliminate choice (E) as well. Looking more closely at rule 2 and choice (D), however, you can see that if s is trained on Monday, it has to be trained with R or else rule 2 has been violated. This means choice (D) is not possible and therefore must be the answer. **Choice (D) is the credited response.**

The final General question is question 6.

Question 6 asks you to find four choices that work and eliminate them. The right answer will be something that must be false. Since you don't have much past work on your diagram from previous questions, you'll have to try out some choices. Start with choice (A). If R and b are trained on Friday, this means Friday is the first day R is trained (rule 4). However, this leaves no room to include s, who must either be with R for the first day of training or be trained after it (rule 2). Because it isn't possible to satisfy both these rules at once, this answer choice doesn't work. The question asks for what cannot be true, so choice (A) is your answer; no need to check the rest. **Choice (A) is the credited response.**

Your last remaining question is a Complex one, question 5.

Question 5 stipulates that each day exactly one veteran and one non-veteran will be trained. It asks you to determine which answer choice would make it possible to figure out the entire week's schedule of training. You'll have to go through the answer choices and test them out. Start with choice (A). While it gives you information about Monday, it doesn't help you to determine anything about the other four days of the week, so eliminate it. Choice (B) tells you who is on Friday, but because you can't tell whether it's the first time R and s are used, this choice doesn't help much either. Cross it off.

Choice (C) tells you that A is the veteran on both Monday and Thursday. This means that K must be the veteran on Tuesday and Wednesday (rule 5). The only remaining veteran spot is on Friday, and that must be R because it hasn't been used yet. If R shows up first on Friday, s must accompany it (rule 2). Finally, you have to consider b, which can only go with an element on its first day (rule 4); this means b must be on Monday. The only remaining spot is the non-veteran on Thursday. Neither b nor s can fill that slot, thanks to rules 2 and 4, so that leaves l.

Here is your diagram:

		M	T ~b ~s	W ~b ~s	Th	F
5.(c)	v:	A	K	K	A	R
	n:	b	l	l	l	s

Because choice (C) allowed you to determine the entire week's lineup, it must be the right answer; you don't need to try the remaining choices. **Choice (C) is the credited response.**

FERRIS WHEEL FUN

Sandy brought her first-grade class to the amusement park. After putting most of her students onto the Ferris wheel, she notices that the only children left are Adam, Brad, Cary, Dan, Eunice, and Fanny. She places the children in the next three carts. Each of the six children must ride in exactly one of the next three carts, and each of the carts must have at least one and at most three of the children. The following conditions apply:

Adam rides in an earlier cart than Brad.
Dan does not ride in an earlier cart than Brad.
Cary rides in an earlier cart than Eunice.
Brad rides in the same cart as either Eunice or Fanny, but not both.

1. Which one of the following could be an accurate matching of the carts and the children riding in each of them?

(A) first cart: Eunice
second cart: Adam, Cary
third cart: Brad, Dan, and Fanny
(B) first cart: Adam
second cart: Brad, Fanny
third cart: Cary, Dan, and Eunice
(C) first cart: Adam, Cary
second cart: Brad, Dan, and Eunice
third cart: Fanny
(D) first cart: Adam, Brad, and Fanny
second cart: Cary
third cart: Dan, Eunice
(E) first cart: Cary
second cart: Adam, Dan, and Fanny
third cart: Brad, Eunice

2. If Eunice is the only child riding in one of the carts, then which one of the following could be true?

(A) Eunice rides in the first cart.
(B) Fanny rides in the first cart.
(C) Adam rides in the second cart.
(D) Cary rides in the second cart.
(E) Dan rides in the second cart.

3. If Adam rides in the second cart, then which one of the following could be true?

(A) Exactly three children ride in the first cart.
(B) Exactly two children ride in the first cart.
(C) Exactly three children ride in the second cart.
(D) Exactly one child rides in the third cart.
(E) Exactly two children ride in the third cart.

4. If Cary rides in the first cart, then which one of the following could be true?

(A) Adam rides in the third cart.
(B) Dan rides in the first cart.
(C) Brad rides in the first cart.
(D) Adam and Eunice ride in the second cart.
(E) Adam and Dan ride in the second cart.

5. If Fanny rides in the first cart, then which one of the following must be true?

(A) Adam rides in the second cart.
(B) Dan rides in the third cart.
(C) Cary rides in the first cart.
(D) Cary rides in the second cart.
(E) Brad rides in the third cart.

6. Which one of the following is a complete list of children, any one of which could be the only child riding in the first cart?

(A) Adam
(B) Adam, Cary
(C) Adam, Dan
(D) Adam, Cary, Fanny
(E) Adam, Dan, Cary, Fanny

ANSWERS TO FERRIS WHEEL FUN

1. C
2. E
3. B
4. D
5. B
6. D

EXPLANATIONS TO FERRIS WHEEL FUN

Prepare

Ingredient Scan

Task: 2-D Order game, combining order and groups; assign at least 1, but at most 3, children to each of the carts.

Inventory: 6 elements, 3 groups

Rules: Straightforward range rules

Questions: 6 Questions: 1 Grab-a-Rule, 4 Specific, 1 General

Red Flags: It's a bit difficult to figure out whether to think of this as a Group game or a 2-D Order game, but the range rules help you make the decision.

Rank: 2

Diagram and Inventory

You have six elements, A, B, C, D, E, and F. You need three columns numbered 1, 2, and 3, from earliest to latest. Every group must have at least one element and at most three elements. The elements can go only once, but the number of elements in each slot is not known.

Symbolize the Rules and Double-Check

Rule 1: 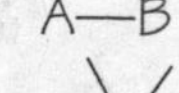

Rule 2: 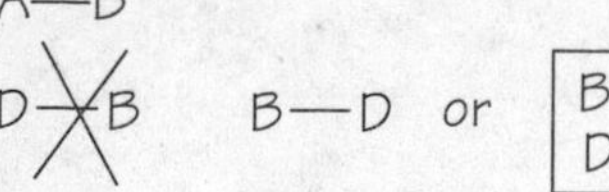

Rule 3: C—E

Rule 4: 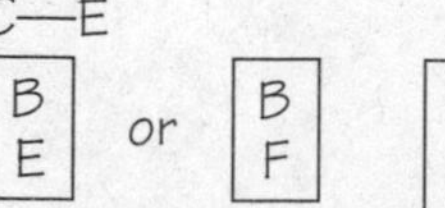

Don't forget to double-check your rules!

Deductions

Links: B is involved in several rules so link rules 1, 2, and 4 together.
Spatial restrictions: From rule 1, A can't go last and B can't go first. From rule 3, C can't go last and E can't go first. Rule 2 says that B must be before D or with D, so that means that D can't go first either. Rule 4 doesn't necessarily rule out E or F from being anywhere since only one of them at a time is ever partnered with B. Move on to the questions.
Most restricted: B is the most important element of the game since it is involved in three of the four rules.
Least restricted: F is the most flexible. If it's not with B, it could go anywhere.

Here is your diagram:

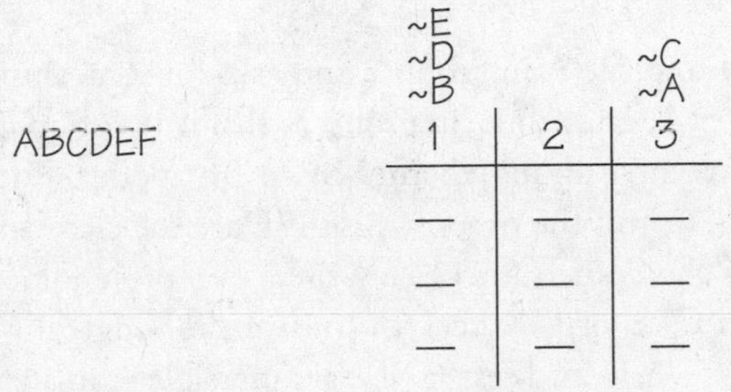

ABCDEF

~E ~D ~B 1	2	~C ~A 3
—	—	—
—	—	—
—	—	—

Assess, Act, Answer

Question 1 is a Grab-a-Rule so do it first.

For question 1, use the rules to eliminate answer choices. Rule 1 eliminates choice (D). Rule 2 eliminates choice (E). Rule 3 eliminates choices (A) and (B). **Because choice (C) is all that remains, it is the credited response.**

Question 2 is a Specific question, so go ahead and do that one.

Question 2 says that E will be alone in one group. What rules relate to E? Rule 3 tells you that E must be in either group 2 or 3. Rule 4 tells you that B will have to be with F. Because there are only two options for E, draw those two scenarios as separate rows and figure out other implications. If E is alone in group 2, then BF will have to go in group 3. Because of rule 2, D will also have to go with B in group 3. That means A and C are forced into group 1 (group 3 is already at its max, and group 2 is being reserved for only E). For the other scenario, in which E is alone in group 3, then BF will have to go in group 2. Again, D must also go with B (since it can't encroach on E's solitude in group 3), and A and C will be forced into group 1 since group 2 will be maxed out at three elements. The question asks for something possible, so the first thing that works with either of your scenarios is the answer. **Choice (E) describes something from one of the two scenarios, so it is the credited response.**

	~E ~D ~B 1	2	~C ~A 3
2.	A C	E	B D F
	A C	B D F	E

Question 3 is your next Specific question.

Question 3 directs you to place A in group 2 and asks for something that *could be true.* Rule 1 tells you that B must be after A, and, thus, in group 3. If B is in group 3, you know that D will have to join it. You still need to worry about whether BF or BE applies. Put an E/F placeholder in group 3. Group 1 is still open. C and the other half of F/E are the elements that are left. E can't ever go in group 1, so the only choices left are C/F. Write a C/F placeholder in group 1. There is one more element to place, either C, F, or E. Check the answers for anything that could be true. If it seems possible, flesh out the scenario and test it. If it's impossible, eliminate it. Choice (A) isn't possible based on your diagram; there aren't enough unassigned elements left to put three of them in group 1. Eliminate Choice (A). Choice (B) seems like it might be possible. Could both C and F go in group 1? That would mean BDE are all in group 3. Check all the rules and make sure they are all obeyed. They are. **Because choice (B) is possible, it is the credited response.**

	~E ~D ~B 1	2	~C ~A 3
5.	F/C	A	B D E/F

Question 4 is also a Specific question, so do that one next.

Question 4 says to place C in group 1 and asks for something that could be true. With C in group 1, not much else is determined. The only rule pertaining to C is rule 3, which just tells you that E must be in group 2 or 3. Because B can only go in group 2 or 3, draw two rows to make a scenario with B in group 2 and one with B in group 3. For the scenario in which B is in group 2, A is forced into group 1. It also means an E/F placeholder can be attached to B in group 2. D is still free to be in group 2 or 3, as is the other half of F/E. For the scenario in which B is in group 3, D is in group 3 as well as the E/F placeholder attached to B. Now, A and the other half of F/E have some flexibility as to whether they end up in group 1 or group 2. Avoid writing in anything unknown, and check the answers for something that seems possible. Choices (A), (B), and (C) describe element positions ruled out by your deductions. Choice (D) might be possible in the second of your scenarios. With C in group 1, test A and E in group 2. That means BDF would be in group 3. Verify this obeys all the rules. **It does; therefore, choice (D) is the credited response.**

	~E ~D ~B		~C ~A
	1	2	3
6.	C A	B E/F	D D/F/E
	C	E/F/A	B D E/F

Question 5 is also a Specific question, so do that one next.

Question 5 says to placc F in the first group and asks what must follow. Only rule 4 relates to F. Because B can't go in group 1, then BF will not apply for this question. BE will have to go into group 2 or 3. Try a scenario with each to flesh out the other implications. In the first scenario, F is in group 1 and BE is in group 2. Rules 1 and 3 will force A and C to be in group 1. That leaves only D and an empty group 3, so D must go in group 3. For the second scenario, F is in group 1 and BE is in group 3. That immediately tells you that D must also be in group 3 since D can't come before B. Group 3 is maxed out, group 2 is empty, and A and C still need to be placed. The question asks for something that *must be true*, which means the answer must be something that occurs in both of your scenarios. The only thing that is constant for both scenarios is that D is in group 3. **Choice (B) identifies this, so it is the credited response.**

	~E ~D ~B		~C ~A
	1	2	3
3.	F C A	B E	D
	F	—	B E D

The General question, question 6, is all you have left.

Question 6 asks for a complete list of all elements that could be the *only* element in group 1. Start by eliminating any answer choices that list elements you know could never be in group 1 (B, D, and E). That eliminates choices (C) and (E). The only difference between the remaining choices deals with C and F. Do you have any scenarios from your previous work with only C or F in group 1? Yes, the second scenario from question 3 and the work from question 5 both lend themselves to working with only C or F in group 1. Because question 5 lists them both as possibilities for group 1, verify that you could complete a viable scenario with C alone in 1 and with F alone in group 1. In each case, it would be possible. Therefore, both C and F should be in your answer choice. **Since, of the remaining choices, only choice (D) has both C and F, choice (D) is the credited response.**

TICK-TOCK

A company has a total of seven conference rooms, numbered 1 through 7. Each room contains one of seven different clocks—J, K, L, M, N, O, and P—each of which must be inspected by the company manager. Each conference room will be inspected exactly once. The manager will inspect the conference rooms in consecutive order according to the conference room number. Any clock that is not working will receive a new battery. The manager will inspect the rooms according to the following conditions:

K is located in conference room 3.
The clock located in conference room 4 does not need a new battery.
M is inspected before J is inspected.
P is inspected before both N and L are inspected.
No batteries are replaced after M is inspected.
Exactly two batteries need to be replaced after K is inspected.

1. Which one of the following could be true?

(A) J is in conference room 6.
(B) M is in conference room 5.
(C) P is in conference room 4.
(D) L is in conference room 2.
(E) N is in conference room 1.

2. If P is the second clock to need a new battery, then which one of the following must be false?

(A) O does not need a new battery.
(B) N needs a new battery.
(C) L does not need a new battery.
(D) K does not need a new battery.
(E) K needs a new battery.

3. Which one of the following clocks must be inspected before K is inspected?

(A) M
(B) P
(C) O
(D) L
(E) N

4. If O is inspected before N but after L, then which one of the following could be true?

(A) N does not need a new battery.
(B) O needs a new battery.
(C) L does not need a new battery.
(D) N is inspected fourth.
(E) P is inspected second.

5. If neither N nor L needs a new battery, then which of the following must be true?

(A) O needs a new battery.
(B) L is in conference room 2.
C) N is in conference room 4.
(D) K needs a new battery.
(E) P does not need a new battery.

6. If N and O both need batteries, then each of the following could be true EXCEPT:

(A) P is in conference room 1.
(B) N is in conference room 5.
(C) O is in conference room 1.
(D) L needs a new battery.
(E) P does not need a new battery.

ANSWERS TO TICK-TOCK

1. D
2. A
3. B
4. C
5. A
6. D

EXPLANATIONS TO TICK-TOCK

Prepare

Ingredient Scan

Task: 2-D Order game; assign clocks to conference rooms (in order) and decide whether they need new batteries

Inventory: 7 elements, plus battery or no battery

Rules: Straightforward range and block rules, with a couple of hard-to-symbolize rules

Questions: 6 total: 4 Specific, 2 General

Red Flags: Rules 5 and 6 are hard to symbolize

Rank: 3/4

Diagram and Inventory

The setup describes seven rooms being inspected in order. Each room—J, K, L, M, N, O, and P—has a clock, and each clock either needs a new battery or does not need a new battery. Because there are two types of elements being assigned, set this up as a two-tiered diagram with one tier for clocks and one tier for battery/no battery.

Symbolize the Rules and Double-Check

Rule 1: Add this to the diagram.

Rule 2: Add this to the diagram.

Rule 3: M—J

Rule 4: P < N, L (P before both N and L)

Rule 5: no batteries after M

Rule 6: K—b—b

The first few rules are straightforward, but clue 5 is tough to symbolize. You could technically make an M—b antiblock, but making a note will also suffice. Clue 6 also looks tricky, but just symbolize it as it would look in the diagram.

Don't forget to double-check your rules!

Deductions

Links: Combine rules 5 and 6 to deduce that K—M, which means that M cannot be first or second. Only O and P are left to go in the first room. Combine rules 5 and 6 with rules 1 and 2 to see that if there must be two batteries after K and 4 does not get a battery, and there are no batteries after M, M must be in slot 6. This means that J is in the last slot and that slots 5 and 6 get batteries while slot 7 does not. Because P needs N and L after it, P must be in slot 1 or slot 2.
Spatial restrictions: From rule 3 you know that M cannot be last and J cannot be first. From rule 4 you know that both N and L cannot be first and that P cannot be sixth or seventh.
Most restricted: P
Least restricted: O

Here is your diagram:

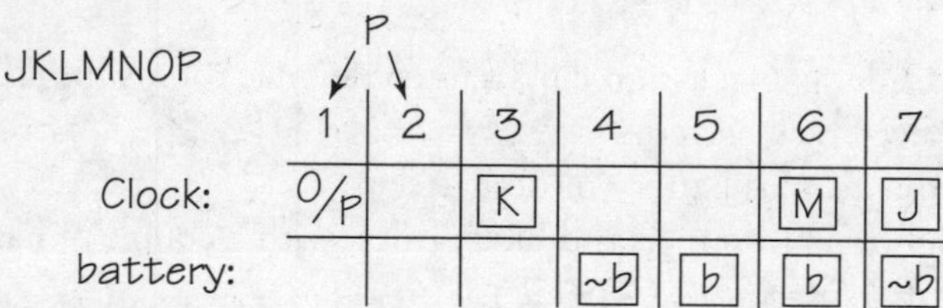

Assess, Act, Answer

There is no Grab-a-Rule question, so go to question 2, the first Specific question.

In question 2, because P must be in slot 1 or 2, if P is to be the second clock to get a battery it must be in slot 2. That means that O is in slot 1, and L and N are interchangeable in slots 4 and 5.

Here is your diagram:

	1	2	3	4	5	6	7
2.	O	P	K	L/N	L/N	M	J
	b	b		~b	b	b	~b

The question asks you to find something that must be false. **The only choice that must be false is choice (A), making it the credited response.**

Move on to question 4, the next Specific question.

If O is inspected before N and after L, then P must be in slot 1, L in slot 2, O in slot 4, and N in slot 5.

Here is your diagram:

	1	2	3	4	5	6	7
4.	P	L	K	O	N	M	J
				~b	b	b	~b

The question asks for something that *could be true.* The only choice that could be true is choice (C). **Choice (C) is the credited response.**

Move on to question 5, the next Specific question.

If N and L do not get new batteries, then neither of them can go in slot 5, which leaves only O to go there. Since O is not in slot 1, P is, and N and L are interchangeable in slots 2 and 4.

Here is your diagram:

	1	2	3	4	5	6	7
5.	P	N/L	K	N/L	O	M	J
		~b		~b	b	b	~b

You are looking for something that *must be true.* From the diagram, you can see that O needs a new battery. **Therefore, choice (A) is the credited response.**

The final Specific question is question 6.

If N and O both need new batteries, then neither can be in slot 4. The only element left for slot 4 is L.

Here is your diagram:

P
/ \

	1	2	3	4	5	6	7
6.			K	L		M	J
				~b	b	b	~b

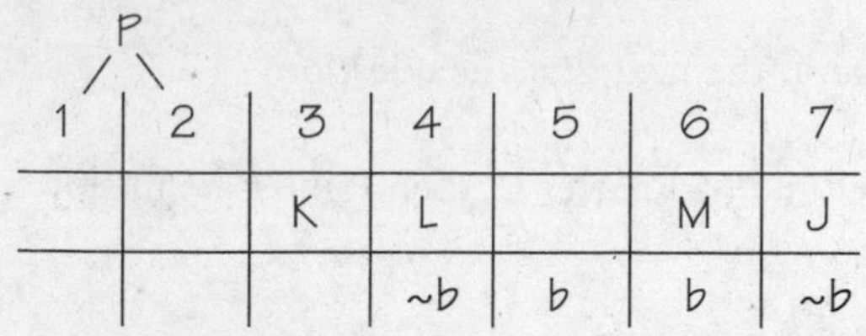

Again, because the question asks for what *could be true EXCEPT*, you are looking for what must be false. Based on the diagram the only choice that has to be false is choice (A). **Choice (A) is the credited response.**

Now that the Specific questions are complete, attack the General questions, starting with question 1.

Question 1 asks for something that *could be true*. You saw L in slot 2 in the work for questions 4 and 5, so you know that can be true. **Choice (D) is the credited response.**

The final General question is question 3.

In question 3 you need to know which clock must be inspected before K. From the deductions, the only clock that has to be before K is P. **Choice (B) is the credited response.**

THE RULES OF THE ANCIENTS

The people of Untubtu are making offerings to their deities—Prasata, Quisan, Ragnack, Xuo, Yuknl, and Zossoz. Each deity is given either one, two, three or four offerings, according to the status the Untubtu people have accorded them. The offerings must comply with the following rules of the ancients:

Each possible number of offerings is given to at least one deity.
At most one deity is given more offerings than Quisan is.
Ragnack is given exactly one fewer offering than Prasata is.
No three deities are given the same number of offerings.
Xuo is given as many offerings as either Prasata or Yuknl is.

1. Which of the following could be an accurate matching of deities to number of offerings?

(A) one offering: Xuo, Yuknl; two offerings: Ragnack; three offerings: Prasata; four offerings: Quisan, Zossoz
(B) one offering: Xuo, Yuknl; two offerings: Quisan, Zossoz; three offerings: Ragnack; four offerings: Prasata
(C) one offering: Zossoz; two offerings: Yuknl; three offerings: Ragnack, Quisan; four offerings: Prasata, Xuo
(D) one offering: Ragnack; two offerings: Prasata; three offerings: Xuo, Zossoz; four offerings: Quisan, Yuknl
(E) one offering: Ragnack, Zossoz; two offerings: Xuo, Yuknl; three offerings: Quisan; four offerings: Prasata

2. If Yuknl is the only deity that is given one offering, then which of the following could be true?

(A) Xuo is given two offerings.
(B) Zossoz is given two offerings.
(C) Quisan is given three offerings.
(D) Ragnack is given three offerings.
(E) Prasata is given four offerings.

3. Which of the following CANNOT be true?

(A) Yuknl is the only deity that is given two offerings.
(B) Yuknl is the only deity that is given three offerings.
(C) Yuknl is the only deity that is given four offerings.
(D) Quisan is the only deity that is given three offerings.
(E) Quisan is the only deity that is given four offerings.

4. If Prasata is the only deity that is given two offerings, then which of the following must be true?

(A) Yuknl is given one offering.
(B) Zossoz is given one offering.
(C) Quisan is given three offerings.
(D) Xuo is given three offerings.
(E) Ragnack is given three offerings.

5. If Yuknl is given the same number of offerings as Zossoz, then which of the following must be true?

(A) Yuknl is given one offering.
(B) Zossoz is given one offering.
(C) Quisan is given three offerings.
(D) Xuo is given three offerings.
(E) Ragnack is given three offerings.

6. If Ragnack and Yuknl are each given one offering, then which of the following could be true?

(A) Zossoz is given two offerings.
(B) Prasata is given three offerings.
(C) Xuo is given three offerings.
(D) Zossoz is given three offerings.
(E) Prasata is given four offerings.

7. Which of the following can be given, at most, three offerings?

(A) Xuo
(B) Prasata
(C) Quisan
(D) Zossoz
(E) Yuknl

ANSWERS TO THE RULES OF THE ANCIENTS

1. A
2. B
3. A
4. D
5. E
6. D
7. A

EXPLANATIONS TO THE RULES OF THE ANCIENTS

Prepare

Ingredient Scan

Task: 2-D Order game; assign 6 deities according to the number of offerings they each are given

Inventory: 6 deities; 4 options for amounts of offerings

Rules: The rules don't sound exactly like an ordinary Order or Group game. You may have to consider how you would symbolize them in order to determine how you would like your diagram to look. Rule 2 is a bit weird; it might be a challenge to symbolize.

Questions: 7 total: 1 Grab-a-Rule, 4 Specific, 2 General

Red Flags: Determining a good diagram and paraphrasing some of the rules to make them more lucid are the biggest hurdles here

Rank: 2

Diagram and Inventory

Although the setup makes it sound like you're assigning a number of offerings to each deity, this game will function more like a 2-D Order game if the number of offerings are the core. Your elements are P, Q, R, X, Y, and Z, and your columns are 1, 2, 3, and 4. Each element must be used and can be used only once.

Symbolize the Rules and Double-Check

Rule 1: This just tells you that there is at least one element in each column. You can add a placeholder to each column to remind yourself that there must always be at least one in each group.

Rule 2: Q—(max 1)

Rule 3: [RP]

Rule 4: Maximum 2 per group

Rule 5: [X over P] or [X over Y]

The second rule is the most confusing to symbolize. It helps to think about what it means in a specific game scenario to determine how to symbolize it.

Don't forget to double-check your rules!

Deductions

Spatial restrictions: If there can only be at most one element in a higher numbered group than Q (rule 2), then Q must not be in a low group; groups 1 and 2 would be impossible for Q. Group 3 could work, with the caveat that only one element could be in group 4. Rule 3 looks like a normal block rule, so you can exclude P from being in the first group and R from being in the last group. Put a ~P over group 1 and a ~R over group 4. The RP block has 3 options. Because XP or XY will be a vertical block, consider where it could go. It seems like it could go anywhere except for maybe group 4, since that will either be Q or only have room for one element. (If XP or XY were in group 4, it would force Q to be in group 3, and then there would be two elements higher than Q, breaking rule 2). Therefore, the XP/XY block could never be in group 4 and you can add a ~X above group 4.
Most restricted: Q
Least restricted: Z is a free agent.

Here is your diagram:

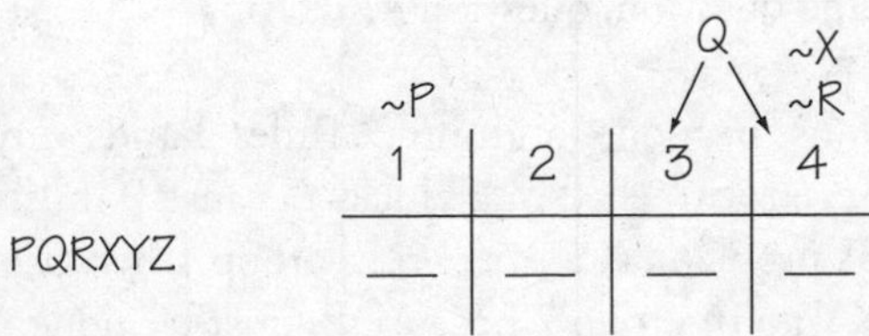

Assess, Act, Answer

The first question is a Grab-a-Rule, so do that one first.

For question 1, use the rules to eliminate answer choices. Rule 1 eliminates nothing. Since there are five rules and only four answer choices to be eliminated, it shouldn't surprise you when a rule does not eliminate an answer choice. Rule 2 eliminates choices (B) and (C). Rule 3 eliminates choice (E). Rule 4 eliminates nothing. Rule 5 eliminates choice (D). **Because choice (A) is all that remains, it is the credited response.**

Question 2 is your first Specific question, so do it next.

Question 2 asks you to place Y alone in group 1. Because Y must be alone, the X vertical block for this question will be XP (rule 5). Your RP block can go in either 2/3 or 3/4. Draw two rows to flesh out each of these options. The first scenario has Y in 1, R in 2, and XP in 3. The second scenario has Y in group 1, R in group 3, and XP in group 4. As you deduced earlier, X cannot go in group 4 because XP or XY would fill up that group and make Q's position impossible. Draw a line through the second scenario to show it's broken. Looking back at the first scenario, Q will be forced into group 4. Only Z remains, and it is a free agent. It can't go in group 1 because Y must be alone for this question, and it can't go in group 3 because that group already has two elements. Z can go in 2 or 4. You can either write those possibilities in parenthetically or write a Z off to the side to remind yourself that it still must be placed. The question asks for something that *could be true,* so the credited response is anything that is possible. Choice (A) is impossible because X is in group 3. Eliminate it. Choice (B) is possible because Z can go in group 2 or 4. **Therefore, choice (B) is the credited response.**

	~P 1	2	Q (3/4) 3	~X ~R 4
2.	Y	R	X P	Q
	~~Y~~		~~R~~	~~X~~ P

Move to your next Specific question, question 4.

Question 4 says that P must be alone in group 2. Rules 3 and 5 involve P. Place P in group 2 and R in group 1 because they are attached in a block. Because P must be alone, you'll have to use the XY vertical block for this problem. XY can't go in group 1 because that would put three elements in that group, nor can XY go in group 2 because P must be alone. X cannot go in group 4 ever, so XY must go in group 3. That means Q must go in group 4. You are left with Z, the free agent. This time Z can either go in group 1 or group 4; note that on the side. The question asks for something that *must be true,* so it is unlikely to deal with Z. Everything else is set in stone so just compare the answers to your diagram. **Choice (D) applies so it is the credited response.**

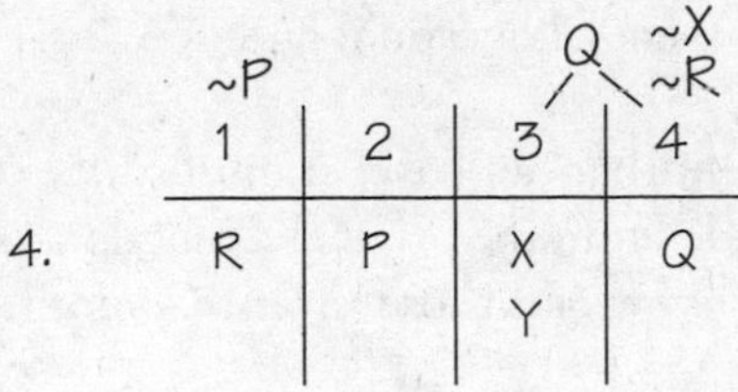

Question 5 is also a Specific question, so move to that question next.

For question 5, symbolize the condition it gives you: a YZ vertical block. You will use the XP vertical block for this problem (rule 5). YZ and XP fill up two of the four groups, which means R and Q will be assigned to the other two groups. From all you've done up until now, it should be clear that Q will have to be in group 4 for this scenario. X cannot be in group 4, and YZ can't fill up group 4 without breaking rule 2. Because the question asks for something that *must be true*, check the answers for anything relating to Q. **Choice (E) describes something you know is unavoidable, so it is the credited response.**

Question 6 is also a Specific question, so do that one next.

Question 6 places YR together in group 1. Your RP block places P in group 2 automatically. X will join P in group 2, because it can no longer be with Y. That leaves Q and Z for groups 3 and 4. Neither combination of those two would break any rules, so put a Q/Z in group 3 and a Z/Q in group 4. The question asks for something that *could be true*, so the answer likely has to do with your possibilities, Z and Q. Scan the answers for those letters. **Choice (D) is possible, so it is the credited response.**

	~P 1	2	Q 3	~X ~R 4
6.	R	P	Z/Q	Q/Z
	Y	X		

Go back to your first General question, question 3.

Question 3 asks for something impossible, so use your previous work to get rid of any choices that describe something you've already seen. Choices (D) and (E) should be eliminated based on the work from questions 4 and 6. The other three choices deal with putting Y alone in group 2, 3, or 4, so try to figure out which one would pose a problem. If Y is alone in group 2, it's going to force the RP block to go in groups 3 and 4. This could be trouble. How does this interact with Q and the XP/XY block? You would have to use XP since you're trying to see if Y can be alone. That means you'd have XP in group 4, which you know is not valid.
Because choice (A) describes something impossible, it is the credited response.

Finally, move on to the next General question, question 7.

Question 7 asks for an element that can have, at most, three offerings; in other words, which element cannot go in group 4? From the original deductions, you ruled out R and X from ever being in group 4. Scan the answers for those letters. **Choice (A) is the credited response.**

THURSDAY NIGHT COMEDY

Channel 1 and Channel 2 each offer several comedy shows as part of their Thursday night lineup. Three of the shows—*Smackdown*, *Thrashing*, and *Ultra-blather*—are political spoofs, and three of the shows—*Whimsy*, *Yorick's Hour*, and *Zany*—are sketch comedies. Each channel has three one-hour time slots in which to air these shows: Channel 1 at 8, 9 and 10; Channel 2 at 9, 10 and 11. Each show is aired exactly once, and no other show is aired. The following conditions must obtain:

Each channel airs one program at a time.
If any sketch comedy show is aired at 10, then no political spoof is aired at 10.
Thrashing is aired at some time after Smackdown.
Ultra-blather and Zany are not shown on the same channel.
Yorick's Hour is aired immediately after a political spoof, though not necessarily on the same channel.
Whimsy is aired at 8 or 11.

1. Which of the following could be a complete and accurate list of the shows aired on Channel 1, from 8 to 10?

   (A) *Smackdown, Yorick's Hour, Thrashing*
   (B) *Whimsy, Yorick's Hour, Ultra-blather*
   (C) *Thrashing, Yorick's Hour, Whimsy*
   (D) *Smackdown, Ultra-blather, Yorick's Hour*
   (E) *Whimsy, Ultra-blather, Zany*

2. If a political spoof is shown at 10, then each of the following could be false EXCEPT:

   (A) A political spoof is shown at 8.
   (B) A sketch comedy show is shown at 8.
   (C) A sketch comedy show is shown at 9.
   (D) A political spoof is shown at 11.
   (E) A sketch comedy show is shown at 11.

3. If *Yorick's Hour* is shown at 11, then which of the following could be an accurate lineup of the shows on Channel 1, from first to last?

   (A) *Whimsy, Zany, Ultra-blather*
   (B) *Whimsy, Zany, Thrashing*
   (C) *Whimsy, Zany, Smackdown*
   (D) *Whimsy, Thrashing, Zany*
   (E) *Smackdown, Ultra-blather, Yorick's Hour*

4. Each of the following shows could be aired at 10 or later EXCEPT:

   (A) *Zany*
   (B) *Whimsy*
   (C) *Ultra-blather*
   (D) *Thrashing*
   (E) *Smackdown*

5. The show that is aired at 8 could be

   (A) *Ultra-blather*
   (B) *Zany*
   (C) *Smackdown*
   (D) *Yorick's Hour*
   (E) *Thrashing*

6. Which of the following shows CANNOT be aired at 11?

   (A) *Thrashing*
   (B) *Ultra-Blather*
   (C) *Yorick's Hour*
   (D) *Smackdown*
   (E) *Zany*

ANSWERS TO THURSDAY NIGHT COMEDY

1. D
2. E
3. B
4. E
5. C
6. D

EXPLANATIONS TO THURSDAY NIGHT COMEDY

Prepare

Ingredient Scan

Task: 2-D Order game; assign each of 6 comedy shows to exactly 1 combination of channel and time slot
Inventory: 6 elements for 8 total spaces
Rules: Rules relating to both specific elements and to element type in general
Questions: 6 total: 1 Grab-a-Rule, 2 Specific, 3 General
Red Flags: Not strictly a 1:1 ratio, but by blocking out the unused spaces it works like a 1:1 game
Rank: 3

Diagram and Inventory

The setup describes a two-tiered Order game in which you must place 6 shows into different time slots—8, 9, 10, and 11—on two different channels—Channel 1 and Channel 2. There are three political spoofs—S, T, and U—and three sketch comedies—w, y, and z. Each show only airs once, and every show must air.

Symbolize the Rules and Double-Check

Rule 1: 1 program per channel per slot This should be reflected in your diagram.

Rule 2: sketch comedy$_{10}$→~political spoof$_{10}$; political spoof$_{10}$→~sketch comedy$_{10}$

Rule 3: S—T

Rule 4: $U_1 z_2$/ $U_2 z_1$

Rule 5: | S/T/U y | regardless of channel

Rule 6: w = 8/11

Note the use of capital letters for political spoofs and lowercase ones for sketch comedies.

Don't forget to double-check your rules!

Deductions

Links: From rule 2, you learn that the shows aired at 10 will have to be the same type of show, both sketch comedies or both political spoofs. Since rule 5 requires y to air immediately after a political spoof, what gets aired at 10 will likely affect where y can be placed.
Spatial restrictions: From the original information in the setup, you know that nothing is aired on Channel 1 in slot 11 or on Channel 2 in slot 8, so block those spaces out. From rule 3, T cannot be in slot 8, and S cannot be in slot 11. From rule 5, y cannot be in slot 8. From rule 6, w cannot be in slot 9 or 10.
Most restricted: Figuring out what airs in slot 10 will determine where most of the other elements go.
Least restricted: Aside from not being on the same channel as each other, U and z have no restrictions on where they can go in the diagram.

Here is your diagram:

PS: STU

sc: wyz

	~T~y 8	~w 9	~w 10	~S 11
1				X
2	X			

Question 1 is a Grab-a-Rule, so start there.

For question 1, use the rules to eliminate answer choices. Rule 3 eliminates choice (C), rule 4 eliminates choice (A) and choice (E), and rule 5 eliminates choice (B). **The only choice left, and therefore the credited response, is choice (D).**

Move on to the Specific questions. The first Specific question is question 2.

For question 2, indicate in your diagram that both slots in slot 10 will be political spoofs (rule 2). You now need to think about where y could go. One possibility is slot 11 on Channel 2; another is slot 9 on either channel, but only if the third political spoof airs in slot 8 (rule 5). Since w needs one of slots 8 and 11 (rule 6), you have two possible scenarios.

Here is your diagram:

		~T~y	~W	~W	~S
		8	9	10	11
2.	1	w		p	X
	2	X		p	y
	1	p	y	p	X
	2	X		p	w

The question asks you to identify four choices that could be true and eliminate them, which means the credited response will be something that must be true. Based on your diagram, the only statement that must be true is choice (E). **Choice (E) is the credited response.**

The final Specific question is question 3.

For question 3, place y in slot 11. This means there will be political spoofs in slot 10 (rule 5), and w will be in slot 8 (rule 6). From rule 3, you know that S will have to take one of the two 9 time slots and T one of the two 10 time slots. This leaves z and U for the remaining 9 and 10 slots, respectively; be sure to split them up as per rule 4.

Here is your diagram:

		~T~y	~W	~W	~S
		8	9	10	11
3.	1	w	z/S	T/U	X
	2	X	S/z	U/T	y

The question asks for the lineup on Channel 1. The only choice that doesn't contradict the diagram or one of the rules is choice (B). **Choice (B) is the credited response.**

Move on to the General questions. The first General question is question 4.

Question 4 asks which show cannot be aired in either slot 10 or 11. Use your past work and deductions to eliminate answer choices. From question 2 you can eliminate choice (B); from question 3 you can eliminate choice (C) and choice (D). This leaves you with two remaining choices. Since you have more restrictions on where S can go, start with that. You know S cannot be in slot 11 from your earlier deductions, but can it go in slot 10? If S is in slot 10, then T would have to be in slot 11 (rule 3) and U would have to be in slot 10 as well (rule 2). But this would make it impossible to satisfy rule 5, so S cannot be in slot 10. **Therefore choice (E) is the credited response.**

The next General question is question 5.

Question 5 asks which show can go in slot 8. From your deductions you can eliminate choice (D) and choice (E). You're left with three choices. As in question 4, it makes more sense to try out S because you have more information about where it can't go in the diagram. Try S in slot 8. This puts w in slot 11 (rule 6). In order to satisfy rule 2, you'll need to pair y and z and then U and T, but either pair could go in slot 9 or 10 and still satisfy rule 5 as well.

Here is your diagram:

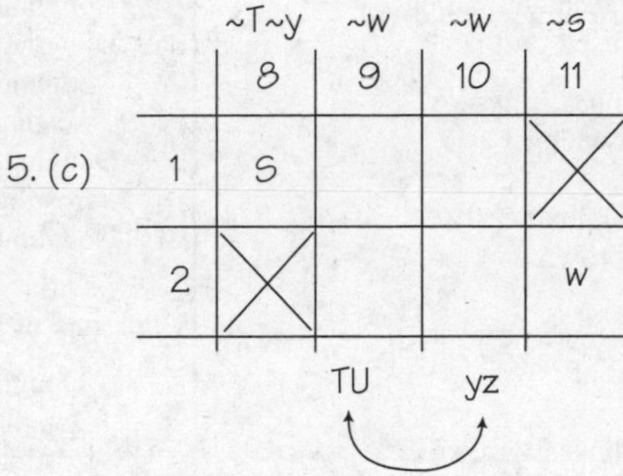

Since this choice appears to work, it must be the right answer; there is no need to try choice (A) or choice (B). **Choice (C) is the credited response.**

The final General question is question 6.

Question 6 asks which show cannot be aired in slot 11; from your earlier deductions related to rule 3, you know S cannot be in slot 11. **Choice (D) is the credited response.**

DELICIOUS DOUGHNUT SHOP

Tom works at the Delicious Doughnut Shop. His job is to put frosting on the doughnuts. Each side of each of four different doughnuts—doughnuts 1, 2, 3, and 4—contains exactly one of the following four colors of frosting: brown, orange, red, and white. The following must obtain:

Doughnut 2 does not contain red frosting.

Each color frosting is used on exactly two sides of the four doughnuts.

Doughnut 1 has red frosting on at least one side, but contains neither orange nor white frosting.

Brown frosting is not on either side of a doughnut numbered exactly one higher than a doughnut that has any white frosting on it.

1. Which one of the following could be an accurate pairing of doughnuts with the colors of frosting used on them?

    (A) Doughnut 1: brown and red; Doughnut 2: brown and red; Doughnut 3: orange and white; Doughnut 4: orange and white
    (B) Doughnut 1: orange and white; Doughnut 2: brown and orange; Doughnut 3: brown and red; Doughnut 4: two sides of white
    (C) Doughnut 1: brown and red; Doughnut 2: brown and white; Doughnut 3: two sides of red; Doughnut 4: two sides of orange
    (D) Doughnut 1: brown and red; Doughnut 2: brown and white; Doughnut 3: orange and red; Doughnut 4: orange and white
    (E) Doughnut 1: two sides of red; Doughnut 2: brown and white; Doughnut 3: orange and white; Doughnut 4: brown and orange

2. Which one of the following CANNOT be true?

    (A) Doughnut 2 has white frosting on both sides while Doughnut 3 has orange frosting on both sides.
    (B) Doughnut 3 has white frosting on both sides while Doughnut 2 has orange frosting on both sides.
    (C) Doughnut 3 has white frosting on both sides while Doughnut 4 has orange frosting on both sides.
    (D) Doughnut 4 has white frosting on both sides while Doughnut 2 has orange frosting on both sides.
    (E) Doughnut 4 has white frosting on both sides while Doughnut 3 has orange frosting on both sides.

3. Which one of the following could be true?

    (A) Doughnut 1 has red frosting on both sides while Doughnut 4 has brown and orange frosting.
    (B) Doughnut 3 has brown frosting on both sides while Doughnut 4 has red and white frosting.
    (C) Doughnut 2 has orange frosting on one side while Doughnut 3 has orange and red frosting.
    (D) Doughnut 3 has red frosting on one side while Doughnut 4 has brown frosting on both sides.
    (E) Doughnuts 2 and 3 each have red frosting on one side.

4. Which one of the following could be true?

    (A) Doughnut 1 has two sides of brown frosting.
    (B) Doughnut 2 has both orange and red frosting.
    (C) Doughnuts 3 and 4 each have a side of brown frosting.
    (D) Doughnuts 1 and 4 each have a side of orange frosting.
    (E) Doughnut 4 has both brown and white frosting.

5. Which one of the following must be true?

    (A) If Doughnut 1 has two sides of red frosting, Doughnut 4 has at least one side of white frosting.
    (B) If Doughnut 2 has two sides of brown frosting, Doughnut 3 has at least one side of orange frosting.
    (C) If Doughnut 3 has two sides of brown frosting, Doughnut 2 has at least one side of red frosting.
    (D) If Doughnut 2 has two sides of white frosting, Doughnut 4 has at least one side of brown frosting.
    (E) If Doughnut 4 has two sides of orange frosting, Doughnut 3 has at least one side of brown frosting.

6. If neither Doughnut 3 nor Doughnut 4 has any brown frosting, then which one of the following must be true?

    (A) Doughnut 2 has at least one side of brown frosting.
    (B) Doughnut 2 does not have white frosting.
    (C) Doughnut 3 has at least one side of white frosting.
    (D) Doughnut 3 has at least one side of red frosting.
    (E) Doughnut 3 does not have white frosting.

ANSWERS TO DELICIOUS DOUGHNUT SHOP

1. D
2. B
3. C
4. E
5. D
6. A

EXPLANATIONS TO DELICIOUS DOUGHNUT SHOP

Prepare

Ingredient Scan

Task: 2-D Order game, combining order with groups; assign 2 colors to each of 4 doughnuts in order
Inventory: 4 elements total for 8 spaces, every element gets used twice, creating a 1:1 ratio
Rules: Some tricky wording on otherwise straightforward rules
Questions: 6 total: 1 Grab-a-Rule, 1 Specific, 4 General
Red Flags: Multiple uses of elements, not a 1:1 ratio initially
Rank: 4

Diagram and Inventory

The setup describes an Order game in which four colors of frosting—b, o, r, and w—must be assigned to both sides of four doughnuts—1, 2, 3, and 4.

Symbolize the Rules and Double-Check

Rule 1: $2 \neq r$ Put this in your diagram.

Rule 2: b,b, o, o, r, r, w, w

Rule 3: $1 = r^{+}$; $1 \neq o$, w Put this in your diagram.

Rule 4: ~~wb~~

Don't forget to double-check your rules!

Deductions

Links: Combining rule 3 with rule 1, you know that if b is in Doughnut 1, then r must go in either Doughnut 3 or Doughnut 4.
Spatial restrictions: From rule 3 you know that only b or r can go in the remaining open space in Doughnut 1.
Most restricted: Doughnut 1 has one side of red frosting, but can only have either b or r on its remaining side (rule 3). Since r cannot be in Doughnut 2 (rule 1) and b is restricted by where w goes (rule 4), the open space in Doughnut 1 is the most restricted aspect of the game and will determine where other elements can be placed.
Least restricted: The rules never mention o; it is the least restricted aspect of the game.

Here is your diagram:

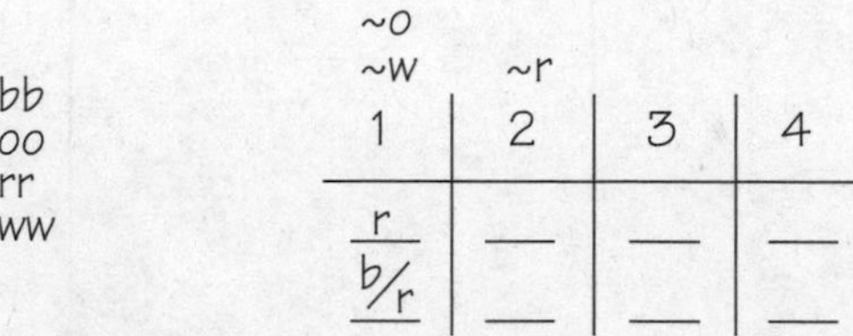

Assess, Act, Answer

Question 1 is a Grab-a-Rule, so begin there.

For question 1, use the rules to eliminate answer choices. Rule 1 eliminates choice (A), rule 2 eliminates choice (C), rule 3 eliminates choice (B), and rule 4 eliminates choice (E). **The only choice left, and therefore the credited response, is choice (D).**

Move on to the Specific question, which is question 6.

Question 6 tells you that the b's have to be in Doughnuts 1 and 2. Since there are two possible ways to do this, you'll need to construct two different scenarios. From your earlier deductions, you know that the open space in Doughnut 1 can be either b or r. Try each. If Doughnut 1 has both r's, then both sides of Doughnut 2 are b. If b is in the open space in Doughnut 1, then Doughnut 2 has the other b and one of either o or w (rule 1).

Here is your diagram:

	~o ~w 1	~r 2	3	4
6.	r	b	__	__
	r	b	__	__
	r	b	__	__
	b	o/w	__	__

The question asks for something that *must be true*. From your diagram, the only choice that must be true is choice (A). **Choice (A) is the credited response.**

Move on to the General questions, beginning with question 2.

Question 2 asks for something that cannot be true. Use the rules and your deductions to eliminate any choices you can. In this case, none of the answer choices can be eliminated immediately, so you'll have to try a few. Choice (A) seems possible, as either option is still available for the open space in Doughnut 1 and rule 4 won't be violated by this arrangement. Eliminate it, since it can be true. For choice (B), filling all the spaces in Doughnuts 2 and 3 with o and w, respectively, means that at least 1 of the b's will have to go in Doughnut 4. This violates rule 4, which means this choice isn't possible and is therefore our answer. No need to go through the rest of the choices. **Choice (B) is the credited response.**

The next General question is question 3.

Question 3 asks for something that *could be true*. Use the rules and your deductions to eliminate answer choices. Rule 1 eliminates choice (E). From your earlier deductions, you know that either r or b must be in the open space in Doughnut 1. This, in conjunction with rules 2 and 3, allows you to eliminate choice (B) and choice (D). You're left with choice (A) and choice (C). Try choice (A). If you put both r's in Doughnut 1 and b and o in Doughnut 4, that leaves both w's, the other b, and the other o for Doughnuts 2 and 3. There is no way to accommodate rule 4 in this instance, so this cannot be right. Eliminate choice (A). **The credited response must therefore be choice (C).**

The next General question is question 4.

Question 4 also asks for something that could be true. Again, use the rules and your deductions to eliminate answer choices. Rule 1 eliminates choice (B). Rule 3 eliminates choice (A) and choice (D). Rule 4 in conjunction with rule 3 eliminates choice (C): Because w cannot go in Doughnut 1, splitting up the b's between Doughnuts 3 and 4 makes it impossible to accommodate rule 4 when placing w. This leaves only choice (E) remaining; it therefore must be the answer. **Choice (E) is the credited response.**

The final General question is question 5.

Question 5 asks for something that *must be true*. Again, use the rules and your deductions to eliminate answer choices. Rule 1 eliminates choice (C). Unfortunately, you still have four choices left, so you'll have to try them out. Because the choices are phrased as "if… then" statements, try the first part of the choice to see whether the second part must follow from that information. For choice (A), knowing that both r's are in Doughnut 1 does not tell you anything further about the rest of the doughnuts, so eliminate it. For choice (B), knowing that both b's are in Doughnut 2 does tell you that Doughnut 1 has both r's (rule 3 and earlier deductions), but again you know nothing about how w and o are assigned to the remaining slots. Eliminate choice (B). Choice (D) tells you that Doughnut 2 has both w's. This means that b cannot go in Doughnut 3 (rule 4), so either both b's are in Doughnut 4, or one is in Doughnut 4 while the other takes the open space in Doughnut 1.

Here is your diagram:

	~o ~w 1	~r 2	3	4
5.(c)	r	w	___	b
	___	w	___	b
	r	w	___	b
	b	w	___	___

In either case, it must be true that at least one b ends up in Doughnut 4, so this choice as a whole must be true. No need to check choice (E). **Choice (D) is the credited response.**

U.N. FOOD TRUCK

One afternoon, a United Nations supply truck visits exactly five villages—Asani, Bogawa, Crafre, Dengal, and Echu—dropping off food rations. The only rations the truck is carrying that afternoon are rice and beans. The truck drops off supplies at each village exactly once. The following constraints apply:

The truck supplies rice to any village that it supplies beans to.

The truck supplies beans to the second village it visits.

The truck supplies beans to both Bogawa and Dengal.

The third village the truck supplies is Echu.

The truck supplies Asani at some time after it supplies Bogawa and supplies Crafre at some time before it supplies Asani.

The truck supplies only rice to Crafre.

1. Which one of the following could be the order in which the supply truck visits the villages?

(A) Bogawa, Crafre, Echu, Dengal, Asani
(B) Crafre, Echu, Bogawa, Dengal, Asani
(C) Bogawa, Dengal, Echu, Crafre, Asani
(D) Crafre, Asani, Echu, Dengal, Bogawa
(E) Crafre, Dengal, Echu, Asani, Bogawa

2. If the supply truck visits Dengal at some time before it visits Asani, then which of the following must be false?

(A) The first village the supply truck visits is Dengal.
(B) The fifth village the supply truck visits is Asani.
(C) The fourth village the supply truck visits is Asani.
(D) The fourth village the supply truck visits receives rice and beans.
(E) The fifth village the supply truck visits receives only rice.

3. If the supply truck visits Crafre at some time before it visits Bogawa, then which one of the following must be true?

(A) The first village the supply truck visits receives only rice.
(B) The fourth village the supply truck visits receives only rice.
(C) The fourth village the supply truck visits receives beans.
(D) The fifth village the supply truck visits receives only rice.
(E) The fifth village the supply truck visits receives beans.

4. If the supply truck supplies Asani at some time before it supplies Dengal, then which one of the following must be false?

(A) The supply truck supplies Bogawa at some time before it supplies Crafre.
(B) The supply truck supplies Bogawa at some time before it supplies Dengal.
(C) The supply truck supplies Crafre at some time before it supplies Dengal.
(D) The fourth village the supply truck visits receives beans.
(E) The fifth village the supply truck visits receives beans.

5. If the truck supplies beans to each village it visits after supplying Bogawa, then which one of the following must be true?

(A) The fifth village the supply truck supplies is Asani.
(B) The fourth village the supply truck supplies is Bogawa.
(C) The fourth village the supply truck supplies is Crafre.
(D) The second village the supply truck supplies is Bogawa.
(E) The first village the supply truck supplies is Crafre.

ANSWERS TO U.N. FOOD TRUCK

1. C
2. C
3. A
4. A
5. E

EXPLANATIONS TO U.N. FOOD TRUCK

Prepare

Ingredient Scan

Task: 2-D Order game; assign a village and a type of ration to each of 5 ordered slots.
Inventory: 5 towns and 2 types of rations for 5 slots, no 1:1 correspondence for the rations
Rules: Straightforward block and range rules and one conditional rule.
Questions: 5 total: 1 Grab-a-Rule, 4 Specific
Red Flags: The first rule might be complicated to work with
Rank: 2/3

Diagram and Inventory

The setup describes an order game in which you must place five towns—A, B, C, D, and E—in the order they receive food rations b and r. Because you are assigning rations as well as towns, and the rules present us with horizontal and vertical relationships, draw a 2-dimensional diagram with one line for towns and one for rations.

Symbolize the Rules and Double-Check

Rule 1: b→br; ~br→r

Rule 2: Place this information directly into your diagram.

Rule 3: [B / br] [D / br]

Rule 4: Place this information directly into your diagram.

Rule 5: B > A; C > A

Rule 6: [C / r]

The rules are relatively straightforward to symbolize. Notice that rule 1 is really a conditional that lets you know that if you have beans you must also have rice. This does not mean, however, that you have a beans-rice block! You can have rice alone, so if you only have one ration delivered to a town it must be rice.

Don't forget to double-check your rules!

Deductions

Links: Because E is already in slot 3, you know from rule 5 that since B and C must both come before A, that means that neither B nor C can be in slot 5 and A cannot be in slots 1, 2, or 3. A must go in either slot 4 or slot 5. You can combine rules 2 and 6 as well. Since C receives only C, it cannot go in slot 2. Because it cannot go in slot 3
(E is already there) or slot 5 (rule 5), that means C must go in either slot 1 or slot 4. Since A, C, and E cannot go in slot 2, that means slot 2 must be either B or D.
Most restricted: Because A and C each only have two slots they can go in, they are the most restricted elements.
Least restricted: b and r are fairly unrestricted overall.

Here is your diagram:

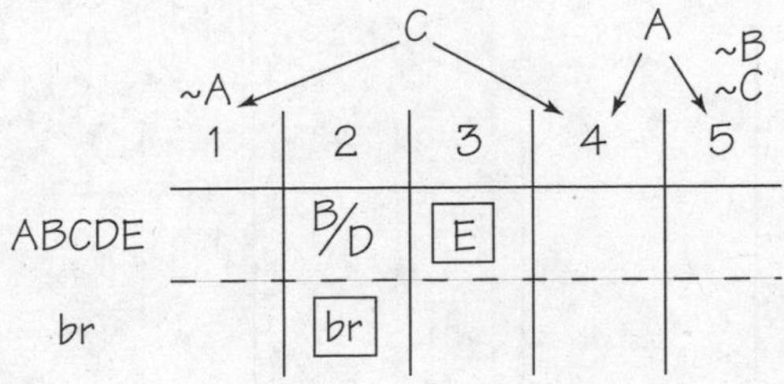

Assess, Act, Answer

Question 1 is a Grab-a-Rule question, so start there.

For question 1, use the rules to eliminate answer choices. Rule 2 eliminates choice (B), rule 5 eliminates choice (D) and choice (E), and rule 6 eliminates choice (A). **The only choice left, and therefore the credited response, is choice (C).**

Question 2 is a Specific question, so answer that one next.

For question 2, since D must come before A, that means there are now 3 elements that must come before A (rule 2), so A must be in slot 5.

Here is your diagram:

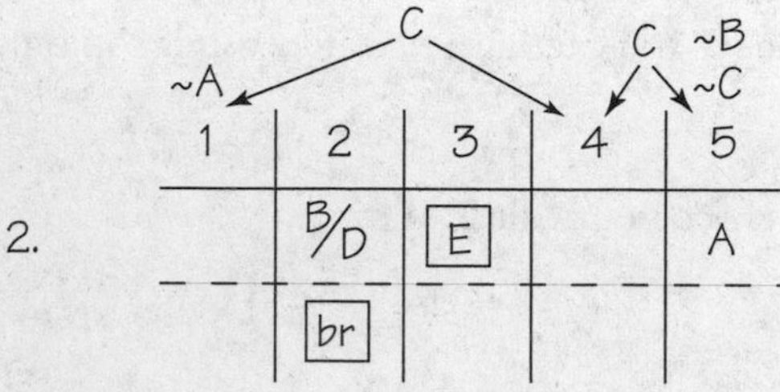

The question asks for something that *must be false*. The only choice that is false according to the diagram is that A is the fourth village visited. **Choice (C) is the credited response.**

Move on to question 3, the next Specific question.

For question 3, because C has to come before B, that means that C must be in slot 1 (deductions.) There are only two possible scenarios if C is in slot 1. If D is in slot 2, then B is in slot 4 and A is in slot 5, or if B is in slot 2, then D and A are interchangeable in slots 4 and 5.

Here is your diagram:

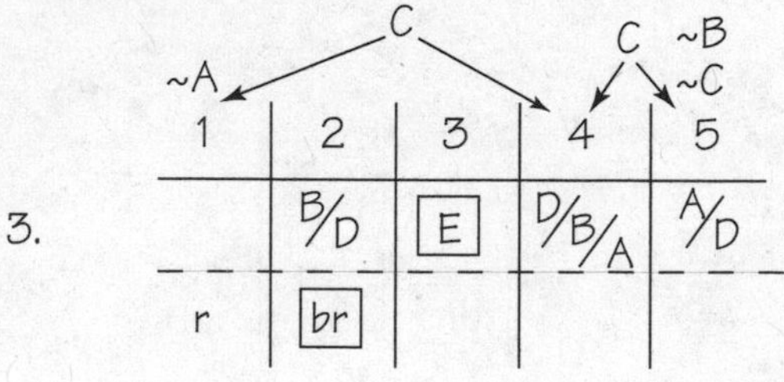

This question asks for something that *must be true*. The only possibility that must be true is that the first village receives r, not rice, because C must be the first village (rule 6.) **That makes choice (A) the credited response.**

Move on to question 4, the next Specific question.

Question 4 stipulates A before D. Since A must already be in slot 4 or 5 (deductions) that means that A is in slot 4 and D is in slot 5. This also means that B is in slot 2 (deductions) and C is in slot 1, the only slot left.

Here is your diagram:

1	2	3	4	5
C	B	[E]	A	D
r	[br]			br

The question asks for something that *must be false*. The only item in this list that must be false is that B is supplied before C. **Choice (A) is the credited response.**

Move on to question 5, the final Specific question.

This question stipulates that all the villages after B must receive beans and rice. Since C can only receive rice, that means that C must come before B, and because C can only be in slots 1 or 4 (deductions) then C must be in slot 1. If C is in slot 1, then B or D can be in slot 2, B, D, or A can be in slot 4, and A or D can be in slot 5.

Here is your diagram:

1	2	3	4	5
C	B/D	[E]	D/B/A	A/D
r	[br]			

Because the question asks for something that *must be true*, the answer should be in the diagram. The only item in this list that matches the diagram is that the first village to receive supplies is C. **Therefore, choice (E) is the credited response.**

There is one subset of Group games that is so important that it deserves its own chapter. When games involve sorting elements into only two groups, we call them In-Out games.

In one version of In-Out games, the setup stipulates that a list of elements must be sorted into one of two groups. When there are only two groups, knowing that an element is in one group means it's out of the other group. Similarly, knowing that an element is out of one group means it's in the other group. Here is how those diagrams look:

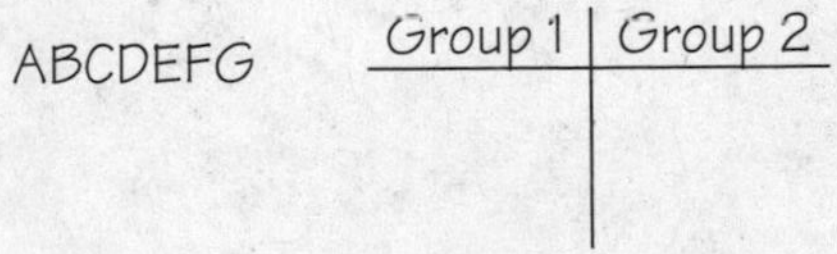

ABCDEFG

Group 1	Group 2

Other In-Out games have setups that list elements and say that only some elements will be selected or included. By implication other elements will be excluded. Thus, though the setup doesn't name the groups, there are still two groups—an In group and an Out group. Those diagrams look like this:

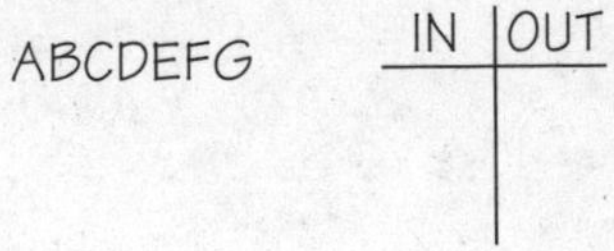

ABCDEFG

IN	OUT

When preparing an In-Out game, make use of placeholders to keep track of the bare minimum requirements for each column. For example, if two elements can't be In together, you know at least one of those elements has to be Out, so add a placeholder to the Out column to represent that. Keeping track of the minimums and maximums for each column will help you get through these games swiftly.

For some games, you will have to keep track not only of the names of elements, but groups to which those elements belong. We call these 2-D In-Out games, because you are working with two different dimensions for every element, similar to combining order and groups in 2-D Order games. For these games, keep track of the group letters below the spaces in your diagram. Here is an example:

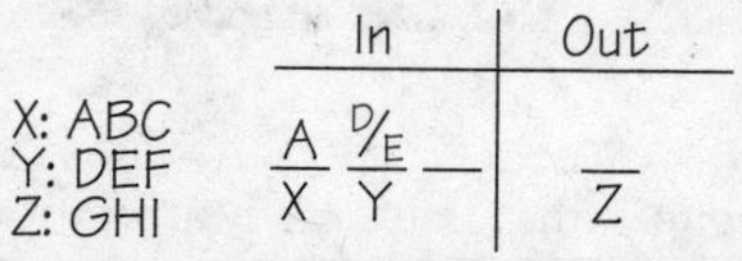

X: ABC
Y: DEF
Z: GHI

In			Out
A	D/E	__	__
X	Y		Z

A PERFECT STORM

There are seven tropical storms brewing in the Atlantic Ocean: Hildegarde, Ibrahim, Jorgina, Kevin, Lanikai, Marley, and Niharika. The tropical storms may develop into hurricanes, consistent with the following conditions:

If Kevin develops into a hurricane, so does Ibrahim.

If Marley does not develop into a hurricane, Hildegarde develops into a hurricane.

If Ibrahim develops into a hurricane, so does Lanikai.

If Lanikai develops into a hurricane, neither Jorgina nor Hildegarde develops into a hurricane.

1. Which one of the following could be a complete and accurate list of the tropical storms that develop into hurricanes?

   (A) Hildegarde, Jorgina, Marley, Niharika
   (B) Hildegarde, Lanikai, Marley, Niharika
   (C) Hildegarde, Ibrahim, Jorgina, Lanikai
   (D) Ibrahim, Jorgina, Kevin, Niharika
   (E) Ibrahim, Jorgina, Kevin, Marley

2. If both Kevin and Niharika develop into hurricanes, then exactly how many of the other tropical storms must also develop into hurricanes?

   (A) zero
   (B) one
   (C) two
   (D) three
   (E) four

3. If exactly three tropical storms develop into hurricanes, then each of the following could be true EXCEPT:

   (A) Jorgina and Marley both develop into hurricanes.
   (B) Niharika and Hildegarde both develop into hurricanes.
   (C) Ibrahim and Niharika both develop into hurricanes.
   (D) Lanikai and Ibrahim both develop into hurricanes.
   (E) Marley and Niharika both develop into hurricanes.

4. What is the maximum number of tropical storms that could develop into hurricanes if Marley does not?

   (A) two
   (B) three
   (C) four
   (D) five
   (E) six

5. If both Jorgina and Niharika develop into hurricanes, then which one of the following must be true?

   (A) Lanikai also develops into a hurricane.
   (B) Ibrahim also develops into a hurricane.
   (C) Marley also develops into a hurricane.
   (D) Kevin does not develop into a hurricane.
   (E) Hildegarde does not develop into a hurricane.

6. If Lanikai does not develop into a hurricane, each of the following could be true EXCEPT

   (A) Both Jorgina and Niharika develop into hurricanes.
   (B) Both Jorgina and Marley develop into hurricanes.
   (C) Exactly three tropical storms develop into hurricanes.
   (D) Exactly four tropical storms develop into hurricanes.
   (E) Both Kevin and Hildegarde develop into hurricanes.

ANSWERS TO A PERFECT STORM

1. A
2. D
3. C
4. B
5. D
6. E

EXPLANATIONS TO A PERFECT STORM

Prepare

Ingredient Scan

Task: In-Out game; select which of 7 storms become hurricanes
Inventory: 7 tropical storms
Rules: Like most In-Out games, all the rules are conditionals
Questions: 6 questions: 1 Grab-a-Rule, 4 Specific, 1 General
Red Flags: Make sure you diagram your conditionals correctly
Rank: 3

Diagram and Inventory

Make two columns, In and Out. You may want to label the In column "hurricane" to prevent any confusion. There are seven storms—H, I, J, K, L, M, and N. There is no limit on how many storms may be In or Out.

Symbolize the Rules and Double-Check

Rule 1: K→I; ~I→~K
Rule 2: ~M→H; ~H→M
Rule 3: I→L; ~L→~I
Rule 4: L→~J and ~H; J or H → ~L

Remember that "neither this nor that" means "not this AND not that." Also, remember "and" changes to "or" when you write out the contrapositive, and "or" switches to "and" as well.

Don't forget to double-check your rules!

Deductions

Links: Note conditional statements that have links with each other. Don't take the time to write them all out—it's a waste of space and is redundant with the rules you already have written, but keep in mind where the links exist because it will help you later.
Spatial restrictions: At least one of M/H must always be Out. Add a M/H placeholder to the Out column.
Most restricted: K sets off a significant chain of events.
Least restricted: N is a free agent.

Here is your diagram:

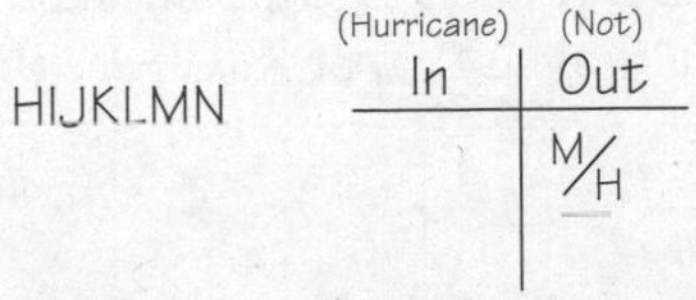

HIJKLMN	(Hurricane) In	(Not) Out
		M/H

Assess, Act, Answer

Question 1 is a Grab-a-Rule, although in In-Out games, Grab-a-Rule questions only show you half of the diagram (in this case, the In column).

For question 1, if it helps, you can draw the implied corresponding Out column next to each answer choice. When you are testing conditional rules, remember to look only for the answer choices that satisfy the left side of the statement. For instance, for rule 1, scan the answer choices for those that include K. Only choices (D) and (E) apply. Verify that I is also present. Both choices satisfy the rule, so move on to rule 2. For rule 2, examine only choices that don't have M and make sure those choices do have H. This eliminates choice (D). Rule 3 eliminates choice (E). Rule 4 eliminates choices (B) and (C). **Since choice (A) is all that remains, it is the credited response.**

Question 2 is a Specific question so do that one next.

For question 2, place K and N into the In column and check your conditionals to see what results. N is a free agent, but K forces I, L, and M to be In and forces J and H to be Out. The question asks how many storms also must be In. **Since 3 storms were added to the In column, choice (D) is the credited response.**

	(Hurricane) In	(Not) Out
2.	KNILM	JH

Question 3 is also a Specific question.

Question 3 only says that three elements are In, which means four must be Out. The question asks for something that *must be false*. As you just worked out in question 2, if K is In, then 4 storms will be In. That means K can't be In, but that is not an answer choice. Start testing the answer choices to see if they are possible. Choice (A) forces three elements Out. This seems fine. Choice (B) also forces three elements Out. Seems fine. Choice (C) forces L and M to be In. The answer choice says I and N are In, so by adding L and M as well, there are now four storms In. **Choice (C) cannot work with exactly three elements In as the question specifies, so it is the credited response.**

Question 5 is the next Specific question.

For question 5, place J and N into the In column and look at the conditionals. N is a free agent so it does nothing. J forces L, I, and K to be all Out. Since the question asks what *must be true*, scan the answers for anything pertaining to L, I, or K. **Choice (D) correctly states that K cannot be In, so it is the credited response.**

	(Hurricane) In	(Not) Out
5.	JN	LIK M/H

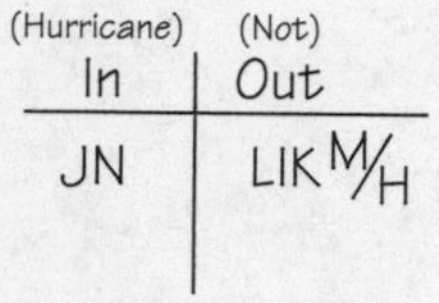

Question 6 is also a Specific question.

For question 6, place L into the Out column and look at the conditionals. L being Out forces I and K to also be Out. The question asks for something that *must be false*, so scan the answers for something false relating to I or K. **Choice (E) describes something impossible, so it is the credited response.**

	(Hurricane) In	(Not) Out
6.		LIK M/H

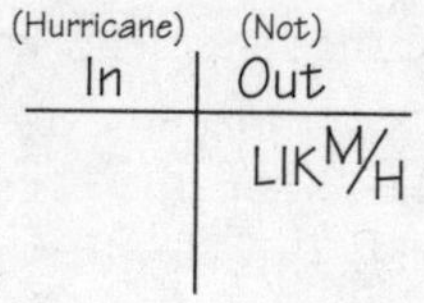

Question 4 looked like a General question, but it turns out to be Specific (the "if" just happens to be later in the sentence).

For question 4, place M in the Out column and determine the maximum number of elements that could be In. M being Out forces H to be In and forces L, I, and K to be Out. Since your diagram currently shows four elements (M, L, I, and K) in the Out column, the maximum that could be In is 3. Verify that adding the remaining two elements (N and J) does not force any rules to be broken. It doesn't. **Therefore, choice (B) is the credited response.**

	(Hurricane) In	(Not) Out
4.	H J N	MLIK

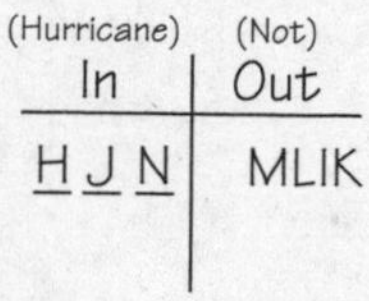

THE JUGGLER

A juggler has exactly five items to juggle: a bowling pin, a chainsaw, a flammable stick, a knife, and a lamp. Due to the uneven weight of the items, the juggler must juggle the items only in accordance with the following rules:

The juggler cannot juggle both the bowling pin and the flammable stick at the same time.

The juggler cannot juggle both the bowling pin and the lamp at the same time.

When the juggler juggles the knife, he cannot juggle any of the following items: the bowling pin, the flammable stick, or the lamp.

1. Which of the following is a pair of items the juggler could juggle at the same time?

    (A) the bowling pin and the flammable stick
    (B) the bowling pin and the lamp
    (C) the flammable stick and the lamp
    (D) the flammable stick and the knife
    (E) the lamp and the knife

2. If the juggler juggles exactly two items, and one is not the chainsaw, which of the following is a list of all the items, aside from the chainsaw, that the juggler CANNOT be juggling?

    (A) the knife
    (B) the flammable stick
    (C) the bowling pin
    (D) the bowling pin, the knife
    (E) the bowling pin, the flammable stick

3. Which of the following statements must be true?

    (A) The juggler juggles at most one other item while juggling the chainsaw.
    (B) The juggler juggles at least two other items while juggling the bowling pin.
    (C) The juggler juggles at most one other item while juggling the flammable stick.
    (D) The juggler juggles at most three items.
    (E) The juggler juggles at most four items.

4. If the juggler were to juggle exactly 3 different items, then how many possible combinations of items are possible?

    (A) one
    (B) two
    (C) three
    (D) four
    (E) five

5. Which of the following CANNOT be true?

    (A) The juggler juggles the bowling pin while juggling the chainsaw.
    (B) The juggler juggles the chainsaw while juggling the flammable stick.
    (C) The juggler juggles the knife while juggling two other items.
    (D) The juggler juggles the lamp while juggling two other items.
    (E) The juggler juggles the chainsaw while juggling two other items.

6. Which one of the following statements, if true, would guarantee that the juggler is juggling no more than one of the following items: the bowling pin, the flammable stick, the lamp?

    (A) The juggler is juggling the bowling pin.
    (B) The juggler is juggling the lamp.
    (C) The juggler is not juggling the bowling pin.
    (D) The juggler is not juggling the chainsaw.
    (E) The juggler is not juggling the knife.

ANSWERS TO THE JUGGLER

1. C
2. D
3. D
4. A
5. C
6. A

EXPLANATIONS TO THE JUGGLER

Prepare

Ingredient Scan

Task: In-Out game; select which of 5 items will be juggled together
Inventory: 5 items
Rules: All conditional statements that keep elements from being together in the In column
Questions: 6 total: 1 Grab-a-Rule, 2 Specific, 3 General
Red Flags: No specified number of In-Out slots
Rank: 3

Diagram and Inventory

The setup describes an In-Out game in which you must decide which of 5 items—b, c, f, k, and l—may be juggled (In) at the same time. There is no set number of items that must be selected.

Symbolize the Rules and Double-Check

Rule 1: 

Rule 2: 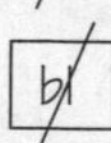

Rule 3: 

In this game, all of the conditional statements can be symbolized as antiblocks. However, it is important to remember that antiblocks apply only to the In column in this game; elements in an antiblock can still be in the Out column together.

Don't forget to double-check your rules!

Deductions

Links: Based on all the antiblocks you've created, if b is selected it must either be alone or paired with c, as b cannot be with f, k, or l. Similarly, if k is selected, it too must either be alone or paired with c, as k cannot be with b, f, or l.
Spatial restrictions: There are no spacial restrictions
Most restricted: b and k each have the greatest number of restrictions.
Least restricted: c is not mentioned in any of the rules.

Here is your diagram:

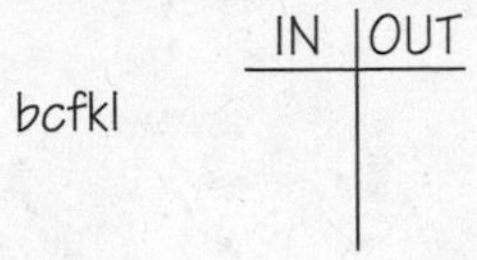

	IN	OUT
bcfkl		

Assess, Act, Answer

Question 1 is a Grab-a-Rule, so begin there.

For question 1, use the rules to eliminate answer choices. Rule 1 eliminates choice (A), rule 2 eliminates choice (B), and rule 3 eliminates choice (D) and choice (E). **The only choice left, and therefore the credited response, is choice (C).**

Question 2 is a Specific question, so answer that one next.

Question 2 asks which items cannot be juggled if two items are juggled and c is not juggled, which means you need to figure out which items end up in the Out column aside from c. Make two spaces in the In column and place c in the Out column of your diagram. From your earlier deductions, you know that b and k can only be selected with c if not selected alone. Since the question states that two items are juggled and that c is not one of them, both b and k must be in the Out column. This leaves only f and l to be selected.

Here is your diagram:

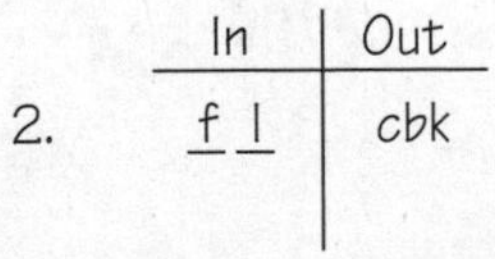

	In	Out
2.	f l	cbk

The only choice that matches what you have in the Out column is choice (D). **Therefore, choice (D) is the credited response.**

The next Specific question is question 4.

For question 4, make three slots in the In column and two slots for the Out column. From rule 3, you know that k cannot be with b, f, or l; this means k must be Out in order for you to select three items. From rules 1 and 2, you know that b cannot be with f or l; rule 3 states that it cannot be with k either. So b must also be placed in the Out column. This leaves only c, f, and l for the three spaces in the In column.

Here is your diagram:

	In	Out
4.	c f l	k b

Since b and k have so many conflicts, it is not possible to create more than this one combination of items when selecting three at a time. **The credited response is choice (A).**

Now that you've finished the Specific questions, move on to the General ones. The first General question is question 3.

Question 3 asks for something that must be true, so refer to your deductions and past work to eliminate answer choices. From question 4, you see that choice (A) and choice (C) don't have to be true, so you can cross them off. Choice (B) can be eliminated based on your deductions; b can be selected with at most one other item, c. You have already seen from question 4 that three items can be selected, but could you have four items, as choice (E) suggests? Based on your deductions, this can't be possible; both b and k can each only be selected with one other item, so there's no way to select four items at once. Eliminate choice (E). **Choice (D) is the credited response.**

The next General question is question 5.

Question 5 asks what cannot be true, which means four of the answer choices will be possible. Use your deductions and past work to eliminate answer choices that do work. From your deductions, you know that it is possible, for b and c to be chosen together, so eliminate choice (A). Choice (B) is possible as you saw it in your work for question 4, so eliminate it. Choice (C) violates your deductions; the only item k can be selected with is c and no others. Since this choice is definitely not true, it must be the credited response. There is no need to check the remaining choices. **Choice (C) is the credited response.**

The final General question is question 6.

Question 6 asks you to find an answer choice that will allow you to determine that only one of b, f, and l is being selected. The best approach here is to go to the answer choices and put the rules and your deductions to work. For choice (A), if you know that b is selected, you also know that neither f (rule 1) nor l (rule 2) can be selected. This ensures that of the three items mentioned in the question, only b is selected, so this must be correct. No need to spend additional time on the remaining choices. **Choice (A) is the credited response.**

ROCK BAND

Mike is auditioning members for an '80s glam band. The members of this band will be selected from among three guitarists—Arnold, Beau, and Corey—three drummers—Killer, Laser, and Madman—and four vocalists—Ursella, Wyette, Xavier, and Zack. In addition, two of the musicians—Beau and Xavier—also audition as keyboardists. The band must have exactly one drummer and each member of the band can be chosen for only one position. The selection of band members must meet the following constraints:

The band will have at least five, and at most six, members.
Arnold and Corey cannot both be selected.
Madman and Zack cannot both be selected.
Ursella and Wyette cannot both be selected.
Wyette is selected only if Corey is also selected.
If Xavier is selected as a keyboardist, then Beau is not selected for the band.

1. Which one of the following could be an accurate list of the band members selected?

(A) Guitarist: Arnold, Beau
Drummer: Killer
Vocalist: Wyette, Xavier
(B) Guitarist: Corey, Beau
Drummer: Killer
Vocalist: Wyette, Zack
(C) Guitarist: Arnold, Beau
Drummer: Killer
Vocalist: Wyette
Keyboardist: Xavier
(D) Guitarist: Arnold, Corey
Drummer: Madman
Vocalist: Ursella
Keyboardist: Xavier
(E) Guitarist: Corey
Drummer: Madman
Vocalist: Ursella, Zack
Keyboardist: Xavier

2. If Xavier is selected as a keyboardist, then which of the following must be true?

(A) Arnold is selected.
(B) Corey is selected.
(C) At most one guitarist can be selected.
(D) At most two guitarists are selected.
(E) At least three vocalists are selected.

3. Which one of the following must be false?

(A) Arnold and Beau are both selected for the band.
(B) Beau and Xavier are both selected for the band.
(C) Madman and Wyette are both selected for the band.
(D) Wyette and Arnold are both selected for the band.
(E) Wyette and Xavier are both selected for the band.

4. If Wyette is selected for the band but Madman is not, then which of the following could be also selected?

(A) Beau and Killer
(B) Killer and Laser
(C) Laser and Ursella
(D) Zack and Arnold
(E) Zack and Ursella

5. If Madman is selected for the band but Arnold is not, then which of the following must be true?

(A) Ursella is selected.
(B) Wyette is selected.
(C) The band must include exactly two vocalists.
(D) The band must include exactly two guitarists.
(E) The band must have exactly six members.

6. If Wyette is selected for a six member band, then which of the following could be true?

(A) Arnold is selected.
(B) Madman is selected.
(C) Zack is not selected.
(D) Beau is selected as a keyboardist.
(E) Xavier is selected as a keyboardist.

ANSWERS TO ROCK BAND

1. B
2. C
3. D
4. A
5. C
6. D

EXPLANATIONS TO ROCK BAND

Prepare

Ingredient Scan

Task: 2-D In-Out game; select which of 10 musicians are chosen for a band
Inventory: 10 musicians for either 5 or 6 spaces
Rules: Rules include complicated conditionals and distribution limitations
Questions: 6 total: 1 Grab-a-Rule, 4 Specific, 1 General
Red Flags: Complex inventory where some elements fall into two groups
Rank: 2/3

Diagram and Inventory

The setup describes a game in which five or six musicians are chosen for a band, and four or five are therefore not. Since you can leave elements out, add an Out column to keep track. The inventory consists of three types of musicians which you should keep track of with subscripts: A_G, B_G, C_G, K_D, L_D, M_D, U_V, W_V, X_V, and Z_V. In addition, two of these elements need an additional subscript: $B_{K/G}$ and $X_{K/V}$.

Symbolize the Rules and Double-Check

Rule 1: Make a note that there are five or six elements, and note this in your diagram.

Rule 2: ~~$A_G C_G$~~

Rule 3: ~~$M_D Z_V$~~

Rule 4: ~~$U_V W_V$~~

Rule 5: $\sim W_V$; $W_V \rightarrow C_V \rightarrow \sim C_G$

Rule 6: $X_K \rightarrow \sim B$; $B \rightarrow \sim X_K$

Rule 5 is a conditional statement that has "only if" in it; note in conditional statements that the requirement goes on the left side of the arrow. Also note that rule 6 only applies when X is selected as a keyboardist. If X is selected as a vocalist, the rule does not matter.

Don't forget to double-check your rules!

Deductions

Links: Rules 1, 3, and 5 combine to make: $W_V \rightarrow C_G$ and $\sim A_G$ and $\sim U_V$; $\sim C_G$ or A_G or $U_V \rightarrow \sim W_V$. From rule 1, A or C must always be Out, so put a placeholder for A/C in your out column. Rule 2 is another antiblock that gives an M/Z placeholder in the Out column, and rule 3 gives a U/W placeholder in the Out column as well.
Spatial restrictions: Exactly one drummer is selected. That means that two drummers must be Out. Note this in your diagram.
Least restricted: B_G, K_D, L_D, and X_V have no restrictions on them from the rules.

Here is your diagram:

G: ABC
D: KLM
V: UWXZ

In	Out
_ _ _ _ _ (_)	_ _ A/C U/W (_) M/Z
D	D D G V

Assess, Act, Answer

Question 1 is a Grab-a-Rule question, so start there.

For question 1, use the rules to eliminate answer choices. Rule 2 eliminates choice (D), rule 3 eliminates choice (E), rule 5 eliminates choice (A), and rule 6 eliminates choice (C). **The only choice left, and therefore the credited response, is choice (B).**

Question 2 is a Specific question, so answer that one next.

For question 2, place X_K in your In column. From rule 6, B must be out. From your deductions, A or C must be Out, U or W must be Out, and M or Z must be Out.

Here is your diagram:

	In					Out				
2.	X	L/K	A/C	U/W	Z	M	K/L	B	C/A	W/U
	K	D	G	V	V	D	D		G	V

Because the question asks for something that *must be true*, look through the answer choices to see if any of them matches the diagram. Choices (A) and (B) both could be true, but don't have to be true, so eliminate them. Because B was selected as a keyboardist and not a guitarist, and A and C cannot both be In, there can be at most one guitarist. **Therefore, choice (C) is the credited response.**

Move on to question 4, the next Specific question.

For question 4, place W_V in the In column and M_D in the Out column. From rule 5, C_G is also In, and from rule 1, A_G must be Out. Rule 3 puts U_V in the Out column as well.

Here is your diagram:

	In					Out				
4.	K/L	W	C	_	_	M	L/K	U	A	(_)
	D	V	G			D	D	V	G	

Since the question asks for who can also be in the band, eliminate any answer choice that includes an element from your Out column. Eliminate choices (C), (D), and (E) this way. You can also eliminate choice (B) since it violates the one drummer rule. **This leaves choice (A) as the credited response.**

Move on to question 5, the next Specific question.

For question 5, put M_D in your In column and A_G in your Out column. From rule 3 we know that Z_V must also be Out, and since there can only be one drummer, that means K_D and L_D are also Out. We need to reserve a space for U_V or W_V, so that makes five spaces in our Out column. Since we need to have at least five members In, that means everyone else must be In.

Here is your diagram:

	In					Out				
5.	M	B	C	U/W	X	L	K	A	Z	W/U
	D	G/K	G	V	V	D	D	G	V	V

Since we are looking for what must be true, look to your diagram. Since X and B must both be In, X must be a vocalist. So now we have exactly two vocalists in the band. **Choice (C) is the credited response.**

The last Specific question is question 6.

For question 6, place W_V in your In column and note that six spaces are In and therefore four are Out. Since W_V is In, from rules 2, 4, and 5 we know that C_G must be In and A_G and U_V must be Out. Our other two spaces in the Out column must be drummers, so one of them must be M_D (rule 3) and the remaining guitarists and vocalists must be In.

Here is your diagram:

	In						Out			
6.	$\frac{W}{V}$	$\frac{C}{G}$	$\frac{L/K}{D}$	$\frac{B}{K/G}$	$\frac{X}{V}$	$\frac{Z}{V}$	$\frac{M}{D}$	$\frac{K/L}{D}$	$\frac{U}{V}$	$\frac{A}{G}$

The question asks for something that *could be true*. The only possibility that is not incompatible with our diagram is that B could be selected as a keyboardist. **Therefore, choice (D) is the credited response.**

Now that the Specific questions are complete, attack the General questions. Question 3 is the only General question.

Question 3 asks for something that *must be false*. From the deductions linking rules 2 and 5, A_G and W_V cannot be In together. **Therefore, choice (D) is the credited response.**

SPICY CHILI

Sasha is selecting at least one of the following seven flavors to add to her chili: beer, cayenne, hickory, Italian seasoning, jalapeno, paprika, and salt. The ingredients are included according to the following constraints:

If Italian seasoning is included, then either hickory or paprika (but not both) are included.

If jalapeno is included or beer is not included, then hickory is not included.

If salt is included or jalapeno is not included, then paprika is not included.

If either cayenne or salt is not included, then beer is not included.

1. Which of the following could be a complete and accurate list of the flavors included in the chili?

(A) cayenne, jalapeno
(B) beer, cayenne, hickory
(C) cayenne, Italian seasoning, jalapeno
(D) hickory, Italian seasoning, jalapeno
(E) cayenne, hickory, Italian seasoning, paprika

2. If Sasha includes Italian seasoning in the chili, then which one of the following must be true?

(A) At most four flavors are included.
(B) At least three flavors are included.
(C) Hickory is included.
(D) Jalapeno is included.
(E) Paprika is included.

3. Which of the following CANNOT be true of the chili?

(A) Both beer and paprika are included.
(B) Both beer and Italian seasoning are included.
(C) Both jalapeno and Italian seasoning are included.
(D) Both cayenne and Italian seasoning are included.
(E) Both beer and jalapeno are included.

4. What is the maximum number of ingredients that could be included in the chili?

(A) 3
(B) 4
(C) 5
(D) 6
(E) 7

5. If Sasha includes hickory in the chili, then which of the following could be true?

(A) Paprika is included.
(B) Cayenne is not included.
(C) A total of two ingredients are included.
(D) Italian seasoning is not included.
(E) Salt is not included.

6. If cayenne is not included in the chili, then which one of the following is another flavor that CANNOT be included?

(A) Italian seasoning
(B) hickory
(C) jalapeno
(D) paprika
(E) salt

ANSWERS TO SPICY CHILI

1. A
2. B
3. A
4. C
5. D
6. B

EXPLANATIONS TO SPICY CHILI

Prepare

Ingredient Scan

Task: In-Out game; select which of 7 flavors are added to chili
Inventory: 7 flavors
Rules: All conditional rules
Questions: 6 total: 1 Grab-a-Rule, 3 Specific, 2 General
Red Flags: Lots of conditional rules to keep track of no specified number of spaces
Rank: 2/3

Diagram and Inventory

The setup describes an In-Out game in which at least one of seven flavors—b, c, h, i, j, p, and s—must be added to chili (the In column). There is no set number of flavors that must be selected.

Symbolize the Rules and Double-Check

Rule 1: i→h or p (not both); ~h and ~p→~i
Rule 2: j or ~b→ ~h; h→ ~j and b
Rule 3: s j or ~b→ ~h; h→ ~j and b
Rule 4: ~c or ~s→ ~b; b→ c and s

Don't forget to double-check your rules!

Deductions

Links: Rule 1 tells you that i requires either h or p but not both. If i is paired with h, p is Out, but in addition b is In and j is Out (rule 2). If b is In, so are c and s (rule 4). On the flip side, if i is selected with p, j is In, h is out, and s is Out (rule 3). If s is Out, b is also Out (rule 4).
Spatial restrictions: There are no spatial restrictions.
Most restricted: Whether h is In or Out determines where a lot of the other elements end up.
Least restricted: c is linked to the fewest elements.

Here is your diagram:

bchijps

IN	OUT

Assess, Act, Answer

Start with the Grab-a-Rule question, which is question 1.

For question 1, use the rules to eliminate answer choices. Rule 1 eliminates choice (C) and choice (E), rule 2 eliminates choice (D), and rule 4 eliminates choice (B). **The only choice left, and therefore the credited response, is choice (A).**

Move on to the Specific questions, of which question 2 is first.

For question 2, place i in the In column. Since you aren't given more information, you'll have to try each of the possibilities associated with i, meaning try h and then try p. You've already worked out these scenarios during your deduction work with finding links, but now you can actually fill them in on your diagram.

Here is your diagram:

	In	Out
2.	inbcs	pj
	ipj	hsb

The question asks for what must be true, which means it must be true in either scenario. The only choice that is true in both cases is choice (B). **Choice (B) is the credited response.**

The next Specific question is question 5.

For question 5, place h in the In column. If h is In, then b is In and j is Out (rule 2). If j is Out, so is p (rule 3). If b is In, then c and s are also In (rule 4). The only flavor unaccounted for is i.

Here is your diagram:

	In	Out
5.	hbcs	jp

The question asks for something that *could be true*. The only choice that could be true based on your diagram is choice (D). **Choice (D) is the credited response.**

The final Specific question is question 6.

For question 6, place c in the Out column. If c is Out, then b is Out (rule 4); if b is Out, then so is h (rule 2).

Here is your diagram:

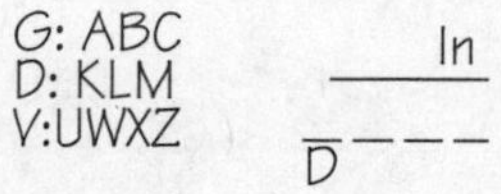

G: ABC
D: KLM
V:UWXZ

In

D̄ – – –

Although you don't have anything in the In column, the question asks for what else cannot be included, so you have enough work to answer the question. Neither h nor b can be included, and h is one of the answer choices. **Choice (B) is the credited response.**

Now that the Specific questions are done, continue on to the General questions. The first General question is question 3.

Question 3 asks for what cannot be true, which means that four choices will be possible; use your deductions and past work to eliminate these. If you look at your work for question 2, you can eliminate choice (B), choice (C), and choice (D), since all these are possible. Neither choice (A) nor choice (E) appears in prior work. However, both choices involve b, so you should look back at the rules involving b. If b is selected, then so are c and s (rule 4). If s is selected, then p cannot be (rule 3). This means that choice (A) cannot be true. There is no need to try choice (E). **Choice (A) is the credited response.**

The final General question is question 4.

Question 4 asks for the maximum number of ingredients that could be selected at one time. From question 2, you know that you can have five ingredients selected, so eliminate choice (A) and choice (B). If you tried to put all seven ingredients together, rule 1 would knock the number down to 6; eliminate choice (E). Even then, though, whether you chose h or p to be selected with i, each will eliminate another ingredient—h eliminates j (rule 2) and p eliminates s (rule 3). Therefore choice (D) is not possible either. **Choice (C) is the credited response.**

The term *distribution game* is a bit of a misnomer. All games involve distributing elements among spaces. However, some games can be "solved" by deducing only a few possible scenarios. These are often Group games, though there are some Order games that can be boiled down to two or three scenarios. Notice here that a *distribution game* is a type of Order or Group game.

How do you know when it is wise to take time to try out possible scenarios? Here are a few clues:

- The setup or rules provide hints about possible arrangements, such as limitations on the number of spaces in a group.
- Many or most of the questions associated with the game ask about the possible distribution of spaces in the diagram.
- You have a block or chunk of elements that can only go one of two ways and will likely set off other deductions.

If you successfully deduce the two or three possible arrangements of the diagram for these games, most of your work will be done. Even though you may take longer to diagram, symbolize, and deduce than you do on more straightforward games, you can usually work the questions rapidly.

If you are working a distribution game and are worried that you have not found all of the possible distributions, don't worry. Do your best to make sure you have exhausted all the variations you can see, but don't panic about missing something. If necessary, you can find it when you work the questions.

Once you see the benefits of taking time to set up distribution games, you might think, "Why shouldn't I map out scenarios for every game?" For most games, it's impractical and needlessly time-consuming to try every iteration. It would take you longer than just going through the questions, whereas for most distribution games, without seeing the distributions first, your only strategy for answering questions would be to try out most or all of the answer choices. *Don't map out scenarios in your setup unless you are confident you can break your game into two or three possible distributions.*

PIPELINE

Exactly five countries—A, I, K, R, and T—surround a sea that contains significant deposits of natural resources. Three different proposed pipelines routes—pipeline 1, pipeline 2, and pipeline 3—have been drawn up, each of which passes through at least one of the five proposed pipelines. Every country is included at least one of these countries, and each country is included in no more than one proposal. The routes must conform to the following conditions:

Pipeline 1 does not pass through either I or K.

The pipeline that passes through A also runs through at least one additional country.

If pipeline 3 passes through I, then pipeline 2 passes through R.

1. Which one of the following could be a complete and accurate matching of countries to the pipelines that might pass through them?

   (A) Pipeline 1: A, T
   Pipeline 2: I
   Pipeline 3: K

   (B) Pipeline 1: A, R
   Pipeline 2: I, K
   Pipelinc 3: T

   (C) Pipeline 1: K, T
   Pipeline 2: A, I
   Pipeline 3: R

   (D) Pipeline 1: T
   Pipeline 2: A, K
   Pipeline 3: I, R

   (E) Pipeline 1: T
   Pipeline 2: I, K, and R
   Pipeline 3: A

2. Which one of the following is a complete and accurate list of the countries, any one of which could be the only country through which pipeline 2 passes?

   (A) I, K, and R
   (B) K, T
   (C) I, T
   (D) I, R
   (E) R

3. If pipeline 3 passes through exactly three countries, then which one of the following must be false?

   (A) Pipeline 2 passes through R.
   (B) Pipeline 3 passes through A, I, and K.
   (C) Pipeline 3 passes through A, K, and R.
   (D) Pipeline 3 passes through A, R, and T.
   (E) Pipeline 3 passes through A, K, and T.

4. Which one of the following CANNOT be a complete and accurate list of the countries through which pipeline 3 passes?

   (A) K, R
   (B) I, K
   (C) I, T
   (D) A, K
   (E) A, I

5. If the same pipeline passes through both K and T, which one of the following could be true?

   (A) Pipeline 1 passes through T.
   (B) Pipeline 3 passes through R.
   (C) Pipeline 2 passes through K.
   (D) Pipeline 3 passes through I.
   (E) Pipeline 2 passes through A.

6. Which one of the following CANNOT be a complete and accurate list of the countries through which pipeline 2 passes?

   (A) A, I, and K
   (B) A, I, and R
   (C) A, I, and T
   (D) A, K, and R
   (E) A, K, and T

ANSWERS TO PIPELINE

1. B
2. D
3. D
4. C
5. E
6. E

Prepare

Ingredient Scan

Task: Group game with variable assignments; assign each of 5 countries to exactly 1 of 3 different pipelines
Inventory: 5 countries
Rules: Mostly straightforward and okay to symbolize, but there aren't many rules
Questions: 6 total: 1 Grab-a-Rule, 2 Specific, 3 General
Red Flags: Variable distribution among the groups
Rank: 3/4

Diagram and Inventory

The setup describes a Group game in which the number of elements can vary within the groups, but the number of spaces is always five. Since the countries are being assigned to the pipelines, the pipelines form the core of the diagram.

Symbolize the Rules and Double-Check

Rule 1: Enter this information directly into your diagram.
Rule 2: [A —] or [A — —]
Rule 3: $I_3 \rightarrow R_2$; $\sim R_2 \rightarrow I\sim_3$

These rules are relatively straightforward to symbolize. Rule 2 can be tricky, but since there are 5 elements dispersed among the 3 groups, and every group must have at least one element in it, that means that A will be with either one or two other countries.

Don't forget to double-check your rules!

Deductions

Spatial restrictions: Again, since we are assigning the five countries to three pipelines, and every pipeline goes through at least one country, that means that if we put one country per pipeline, we have two countries left over to assign. Those two can go into one group, or into two separate groups. So, now we know that our two possible distributions are 1–1–3 or 1–1–2, though not necessarily in that order, which adds to the complexity of this game.
Most restricted: Since A cannot be alone, it is the most restricted element.
Least restricted: There are no restrictions on T.

Here is your diagram:

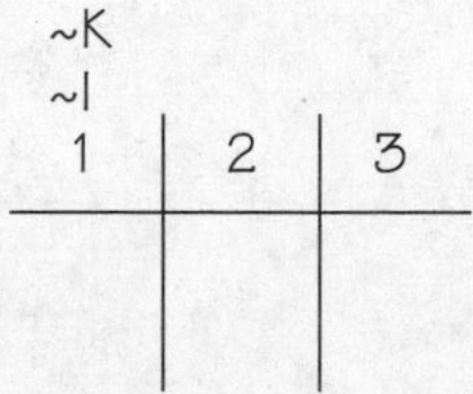

Assess, Act, Answer

Question 1 is a Grab-a-Rule question, so start there.

For question 1, use the rules to eliminate answer choices. Rule 1 eliminates choice (C), rule 2 eliminates choice (E), and rule 3 eliminates choice (D). Since there are only four countries in choice (A), eliminate that one as well. **The only choice left, and therefore the credited response, is choice (B).**

Question 3 is the first Specific question, so answer that one next.

For question 3, place A and two more spaces in group 3, and one space each in groups 1 and 2. Since I cannot be in group 1, it must be in group 2 or 3. If I is in group 2, then K must be in group 3 (rule 1) and the remaining 2 spaces can be either T or R. If I is in group 3, then R must be in group 2 (rule 3) and K must be in group 3 (rule 1), leaving T in group 1.

Here is your diagram:

	~K ~I 1	2	3
3.	T	R	A I K
	T/R	I	A K R/T

Since the question asks for something that *must be false,* look for an answer that cannot work with our diagram. **Choice (D) is the only one that does not work with either scenario and is therefore the credited response.**

Move on to question 5, the next Specific question.

Since question 5 stipulates that K and T need to be together, this means that I, K, and T cannot be in group 1. So, group 1 is composed of either R or AR. Since R is in group 1, then I cannot be in group 3 (rule 3) so I must be in group 2. K and T must now be in group 3, either alone or with A.

Here is your diagram:

	~K ~I 1	2	3
5.	AR	I	KT
	R	I	KTA

The question asks for what could be true. The only choice that could be true is choice (E). **Choice (E) is the credited response.**

Now that the Specific questions are complete, attack the General questions, starting with question 2.

Question 2 asks for a list of countries each of which could be the only country in group 2. In question 3, I was in group 2 alone, so cross off choices (B) and (E) since they don't include I. In question 2, R was also alone, so cross off choice (C). Now we just need to try K. If K is alone in group 2, then I must be in group 3 (rule 1), but if I is in group 3, then R must be in group 2, which means that K cannot be alone. Cross off choice (A). **That leaves choice (D) as the credited response.**

Move on to question 4, the next General question.

Question 4 asks for a list of countries that cannot be the complete list of countries in group 3. Choices (A) and (B) were both seen in question 2, so cross them off. None of the choices match the information in question 5, so we are left to try the remaining choices. Let's just start with choice (C). Put I and T into group 3. Put R in group 2 (rule 3) and K in group 2 (rule 1).

Here is your diagram:

	~K ~I 1	2	3
4.		~~RK~~	~~IT~~

That leaves A for group 1, but A has to be in a group of two or more, so this arrangement cannot work. **Choice (C) is the credited response.**

Move on to question 6, the final General question.

Question 6 is very much like question 4, but for group 2 instead of group 3. None of our prior work has three countries in group 2, so we are going to have to work this one out. Since A is in all the answers, put A and two spaces in group 2. That means that groups 1 and 3 have one space each. What do we know? Since group 1 cannot have I or K and now not A, that leaves T or R for that group. I and K have to go in group 2 or 3. We now have two possible scenarios based on I. If I is in group 3, then R is in group 2 and T is in group 1. If I is in group 2, then K, T, and R are interchangeable in groups 2 and 3.

Here is your diagram:

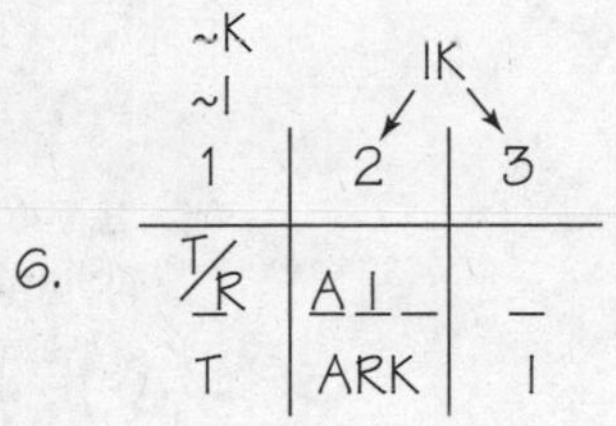

	~K ~I	IK ↙	↘
	1	2	3
6.	T/R	A I _	_
	T	ARK	I

The only arrangement that cannot be made in group 2 is choice (E), since if A, K, and T are in group 2 then I must be in group 3, and that violates rule 3. **The credited response is choice (E).**

MAGIC

Three wizards—Abernethy, Bardolph, and Cynfor—are training five flying carpets—Petara, Quorra, Rumer, Seirian, and Vevay. Each wizard will train at least one flying carpet. Each flying carpet will be trained by exactly one wizard. The assignment of flying carpets to wizards must conform to the following conditions:

Vevay and Seirian are trained by the same wizard.
Rumer and Seirian are not trained by the same wizard.
If Cynfor trains Petara, Cynfor also trains Quorra.
Rumer is trained by Abernethy.

1. Which of the following could be a complete and accurate matching of flying carpets to the wizards that train them?

(A) Abernethy: Rumer
Bardolph: Quorra
Cynfor: Petara, Seirian, Vevay
(B) Abernethy: Rumer
Bardolph: Petara, Quorra
Cynfor: Seirian, Vevay
(C) Abernethy: Rumer
Bardolph: Petara, Seirian
Cynfor: Quorra, Vevay
(D) Abernethy: Seirian, Vevay
Bardolph: Rumer
Cynfor: Petara, Quorra
(E) Abernethy: Rumer, Seirian, Vevay
Bardolph: Petara
Cynfor: Quorra

2. If Quorra and Rumer are trained by the same wizard, which of the following statements could be true?

(A) Abernethy trains exactly three of the flying carpets.
(B) Quorra is trained by Cynfor.
(C) Seirian and Quorra are trained by the same wizard.
(D) Cynfor trains exactly two of the flying carpets.
(E) Vevay and Petara are trained by the same wizard.

3. Which one of the following could be true?

(A) Quorra is the only flying carpet trained by Cynfor.
(B) Rumer, Seirian, and Vevay are all trained by Bardolph.
(C) Rumer and Vevay are trained by the same wizard.
(D) Vevay is the only flying carpet trained by Cynfor.
(E) Three of the flying carpets are trained by Abernethy.

4. Which one of the following must be true?

(A) Quorra and Vevay are not trained by the same wizard.
(B) Quorra is not trained by Abernethy.
(C) Abernethy trains the same number of flying carpets as Cynfor.
(D) Petara and Quorra are trained by the same wizard.
(E) Abernethy trains at most two of the flying carpets.

5. If Vevay is trained by Cynfor, which one of the following must be false?

(A) Bardolph trains exactly one flying carpet.
(B) Cynfor trains exactly three flying carpets.
(C) Petara is trained by Cynfor.
(D) Quorra is trained by Cynfor.
(E) None of the other flying carpets is trained by the wizard who trains Rumer.

6. The wizard with which each flying carpet trains is completely determined if which one of the following is true?

(A) Petara is trained by Abernethy.
(B) Petara is trained by Cynfor.
(C) Quorra is trained by Bardolph.
(D) Rumer is trained by Abernethy.
(E) Vevay is trained by Bardolph.

ANSWERS TO MAGIC

1. B
2. D
3. A
4. E
5. C
6. B

EXPLANATIONS TO MAGIC

Prepare

Ingredient Scan

Task: Group game with fixed assignments (elements can only go once); assign each of 5 flying carpets to exactly 1 of 3 wizards
Inventory: 5 flying carpets
Rules: Standard group game rules
Questions: 6 total: 1 Grab-a-Rule, 2 Specific, 3 General
Red Flags: NNo major red flags
Rank: 1

Diagram and Inventory

You are assigning five things to three groups. The five elements are P, Q, R, S, and V. Make three columns—A, B, and C—as the core of the diagram. Every group has to have at least one element in it, so there aren't too many ways you can split up five things into three groups. The distribution of groups will have to be either 1–1–3 or 1–1–2.

Symbolize the Rules and Double-Check

Rule 1: [VS]

Rule 2: [RS] (crossed out)

Rule 3: $P_C \rightarrow Q_C$; $\sim Q_C \rightarrow \sim P_C$

Rule 4: R is in group A. Place it in your diagram.

Don't forget to double-check your rules!

Deductions

Links: S appears in two rules so consider if you can link them. V and S will always be together according to rule 1 and R and S can never be together according to rule 2. Therefore, R and V will never be in the same group.

Spatial restrictions: Whenever a game gives you a block, start your deductive process by determining what options you have for the block. Can VS go in any of the three groups? It can't go in group A because R is there and R and S can never be in the same group. So it will have to go in group B or C. You can write out a row for each scenario to see if any other deductions are possible. The only other rule to worry about is the conditional. If P is in group C, then Q must also be. Does that present a problem for either scenario? Yes, in the scenario in which VS is in group C, then adding P and Q to group C would leave nothing for group B. Since that can't happen, P can't be added to group C for that scenario.
Most restricted: The VS block should be your first concern. The conditional rule limits P.
Least restricted: Q is the least restricted. It's the independent part of a conditional rule so it is free to go anywhere with impunity.

Here is your diagram:

PQRSV

	A	B	C
i.	R	VS	
ii.	R		VS ~P

Assess, Act, Answer

Question 1 is a Grab-a-Rule, so do that one first.

For question 1, use the rules to eliminate answer choices. Rule 1 eliminates choice (C), rule 2 eliminates choice (E), rule 3 eliminates choice (A), and rule 4 eliminates choice (D). **Because choice (B) is all that remains, it is the credited response.**

Question 2 is your first Specific question, so do it next.

For question 2, symbolize the condition it gives: QR is now a block. You already know R is in group A, so place Q in there with it. Do you know where the VS block goes? It seems like it could still be group B or C. What about the conditional? Q is not in group C, so P cannot be in group C. Something has to be in group C, so it must be the VS block since that's the only other choice. Because of that, P will have to be in group B because something needs to be in B. The question asks for something that *could be true*, and your scenario shows everything that *must be true*. This just means you have to match up an answer with what you're seeing in this scenario. **Since choice (D) is the only one that matches, it is the credited response.**

	A	B	C
2.	QR	P	VS

Question 5 is the next Specific question, so do that one next.

For question 5, place V into group C. Placing V, of course, means placing the VS block into group C. R is always in group A. Group B is still open and P and Q are left. At least one of them must go in group B. Since VS is in group C, you can refer to your second scenario in which you deduced that P cannot go in group C (as it would force Q to come with it). The question asks for something that *must be false.* **Choice (C) correctly states that P cannot go in group C, so it is the credited response.**

	A	B	C
5.	R		VS ~P

All the Specific questions are done, so go back to your first General question 3.

Question 3 asks for something that *could be true.* Start with choice (A). Could Q be the only element in group C? It doesn't seem to present any problems. That means the VS block would be in group B. Is there a safe spot for P? Sure, putting P in group A or group B doesn't affect any rules. **Since this scenario is possible, choice (A) is the credited response.**

Question 4 is the next General question.

Question 4 asks for something that *must be true.* Therefore, your goal is to eliminate answer choices that don't have to be true. To test whether choice (A) has to be true, ask yourself whether Q and V could be in the same group. Looking at the work for question 2, you could put P in group B and add Q to group C with the VS block. Nothing would be amiss, so eliminate choice (A). To test choice (B), determine whether Q can go in group A. It already has in question 2, so eliminate choice (B). Choice (C) says that there will always be an equal amount of things in group A and C. Can you make it otherwise? Looking at the work for question 5, you could put P and Q into group B. That would mean group A has one element and group C has two. That disproves choice (C). Choice (D) says P and Q must be together. The work for question 2 disproves that. **Choice (E) is all that remains, so it is the credited response.**

Even though you've done enough to confidently choose choice (E), you might check it if you're not positive about the work you did to eliminate the previous answer choices. Choice (E) says that A must have at most two elements. To disprove that, try to force A to have three elements. Group A always has R and can never have the VS block, so you would have to use R, P, and Q. That leaves group B and C still open and only a VS block to go in one of those groups. Hence, it is impossible for group A to have three elements.

Question 6 is a General question and the final question of the game.

For question 6, take a second to paraphrase awkward question stems. This type of question, in which you are asked to identify something that allows the diagram to be "completely determined," is basically asking for the answer choice that is the magic domino that makes everything else fall into place. Sketch out the ramifications of each choice. If you have any flexibility, then eliminate the answer. Choice (A) says to place P in group A. You still have VS and Q to fill up groups B and C. That could go either way, so eliminate choice (A). Choice (B) says to place P in group C. That forces Q into group C. That leaves only the VS block and an open group B. VS would have to go in group B or else nothing would. **Because everything fell into place, choice (B) is the credited response.**

SCUBA DIVES

Exactly six people—Doug, Engelberta, Froth, Godiva, Hubert, and Irina—are the only scuba divers investigating a shipwreck by the barrier reef off the coast of Belize. There will be exactly four different dives, one after the other. Exactly two divers will participate in each of the four dives, each person diving at least once, consistent with the following conditions:

Doug dives during the last dive.
Engelberta dives only once, but does not dive with Godiva.
Irina dives neither during the first nor the third dive.
Hubert dives exactly twice, once just before and once just after the only time that Froth dives.

1. Which one of the following could be an accurate list of the divers who dive together during each of the four dives?
   (A) first dive: Engelberta, Hubert; second dive: Engelberta, Froth; third dive: Godiva, Hubert; fourth dive: Doug, Irina
   (B) first dive: Doug, Engelberta; second dive: Hubert, Irina; third dive: Doug, Froth; fourth dive: Godiva, Hubert
   (C) first dive: Doug, Engelberta; second dive: Godiva, Hubert; third dive: Froth, Irina; fourth dive: Doug, Hubert
   (D) first dive: Godiva, Hubert; second dive: Doug, Irina; third dive: Engelberta, Froth; fourth dive: Doug, Engelberta
   (E) first dive: Godiva, Hubert; second dive: Froth, Irina; third dive: Godiva, Hubert; fourth dive: Doug, Engelberta

2. Which one of the following could be true?
   (A) Hubert dives with Froth during the second dive.
   (B) Godiva dives with Doug during the third dive.
   (C) Engelberta dives with Hubert during the fourth dive.
   (D) Godiva dives with Doug during the first dive.
   (E) Godiva dives with Engelberta during the second dive.

3. If Froth dives during the third dive, which one of the following must be true?
   (A) Irina dives during the second dive.
   (B) Godiva dives during the first dive.
   (C) Godiva dives during the third dive.
   (D) Irina dives during the fourth dive.
   (E) Engelberta dives during the third dive.

4. Which one of the following divers could dive in two consecutive dives?
   (A) Froth
   (B) Engelberta
   (C) Doug
   (D) Hubert
   (E) Irina

5. If Irina dives during the fourth dive, then which one of the following could be true?
   (A) Hubert dives during the second dive.
   (B) Engelberta dives during the second dive.
   (C) Engelberta goes on a dive with Doug.
   (D) Godiva goes on a dive with Doug.
   (E) Froth dives during the third dive.

6. Each of the following is a complete and accurate list of the divers who could dive with Irina during any dive EXCEPT:
   (A) Engelberta, Froth
   (B) Froth, Godiva
   (C) Engelberta, Hubert
   (D) Engelberta, Godiva
   (E) Doug, Godiva

ANSWERS TO SCUBA DIVES

1. E
2. D
3. A
4. C
5. B
6. D

EXPLANATIONS TO SCUBA DIVES

Prepare

Ingredient Scan

Task: 2-D Order game, combining order and groups; arrange the order of four pairs of divers
Inventory: 6 divers for 8 spaces
Rules: Straightforward and easy to symbolize
Questions: 6 total: 1 Grab-a-Rule, 2 Specific, 3 General
Red Flags: Having to reuse elements indicates an elevated degree of uncertainty
Rank: 3

Diagram and Inventory

There are four dives occurring in a certain order, so you need four columns numbered 1–4. Each dive consists of two divers, so create a second tier. Use vertical blocks to show divers that go at the same time. Each diver must be used at least once.

Symbolize the Rules and Double-Check

Rule 1: D is in column 4. Add to diagram.
Rule 2: Note the quantity limitation E=1, and make an EG antiblock.

Rule 3: I≠1 or 3. Add to diagram. Since I must be used at least once, you can also add to the diagram that I = 2 and/or 4.

Rule 4: Note the quantity limitation H=2 and F=1, and draw an HFH block

H	F	H
—	—	—

Don't forget to double-check your rules!

Deductions

Links: None of the rules refer to the same elements as each other, so there are no links.
Spatial restrictions: Whenever the rules give you a block (in this case, the HFH block), start your deductions by considering how many different places you could fit the block. The block spans three groups, so it could only go in groups 1–3 or 2–4. Write a row showing each scenario so that you can see any other limitations. If HFH goes into groups 1–3, then there is only one space in each group (since D is already in spacc 4). Looking over the other rules, there are still options for where I might go and how E and G might be split up. If HFH goes into groups 2–4, then group 4 is complete (D and H). Looking at the other rules, rule 3 says I can't go in group 1 or 3, so it must finish group 2. Rule 2 forces you to split up E and G. Since there are only groups 1 and 3 still available, E and G will have to be divided into these groups. Put a G/E placeholder in group 1 and an E/G placeholder in group 3. There is only one more opening to worry about, the second space of group 1. What element(s) could go there? It can't be H, E, or F because their quantity limit has already been met. It can't be I because I can't go in group 1. It can't be G because that would result in either having G with G or having G with E, both of which are unacceptable. The only option is D, so place D in the final space in group 1.
Most restricted: HFH is limited to two scenarios. I is limited to two groups.
Least restricted: D could potentially be in any group.

Here is your diagram:

DEFGHI

I → 2, 4

	~I		~I	
	1	2	3	4
i.	H —	F —	H —	D —
ii.	E/G D	H I	F G/E	D H

Assess, Act, Answer

Question 1 is a Grab-a-Rule, so do that one first.

For question 1, use the rules to eliminate answer choices. Rule 1 eliminates choice (B). Rule 2 eliminates choice (A) because E is only allowed to go once. Rule 3 eliminates choice (C). Rule 4 eliminates choice (D). **Because choice (E) is the only choice remaining, it is the credited response.**

Question 3 is your first Specific question, so do that one next.

For question 3, F must be placed in group 3. Does that lend itself to either scenario 1 or 2? It only works in scenario 2. Since you already have deduced all the limitations of that scenario, you don't need to draw in anything new. Because the question is looking for what must be true, scan the answer choices for the elements that are set in stone in this scenario: I must be in group 2, and D must be in group 1. **Choice (A) says I must go in group 2, so it is the credited response.**

Question 5 is the next Specific question, so do that one next.

Question 5 requires that I be placed in group 4. Does that lend itself to scenario 1 or 2? It only is possible in scenario 1. Make a new row for question 5 on your diagram and copy down the backbone of scenario 1. The HFH block is in groups 1, 2, and 3. Group 4 now has D and I. Look at your rules to see if anything else is forced to happen. E and G still need to be split up, but with three groups still open, you can't deduce which two will have them. I is already being used in group 4, so rule 2 is taken care of. Nothing else must be true, so look at the answer choices for an answer that is possible. Choice (A) is impossible because the two H's are already in groups 1 and 3. Choice (B) seems possible. Since there are only two other open spaces to worry about, attempt to complete a valid scenario. All you have to worry about is a safe spot for G and group 1 or group 3 (or both) would be fine. **Choice (B) is possible, so it is the credited response.**

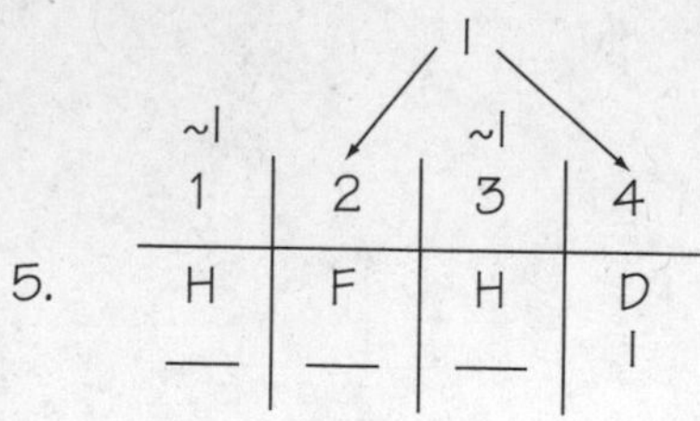

Return to your first General question, question 2.

Question 2 is asking what *could be true,* use your two master scenarios and any specific scenarios on the diagram to assess whether an answer choice is possible. Choice (A) wants H and F to be together, which can never happen since they are forever locked into three consecutive groups. Choice (B) wants GD to fill group 3. In your two master scenarios, the first scenario has H already in group 3, and the second scenario has F already in group 3. Therefore, this is impossible. Choice (C) wants EH in group 4. That is also impossible based on what's already filled in to group 4 for each master scenario. Choice (D) wants to see if I can go in group 4. That seems possible in scenario 1, and you have already worked out that scenario in your work for question 5. **Since this is possible, choice (D) is the credited response.**

The next General question is question 4, so do that one next.

Question 4 asks you to identify an element that could go in two consecutive groups. Start by eliminating any elements you're sure could never go twice in a row. H and F can't because of the HFH block that always must be used. That eliminates choices (A) and (D). E can't go twice in a row because it's only allowed to go once. That eliminates choice (B). D and I are left. I can only go in groups 2 and 4, so I could never go twice in a row. **Because choice (C) is all that remains, it is the credited response.**

Finally, work the final General question, question 6.

Question 6 asks for a list of all elements that can never go with I. Start by thinking of which elements *can* go with I and eliminate any choices that have those. From scenario 1, I could go with D or F. That eliminates choices (A), (B), and (E). From scenario 2, I could go with H. That eliminates choice (C). **Because choice (D) is all that remains, it is the credited response.**

BIOME MAPPING

A cartographer is creating a map of the biomes of six countries: A, B, C, D, E, and F. Each country contains at least one of the following three types of biomes—mangrove, savanna, and taiga—and no other types. The following conditions must be observed:

D and exactly three other countries contain mangrove.
F contains more types of biomes than E does.
C does not contain any type of biome that A does.
B contains exactly two types of biomes.
E contains both savanna and taiga.
A does not contain any type of biome that E contains.

1. Which one of the following must be true?
   (A) Of the types of biomes contained in A there is exactly one type that B also contains.
   (B) Of the types of biomes contained in E there is exactly one type that D also contains.
   (C) Of the types of biomes contained in C there is exactly one type that D also contains.
   (D) There is more than one type of biome that both C and E contain.
   (E) There is more than one type of biome that both B and C contain.

2. It is possible to determine exactly which of the three biomes each country contains for exactly how many of the six countries?
   (A) one
   (B) two
   (C) three
   (D) four
   (E) five

3. Which one of the following must be false?
   (A) Exactly one of the six countries contains exactly one type of biome.
   (B) Exactly two of the six countries contain exactly one type of biome each.
   (C) Exactly three of the six countries contain exactly one type of biome each.
   (D) Exactly one of the six countries contains exactly two types of biomes.
   (E) Exactly three of the six countries contain exactly two types of biomes each.

4. If exactly three countries contain exactly two biomes each, which of the following statements could be true?
   (A) B and C have exactly two biomes in common.
   (B) C and D have exactly one biome in common.
   (C) C and E do not have any biomes in common.
   (D) C and F do not have any biomes in common.
   (E) A and D have exactly two biomes in common.

5. Which one of the following pairs of countries could contain all and only the same types of biomes as each other?
   (A) A and B
   (B) B and E
   (C) B and D
   (D) C and D
   (E) D and E

6. Which one of the following must be true?
   (A) There is exactly one type of biome that both B and C contain.
   (B) There is exactly one type of biome that both B and E contain.
   (C) There is exactly one type of biome that both B and D contain.
   (D) There is exactly one type of biome that both C and E contain.
   (E) There is exactly one type of biome that both D and E contain.

ANSWERS TO BIOME MAPPING

1. A
2. C
3. D
4. B
5. C
6. B

EXPLANATIONS TO BIOME MAPPING

Prepare

Ingredient Scan

Task:	Group game with variable assignments; assign at least 1 but up to 3 types of biomes to each of 6 countries
Inventory:	3 biomes
Rules:	distribution rules as well as blocks and anti-blocks.
Questions:	6 total: 1 Specific, 4 General, 1 Complex
Red Flags:	Assignments are variable, which makes a group game more difficult
Rank:	3/4

Diagram and Inventory

The setup describes six countries that can contain up to three biomes each. It may be tough to decide whether the countries or the biomes should form the core of your diagram. It helps to look at how you might symbolize the rules to make a final determination about your diagram. In this case, since most of the rules are about how many biomes each country can contain, it makes sense to make the countries the core of the diagram.

Symbolize the Rules and Double-Check

Rule 1:	MMMM. Put an M in group D in the diagram.
Rule 2:	F > E
Rule 3:	C≠A
Rule 4:	Put 2 spaces under B in the diagram.
Rule 5:	Add S and T to the E column in the diagram.
Rule 6:	A≠E

The rules are relatively easy to symbolize and indicate a limited number of possible distributions.

You will, therefore have to make some key deductions about the relative distributions of the biomes and how many biomes each country can have in order to keep the questions manageable.

Don't forget to double-check your rules!

Deductions

Spatial restrictions: Because we are told that E contains S and T, and because we know that F must have more biomes than E, we can figure out that E has only S and T, and that F must have all 3 biomes.
Links: The AE antiblock combines with the S and T in E rule to lead to the deduction that A has M, and only M, in it. Additionally, since there is also an AC antiblock, we know that C cannot have M in it. Go back to rule 1 in which we are told there are four countries with M, and that leaves B as the only other country that can have M.

Here is your diagram:

	1 A	2 B	~M 1/2 C	D	2 E	3 F
MST	M	M_	_	M	ST	MST

Assess, Act, Answer

Question 4 is the first and only Specific question.

Question 4 asks for something that *could be true.* You already know that groups B and E have two biomes each, and the other group that has two biomes must be either C or D.

	1 A	2 B	~M 1/2 C	D	2 E	3 F
4.	M	M_	S/T	M S/T	ST	MST

If D is the group with two biomes, it is possible for groups C and D to have the same biome—either S or T. **Thus, choice (B) is the credited response.**

Since there are no more Specific questions, move on to the General questions, starting with question 1.

Question 1 is a General question that asks for something that *must be true.* That means that you are getting rid of anything that could be false. Remember that something that *could be true* is not strong enough to answer a *must be true* question. **In this case, based on your deductions, it is possible to eliminate four of the answer choices and prove that choice (A) is the credited response.**

Question 2 is also a General question.

For question 2, you know that group A must have only M, that group E has exactly S and T, and that group F has all three biomes. While you know that group B has two biomes, you only know for certain that one of them is M. The other one could be S or T, so you don't know exactly which biomes group B has. That means that you know the biomes for three of the groups. **Choice (C) is the credited response.**

Question 3 is another General question, but this one has answer choices about the possible distributions of biomes in the groups.

Question 3 asks for something that *must be false,* so you can eliminate anything that could be true. From our deductions you know that groups B and E both have exactly two biomes which makes choice (D) false. **Choice (D) is the credited response.**

Question 6 is another general question that asks what must be true.

For question 6, use your deductions to eliminate answer choices. The only answer choice that must be true is that there is only one type of biome that groups B and E have in common. **The credited response is choice (B).**

Question 5 is a complex question.

Question 5 asks for two groups that have the same biomes as each other. Again, our deductions come to the rescue.

1 A	2 B	~M 1/2 C	D	2 E	3 F
M	M S/T		M S/T	ST	MST

Since groups B and D already have M in common, it is possible for D to have only two biomes just as B does, and that second space could be either S or T in both groups. **The credited response is choice (C).**

To make the most of the 35 minutes you have for a Games section, you need effective strategies for the section and for individual games.

Becoming a savvy test taker requires developing a thoughtful approach. First, you have to accept that it's the rare test taker who benefits from doing all four games in a section. For any game you attempt, you should be answering every question in that game and be doing so with a high degree of accuracy, close to 100 percent. Only if you can accomplish this on all four games should you be attempting four games. You'll need to do several timed sections to figure out how many games you should be attempting. Start by setting your goal at two games in 35 minutes. If you finish both with a high degree of accuracy, push for two and one-half, then three, and so on.

Here are some other tips for a solid section strategy.

Reorder the Games

LSAT Games include a pair of easier games and a pair of harder games, but the test writers don't present them in that order. Before you start work on a Games section, take about two minutes to evaluate the games. Create your own order of difficulty by ranking the games from easiest to hardest. Games that you understand and can work efficiently count as easier games. Harder games are those that are confusing or will take longer to work. Working the games in order from easiest to hardest assures that you'll correctly answer the maximum number of questions.

Speed Bubble

Increase your efficiency by filling in the answer sheet bubbles in blocks, rather than question by question. When you work a game, mark your answers in your test booklet. Transfer your responses to the answer sheet only after you've finished a game. Catch up on your bubbling when the proctor gives the five-minute warning. After that, bubble each question as you answer it. Don't forget to fill in guesses for any questions you don't have time to work.

Speed bubbling has several benefits. The first advantage is that speed bubbling keeps you from breaking your momentum as you're working a game. You can stay focused on the page instead of moving back and forth between the game and the answer sheet. The second is that speed bubbling minimizes the possibility of error. Because you're answering the questions out of order, you run the risk of bubbling in the wrong spot if you bubble after every question. Bubbling at the end of a game ensures that you will fill the right answer in the right spot. Also, taking a fifteen-second break to fill in the answers at the end of each game gives your brain a much-needed break before it starts up again for the next game.

Stick to Your Approach

No matter how difficult or foreign the game may be, sticking to a systematic approach will get you through the game. You will have to adapt what you know about familiar games, but the process remains the same. When you are working a more difficult game, take time to really understand what the setup asks you to do, and be creative when dealing with rules that are difficult to symbolize. Don't be scared off by what's different about the game; focus on what's familiar and then account for the aspects of the game that are more challenging. Break confusing aspects into smaller pieces.

The following chapters are broken up into timed sections of four games each, followed by the explanations for those games. Give yourself 35 minutes to complete each section. Get used to the directions at the top of the section. By test day, you should have no need to read those directions.

Good luck!

SECTION STRATEGY

Time—35 minutes

24 Questions

Directions: Each group of questions in this section is based on a set of conditions. In answering some of the questions, it may be useful to draw a rough diagram. Choose the response that most accurately and completely answers each question and blacken the corresponding space on your answer sheet.

Questions 1–6

A real estate agent must lease out six adjacent storefronts in a new commercial property. The storefronts are numbered 1 through 6. Six different businesses—a bank, a coffee shop, a dry cleaner, a flower shop, a grocery, and a jewelry store—have expressed interest in leasing a storefront. The agent will lease out the spaces in accordance with the following conditions:

The grocery leases a storefront numbered lower than the one the dry cleaner leases.

The flower shop leases a storefront numbered lower than the one the grocery leases but higher than the one the bank leases.

The coffee shop leases either storefront 3 or storefront 4.

1. Which one of the following could be an accurate list of the businesses leased to storefronts, from storefront 1 through storefront 6 ?

(A) bank, flower shop, grocery, dry cleaner, coffee shop, jewelry store
(B) bank, grocery, coffee shop, flower shop, dry cleaner, jewelry store
(C) jewelry store, bank, dry cleaner, coffee shop, flower shop, grocery
(D) bank, flower shop, coffee shop, jewelry store, grocery, dry cleaner
(E) flower shop, bank, grocery, coffee shop, dry cleaner, jewelry store

2. If storefront 5 is not leased to the grocery, then which of the following must be true?

(A) The bank leases storefront 1.
(B) The coffee shop leases storefront 3.
(C) The grocery leases storefront 4.
(D) The dry cleaner leases storefront 5.
(E) The jewelry store leases storefront 6.

3. If the flower shop leases a storefront numbered exactly one lower than the one the grocery leases, which of the following could be true?

(A) The flower shop leases storefront 3.
(B) The jewelry store leases storefront 3.
(C) The grocery leases storefront 4.
(D) The jewelry store leases storefront 4.
(E) The dry cleaner leases storefront 5.

4. Each of the following could be the business leased to storefront 3 EXCEPT:

(A) the coffee shop
(B) the grocery
(C) the bank
(D) the flower shop
(E) the jewelry store

5. If the grocery leases storefront 3, then what is the lowest numbered storefront that could be leased to the jewelry store?

(A) storefront 1
(B) storefront 2
(C) storefront 4
(D) storefront 5
(E) storefront 6

6. Which one of the following businesses could lease any one of the six storefronts?

(A) flower shop
(B) jewelry store
(C) grocery
(D) dry cleaner
(E) bank

GO ON TO THE NEXT PAGE.

Questions 7–12

A company is putting together a team of five lawyers. The lawyers will be picked from among tax lawyers Aziz, Ciro, and Ezikiel; corporate lawyers Lona, Nell, and Penny; and real estate lawyers Qasim, Sandy, and Ulf. The following conditions must apply:

If more than one tax lawyer is picked, then at most one real estate lawyer is selected.
If either Sandy or Ulf is not picked, Lona cannot be picked.
Penny cannot work on a team with Lona.
Ciro cannot work on a team with Penny.
The team must include at least one lawyer from each of the three groups.

7. Which of the following could be an acceptable team of lawyers selected for the case?

(A) Aziz, Ciro, Lona, Nell, Sandy
(B) Ciro, Lona, Penny, Sandy, Ulf
(C) Aziz, Ezikiel, Nell, Penny, Ulf
(D) Aziz, Ezikiel, Lona, Sandy, Ulf
(E) Lona, Nell, Qasim, Sandy, Ulf

8. If Ciro, Nell, Qasim, and Ulf are among the lawyers picked for the team, who else must be on the team?

(A) Aziz
(B) Ezikiel
(C) Lona
(D) Penny
(E) Sandy

9. If Sandy is picked for the team, and no other real estate lawyer is picked for the team, then which of the following must be true?

(A) If Penny is picked, Aziz cannot be picked.
(B) If Nell is picked, Ciro cannot be picked.
(C) If exactly one corporate lawyer is picked, it must be Penny.
(D) If exactly two corporate lawyers are picked, Ciro cannot be picked.
(E) If exactly two corporate lawyers are picked, Aziz cannot be picked.

10. If Aziz is the only tax lawyer picked for the team, each of the following must be false EXCEPT:

(A) All three real estate lawyers are picked.
(B) Only one real estate lawyer is picked.
(C) Ezikiel and Lona are both picked.
(D) Neither Ulf, nor Penny is picked.
(E) Ciro and Lana are both picked.

11. If Aziz and Ezikiel are picked for the team, the team must include

(A) Ciro or else Lona
(B) Ciro or else Penny
(C) Lona or else Penny
(D) Penny or else Qasim
(E) Sandy or else Qasim

12. If the only corporate lawyer picked for the team is Lona, each of the following could be false EXCEPT:

(A) Aziz and Ciro are both picked.
(B) Ciro and Ezikiel are both picked.
(C) Ezikiel and Sandy are both picked.
(D) Aziz, Sandy, and Ulf are all picked.
(E) Qasim, Sandy and Ulf are all picked.

GO ON TO THE NEXT PAGE.

Questions 13–18

Marlena's school is holding its annual sporting competition. Three track and field events—hurdles, javelin, and relay—and three swimming events—butterfly, freestyle, and medley—will be scheduled for Monday, Tuesday, and Wednesday. On each day, two of the events will take place, one after the other. Each event will take place only once. The following conditions must apply:

On each day, exactly one track and field event and exactly one swimming event will take place.
Relay must take place before freestyle can take place.
Hurdles and javelin must take place before medley can take place.

13. Which one of the following could be an accurate lineup of events for the competition?

(A) Monday: relay before freestyle
Tuesday: javelin before medley
Wednesday: hurdles before butterfly
(B) Monday: javelin before freestyle
Tuesday: relay before butterfly
Wednesday: hurdles before medley
(C) Monday: javelin before butterfly
Tuesday: hurdles before medley
Wednesday: relay before freestyle
(D) Monday: javelin before hurdles
Tuesday: medley before relay
Wednesday: freestyle before butterfly
(E) Monday: hurdles before butterfly
Tuesday: relay before medley
Wednesday: javelin before freestyle

14. If hurdles takes place on Monday, then each of the following must be false EXCEPT:

(A) Freestyle takes place on Monday.
(B) Medley takes place on Tuesday.
(C) Javelin takes place on Monday.
(D) Relay takes place on Monday.
(E) Butterfly takes place on Tuesday.

15. If relay takes place on Wednesday, which of the following must be true?

(A) Hurdles takes place on Tuesday.
(B) Hurdles takes place on Monday.
(C) Butterfly takes place before Javelin.
(D) Butterfly takes place on Monday.
(E) Javelin takes place before Hurdles.

16. If butterfly takes place on Tuesday, then which one of the following could be true?

(A) Medley takes place on Monday.
(B) Freestyle takes place on Tuesday.
(C) Medley takes place on Tuesday.
(D) Javelin takes place on Wednesday.
(E) Relay takes place on Wednesday.

17. Each of the following could be the second event that takes place on Tuesday EXCEPT:

(A) relay
(B) butterfly
(C) javelin
(D) freestyle
(E) hurdles

18. If javelin takes place after freestlye then which of the following must be true?

(A) Hurdles takes place at some time after freestlye.
(B) Hurdles takes place at some time after javelin.
(C) Javelin takes place at some time after butterfly.
(D) Butterfly takes place at some time after freestlye.
(E) Javelin takes place at sometime after relay.

GO ON TO THE NEXT PAGE.

Questions 19–24

Six trapeze artists will perform together in a circus show's grand finale. Each of six performers—Cossette, Dixon, Elonera, Fronde, Havelock, and Kerani—will enter aerially from offstage, one at a time, until all six are on stage. No performer who enters the space will exit until the end of the performance. The sequence of the trapeze artists' entrances must conform to the following conditions:

Kerani enters the stage at some time after Havelock or at some time before Cossette, but not both.

Cossette enters the stage either at some time after Elonera or at some time before Dixon, but not both.

Fronde enters the stage at some time after Havelock and before Elonera.

19. Which one of the following could be a complete and acceptable order in which the trapeze artists enter the stage?
    - (A) Havelock, Fronde, Dixon, Elonera, Cossette, Kerani
    - (B) Dixon, Havelock, Fronde, Cossette, Kerani, Elonera
    - (C) Kerani, Elonera, Dixon, Havelock, Fronde, Cossette
    - (D) Havelock, Dixon, Elonera, Fronde, Cossette, Kerani
    - (E) Havelock, Fronde, Kerani, Cossette, Elonera, Dixon

20. Which one of the following could be an accurate partial list of the trapeze artists?
    - (A) fourth: Havelock; fifth: Elonera; sixth: Dixon
    - (B) second: Fronde; fifth: Cossette; sixth: Dixon
    - (C) second: Cossette; third: Havelock; fourth: Dixon
    - (D) first: Fronde; fourth: Elonera; fifth: Cossette
    - (E) fourth: Kerani; fifth: Cossette; sixth: Elonera

21. If Elonera is the last trapeze artist to enter the space, then each of the following could be false EXCEPT:
    - (A) Cossette enters the space at some time after Kerani.
    - (B) Dixon enters the space at some time after Cossette.
    - (C) Cossette enters the space at some time after Havelock.
    - (D) Fronde enters the space at some time after Dixon.
    - (E) Kerani enters the space at some time after Havelock.

22. Each of the following trapeze artists could be the first to enter the space EXCEPT:
    - (A) Havelock
    - (B) Elonera
    - (C) Kerani
    - (D) Dixon
    - (E) Cossette

23. If Fronde enters the space at some time after Dixon, then which of the following must be false?
    - (A) Elonera is the fifth trapeze artist to enter the space.
    - (B) Dixon is the fifth trapeze artist to enter the space.
    - (C) Havelock is the fourth trapeze artist to enter the space.
    - (D) Havelock is the third trapeze artist to enter the space.
    - (E) Dixon is the second trapeze artist to enter the space.

24. Fronde CANNOT enter the space
    - (A) second
    - (B) third
    - (C) fourth
    - (D) fifth
    - (E) sixth

STOP

IF YOU FINISH BEFORE TIME IS CALLED, YOU MAY CHECK YOUR WORK ON THIS SECTION ONLY. DO NOT WORK ON ANY OTHER SECTION IN THE TEST.

ANSWER KEY

1. D
2. A
3. E
4. C
5. D
6. B
7. C
8. E
9. D
10. A
11. B
12. E
13. C
14. B
15. D
16. D
17. A
18. E
19. A
20. C
21. B
22. B
23. B
24. E

EXPLANATIONS TO SECTION STRATEGY QUESTIONS 1–6

Prepare

Ingredient Scan

Task: 1–D Order; place 6 storefronts in order from 1–6
Inventory: 6 elements, 6 slots, a 1:1 ratio.
Rules: Straightforward and easy to symbolize
Questions: 6 total: 1 Grab-a-Rule, 3 Specific, 2 General
Red Flags: This game looks as straightforward as you can get
Rank: 1

Diagram and Inventory

Create an Order diagram with 6 slots and write out elements B, C, D, F, G, J.

Symbolize the Rules and Double-Check

Rule 1: G—D
Rule 2: B—F—G
Rule 3: C = 3/4. Label this on your diagram.

Don't forget to double-check your rules!

Deductions

Links: Join rules 1 and 2 together for a composite clue: B—F—G—D
Spatial restrictions: Because four of the six elements are chained together in a certain order, there's very little left to worry about. C must go in slot 3 or 4, and J can go anywhere. Take a moment to preview your thought process for each problem: "Is C going in slot 3 or 4? Where is J going?" Those are the only unknowns. Don't worry about marking off every single exclusion (such as "F can't go slot 1, 5, or 6"); instead, ask yourself about the extremities. What's the latest B could come? C needs to fall somewhere in the middle of this chain, so four elements must come after B. B can only be slot 1 or 2. By the same logic, D can only be slot 5 or 6. B or J could be first, and D or J could be last.
Most restricted: Slots 1 and 6 only have two options. B, D, and C each have two options.
Least restricted: J is your free agent. Circle it.

Here is your diagram:

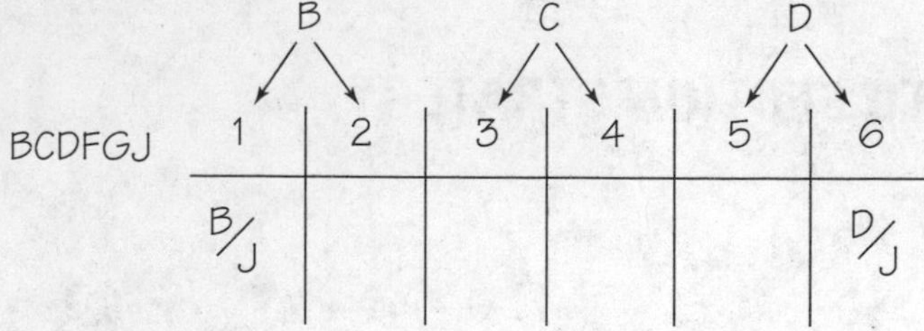

Question 1 is a Grab-a-Rule question so attempt it first.

For question 1, use the rules to eliminate answer choices. Rule 1 eliminates choice (C). Rule 2 eliminates choice (B) and choice (E). Rule 3 eliminates choice (A). **Choice (D) is the only one left, so it is the credited response.**

Question 2 is the first Specific question.

Question 2 stipulates that G can't be in slot 5. How does that narrow down where G can go? Based on the chain, G can't be first, second, or last. That means G can only be in slot 3 or 4. Your work from question 3 already shows what happens if G is in 3. Make a scenario with G in 4. That puts C in slot 3. B and F must come before G so they are in slots 1 and 2, respectively. J and D are left for slots 5 and 6 and are interchangeable, so write in J/D and D/J. Compare the scenario for G in slot 3 with the scenario for G in slot 4. Look for anything that *must* happen in both scenarios. The only constants are B in slot 1 and F in slot 2. Scan the answers for these facts. **Choice (A) is something that must be true in both scenarios, so it is the credited response.**

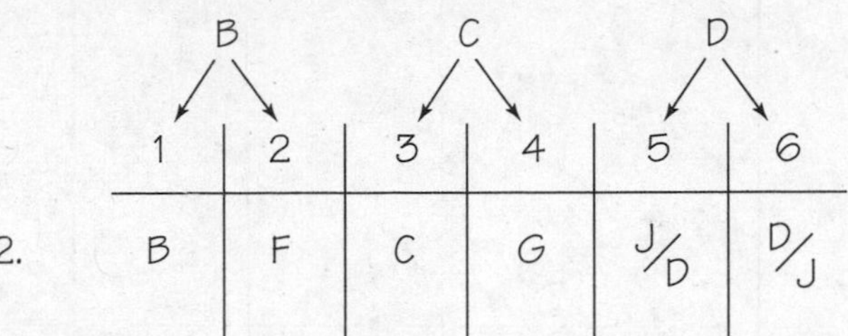

Question 3 is the next Specific question.

Question 3 gives you the condition that G must immediately proceed F. Symbolize that condition next to your row for question 3. Think about how many places that FG block could go. It can't be in slots 1 and 2 because F can't be in slot 1. You can check the answers to see if anything matches the scenario you already have. **Choice (E) is something possible, so it is the credited response.**

Question 5 is a Specific question so go for it.

For question 5, place G in slot 3. That means C must be in slot 4. Where does G fall in the chain? B and F must come before G, so B must be in slot 1 and F must be in slot 2. Slots 5 and 6 remain, and D and J are left. Since J is the free agent, those two are interchangeable. Write in D/J and J/D. The question asks how low J can go. **Slot 5 is your answer, so choice (D) is the credited response.**

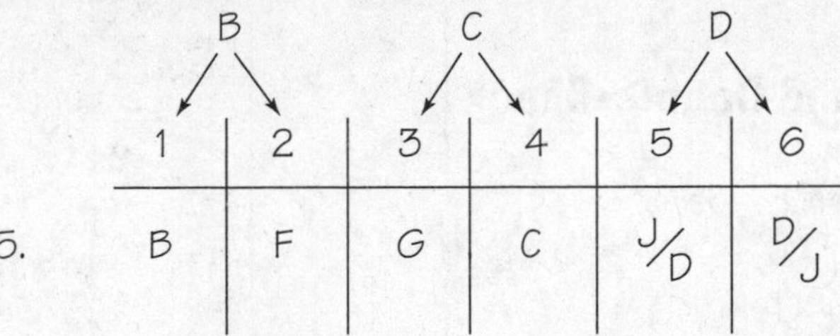

Question 4 is a General question.

Question 4 asks which element can never be in slot 3. Based on the original deductions, you know that neither B nor D can be in slot 3. Look for B or D in the answer choices. **Choice (C) is the credited response.**

Question 6 is a General question.

Question 6 asks which element is free to go anywhere. That's our free agent: J. **Choice (B) is the credited response.**

EXPLANATIONS TO SECTION STRATEGY QUESTIONS 7–12

Prepare

Ingredient Scan

Task: 2-D In-Out game; select a total of 5 lawyers selected in total from 3 different groups of lawyers

Inventory: 9 lawyers

Rules: Mostly conditional rules, some relating to individual elements and one numerical conditional pertaining to the number of elements from a given group

Questions: 6 total: 1 Grab-a-Rule, 5 Specific

Red Flags: Lots of conditional rules, must keep track not only of individual elements but also of the relative number of elements from a given group

Rank: 4

Diagram and Inventory

The setup describes an In-Out Game in which you must select exactly five of nine lawyers for the In column, leaving four for the Out column. There are three different groups of elements: tax lawyers A, C, and E; corporate lawyers L, N, and P; and real estate lawyers Q, S, and U.

Symbolize the Rules and Double-Check

Rule 1: $tt^{+} \rightarrow r$; $rr^{+} \rightarrow t$

Rule 2: $\sim S_r$ or $\sim U_r \rightarrow \sim L_c$; $L_c \rightarrow S_r$ and U_r

Rule 3: $P_c \rightarrow \sim L_c$; $L_c \rightarrow \sim P_c$

Rule 4: $C_t \rightarrow \sim P_c$; $P_c \rightarrow \sim C_t$

Rule 5: Put this into your diagram.

Don't forget to double-check your rules!

Deductions

Links: Because rule 2 involves more than one element from the r group, you can link it to rule 1. If there are two or more t's, there is exactly one r, which means that S and U can't both be In, which means that L must be Out.
Spatial restrictions: In games with multiple groups, it's important to look at rules that involve members of the same group. Rule 3 deals with two member of the c group; since P and L can't both be In, the c group can never have all three members in. This means that there will always be at least one member of the c group in the Out column. Add it to your diagram. Because there will never be more than two c's in at a time, there will always be at least three spaces left for t's and r's, meaning there will always have to be at least two t's or at least two r's, so rule 1 will always be in effect (meaning there will always be exactly one t or exactly one r In).
Most restricted: Rule 1 will always govern the quantities of most of what can be In. P is important because it forces two things Out. L is important because it forces two things In.
Least restricted: A, E, N, and Q have no specific rules attached, so they are very flexible.

Here is your diagram:

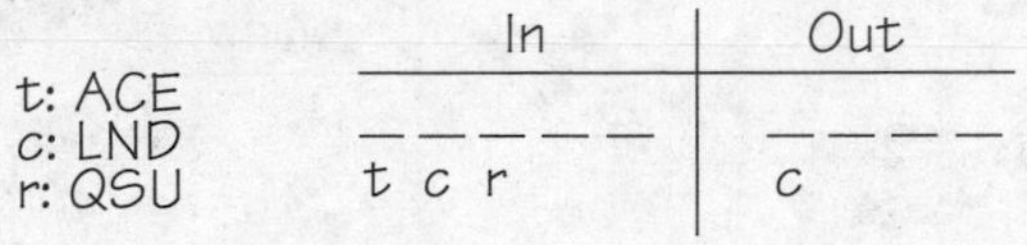

t: ACE
c: LND
r: QSU

In	Out
_ _ _ _ _	_ _ _ _
t c r	c

Assess, Act, Answer

Question 7 is a Grab-a-Rule, so start there.

For question 7, use the rules to eliminate answer choices. Rule 1 eliminates choice (D), rule 2 eliminates choice (A), rule 4 eliminates choice (B), and rule 5 eliminates choice (E). **The only choice left, and therefore the credited response, is choice (C).**

Move on to the Specific questions. Question 8 is a Specific question, so do that next.

For question 8, place C, N, Q, and U in the In column, leaving only one space left to be decided. Since C is In, you now know that P must be Out (rule 4). Since there are two r's, you know that you cannot have more than one t (rule 1). This means that both A and E are out. The only two elements remaining are S and L. If L is in, then S must also be in (rule 2). Since you only have one more spot in the In column, it is impossible for L to be in. Therefore, S must be in and L must be out. **Choice (E) is the credited response.**

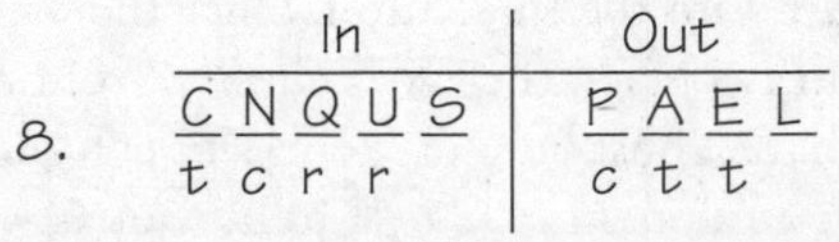

	In	Out
8.	C N Q U S	P A E L
	t c r r	c t t

Question 9 is also a Specific question, so do that next.

In question 9, S is the only member of the r group being picked, so place S in the In column and place Q and U in the Out column. If U is out, then L must also be Out (rule 2). Since you have almost all the spaces in the Out column filled, focus on who might still need to be Out. Rule 3 tells you that you can't have both C and P In; as neither of these is yet in the Out column, you have to reserve that remaining slot for one of them. You also must reserve a space in the In column for either C or P as well. Since the Out column is now full, this means all the rest of the elements must be In, which means you can place A, E, and N in the In column. Now turn to the answer choices. The question ask for something that must be true; because the choices are in conditional form, test the first part of each choice to see whether the second part of the choice must follow from that information. You can eliminate choice (A) and choice (E) right away, as they suggest that A cannot be In, which contradicts your diagram. Choice (B) can be eliminated because you already know that N is In and that it doesn't decide which of C and P must be selected. Eliminate choice (C) because you already have at least one member of the c group, N, in your diagram. This leaves choice (D), which must be true; if two c's are chosen, they will be N and P, pushing C to the Out column. **Choice (D) is the credited response.**

	In	Out
9.	A N S P/C E	Q U L C/P
	t c r t	r r c

Question 10 is a Specific question, so do it next.

For question 10, place A in the In column and place C and E, the other t's, in the Out column. This allows you to eliminate choice (C) and choice (E). Since no additional elements can be placed for certain, try the remaining answer choices to see which one could be true. Choice (A) states that all three r's are selected. If Q, S, and U are all In, then any of the three c's could fit into the remaining space in the In column. Because this is possible, choice (A) is correct; no need to try the other choices. **Choice (A) is the credited response.**

	In	Out
10.(A)	A _ Q S U	_ C E _
	t c r r r	c t t

Question 11 is a Specific question, so do this next.

For question 11, put A and E into the In column. Since there are already 2 t's In, you can only have exactly one r In (rule 1); put two r's in the Out column. From rule 2 and your earlier deduction, having only one r means that L must be Out. Your Out column now has L and two r's in it, but as before, you must leave room for either C or P to be Out as well (rule 4). Only one of them will occupy the remaining space in the Out column, since neither is from the r group; the other must therefore be In. The question asks for which one of two elements must be In; because you know that either C or P must be In, choice (B) is your answer. There is no need to check the other choices. **Choice (B) is the credited response.**

11.

In	Out
A _ _ E P/C	L _ _ C/P
t c r t	c r r

Question 12 is the final Specific question.

For question 12, place L in the In column and N and P in the Out column. Since L is In, S and U must also be In (rule 2). Because you now have at least 2 r's, you must have exactly 1 t (rule 1); the remaining spaces in the Out column must be t's. Since the Out column is now full, the remaining open space in the In column must be from the r group, so Q must be in. You don't know which of the t's is In, so go to the answer choices. The question asks for what must be true. The only choice that you know must be true based on your diagram is choice (E). **Choice (E) is the credited response.**

12.

In	Out
_ L S U Q	N P _ _
t c r r r	c c t t

EXPLANATIONS TO SECTION STRATEGY QUESTIONS 13–18

Prepare

Ingredient Scan

Task: 1-D Order; assign an order to 3 track and field and 3 swimming events over 3 days.
Inventory: 6 events, 6 slots (3 days with ordered pairs on each day), 1:1 ratio.
Rules: These look like straightforward ordering rules.
Questions: 6 total: 1 Grab-a-Rule, 4 Specific, 1 General
Red Flags: Need to keep track of categories of elements
Rank: 2

Diagram and Inventory

The elements are H, J, R, b, f, and m. Use uppercase for track and field events and lowercase for swim events.

T: HJR
s: bfm

Create a diagram with six columns, because each day has two events that happen in order.

Symbolize the Rules and Double-Check

Rule 1: [Xx] (reversible block)

Rule 2: R—f

Rule 3: H, J > m

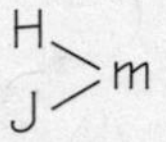

Don't forget to double-check your rules!

Deductions

Links: None of the elements appear in multiple rules, so you can't make any links.
Spatial restrictions: From rule 2, R can't be last and f can't be first. From rule 3, neither H nor J can go last. Because H and J must both come before m and H and J are both track events, H and J cannot both go on Monday. Therefore, the earliest that m could come is the second slot on Tuesday. You can add a ~m to the first three slots.
Most restricted: m is the most limited.
Least restricted: b is the free agent.

Here is your diagram:

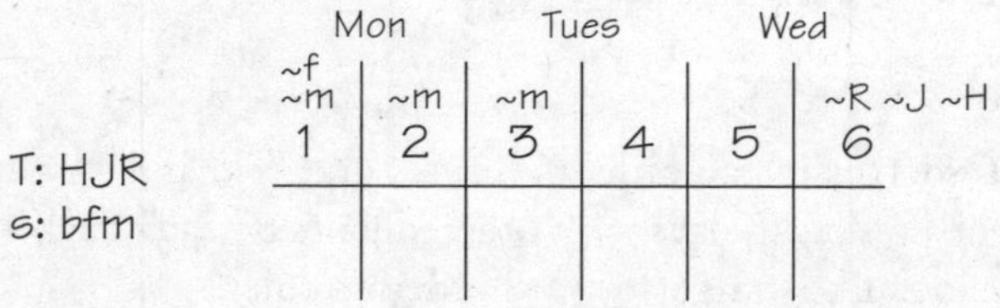

T: HJR
s: bfm

	Mon		Tues		Wed
~f ~m	~m	~m			~R ~J ~H
1	2	3	4	5	6

Assess, Act, Answer

Question 13 is a Grab-a-Rule question, so do it first.

For question 13, use the rules to eliminate answer choices. Rule 1 eliminates choice (D). Rule 2 eliminates choice (B). Rule 3 eliminates choices (A) and (E). **Because choice (C) is all that remains, it is the credited response.**

Question 14 is the first Specific question, so do that one next.

Question 14 requires you to place H on Monday. However, there are two slots on Monday, so you may have to write two scenarios, one with H in the first slot and one with H in the second. Because H is a track event, you know you need the other element in Monday to be a swim event. It can't be f because R hasn't gone yet. It can't be m because J hasn't gone yet. Therefore, b must go on Monday. The question asks for something possible. Scan with an eye for what you already know: Hb fills up Monday. Choices (A), (C), and (D) all tell you impossible things about Monday. Eliminate them. Choice (E) tells you something impossible about b. Eliminate it. **Because choice (B) is all that remains, it is the credited response.**

	Mon		Tues		Wed	
	~f ~m 1	~m 2	~m 3	4	5	~R ~J ~H 6
14.	H	b				
	b	H				

Question 15 is also a Specific question, so do that one next.

For question 15, place R on Wednesday and determine what *must be true*. You've already ruled R out of the very last slot because f must still come after R. Therefore put Rf on Wednesday. Focus on your most limited element, m. You deduced that m could only go in one of the final three slots, and Rf just took up two of those. Therefore, m must be the second Tuesday slot. Only H, J, and b remain. Of these, b is currently the most limited because it is a swim event and the other two swim events have already been used. Therefore, b must go on Monday. Check the answers for something related to b. **Choice (D) is the credited response.**

	Mon		Tues		Wed	
	~f ~m 1	~m 2	~m 3	4	5	~R ~J ~H 6
15.				m	R	f

Question 16 is another Specific question, so go for it.

Question 16 requires b go on Tuesday. Because b is the free agent, it probably shouldn't matter whether b goes in the first or second Tuesday slot. However, by this point in the game, you can see that the swim events are more limited than the track events. By putting a swim event in Tuesday, what is being forced to happen to the other swim events? m can't go on Monday, so m must go on Wednesday. That means f must go on Monday. For f to be on Monday, R would also have to go on Monday. m must go on Wednesday and it has to wait for both H and J, so you know for sure that m has to be the last slot on Wednesday. The order of H and J doesn't matter, and the order of the track event and swim event on Tuesday won't matter. Since the question asks for something that *could be true*, the answer will normally derive from one of your flexible elements. R, f, and m are set in stone, so scan the answers for H, J, or b. **Choice (D) is possible, so it is the credited response.**

	Mon		Tues		Wed	
	~f ~m	~m	~m			~R ~J ~H
	1	2	3	4	5	6
16.	R	f	b	H/J		m

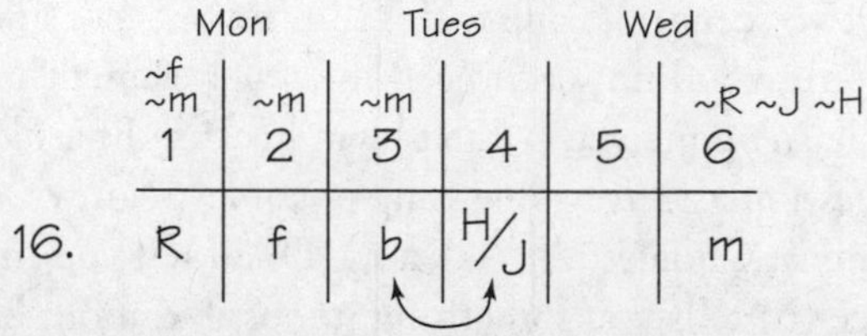

Question 18 is your next Specific question, so do it next.

Question 18 says that f must come before J. You can symbolize this condition and incorporate what you know about f and J. You end up with a pretty comprehensive chain.

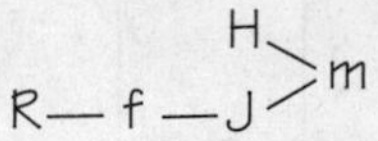

H
R—f—J > m

You probably don't need to write out much since this chain is very useful, but think of the limitations of what could go first and last. R, H, and b (not in the chain) are the only elements eligible to go first. m will have to go last because all three track events must come before m, which requires m to be on Wednesday after the third track event. The question asks for something that *must be true*, so eliminate an answer choice if you can find a counterexample. Choice (A) is not mandatory; f and H are not connected. H could go first and there would be no problem. Eliminate it. Choice (B) is not mandatory for the same reason. Eliminate it. Choice (C) is not mandatory. b could go after J on Tuesday. You could have Rf on Monday, Jb on Tuesday, and Hm on Wednesday. Eliminate it. Choice (D) is not mandatory. You could have bH on Monday, Rf on Tuesday, and Hm on Wednesday. Verify choice (E) is required. Yes, R—J is something you can read off the chain you made for this problem. **Because it must be true, choice (E) is the credited response.**

Go back to Question 17, a General question.

Question 17 asks which element could never be the second Tuesday slot. Use your previous work to make a quick list of elements you already know can be the second Tuesday slot. From your work for questions 3 and 4, you have m, b, H, and J that all were potentially going to be the second Tuesday slot. That eliminates choices (B), (C), and (E). All that remains are R and f. Try R in the second Tuesday slot. That forces f to be in Wed. How do the other rules factor in? m is a swim event that must go in one of the last three slots, but with f already claiming Wednesday's swim event and R blocking m from where it can go on Tuesday, there is no slot left for m. **Because you determined that this scenario is impossible, choice (A) is the credited response.**

EXPLANATIONS TO SECTION STRATEGY QUESTIONS 19–24

Prepare

Ingredient Scan

Task: 1-D Order; assign 6 trapeze artists to 6 ordered slots
Inventory: 6 trapeze artists, 6 slots, 1:1 ratio
Rules: Easy to understand but difficult to symbolize
Questions: 6 total: 1 Grab-a-Rule, 2 Specific, 3 General
Red Flags: The flexible first two rules will make deductions difficult
Rank: 3

Diagram and Inventory

You have six elements—C, D, E, F, H, and K. Create a diagram with slots 1–6 as the core.

Symbolize the Rules and Double-Check

Rule 1: K< H/C *or* H/C >K
Rule 2: C< D/E *or* E/D >C
Rule 3: H—F—E

Don't forget to double-check your rules!

The first two rules are the same kind of language though unusual: Some element must either go before some other element or after some third element, but both relationships can't happen at the same time. Start by symbolizing the first part of each rule. Rule 1 would begin K—C, but you also have to make sure that K is not after H at the same time. If K isn't after H, then K is before H. That means you're really diagramming K—C and K—H as one scenario. Conversely, if K is after H (H—K), then you must prevent K from being before C, which means K will be after C. So the other scenario for rule 1 is H—K and C—K. To keep the symbolization as minimal as possible, you can write K before both C and H and K after both C and H as written above. The same logic applies for rule 2.

Deductions

Links: Although H is common to rules 1 and 3, C is common to rules 1 and 2, and E is common to rules 2 and 3, links between them would be rather confusing because rule 1 and rule 2 each have two different ways of appearing. That means that to properly link all the rules you would have four different possible chains. That amount of work and clutter is more trouble than it's worth.
Spatial restrictions: Since rule 3 is fixed, you can deduce some limitations on its members. F can't be in slots 1 or 6 since something has to come before and after it. H can't be in slots 5 or 6 because two things must come after it. E can't be slots 1 or 2 because two things must come before it.
Most restricted: H and E are each involved in one of the unusual rules and as endpoints in rule 3.
Least restricted: K, C, and D could all theoretically be in any of the six slots.

Here is your diagram:

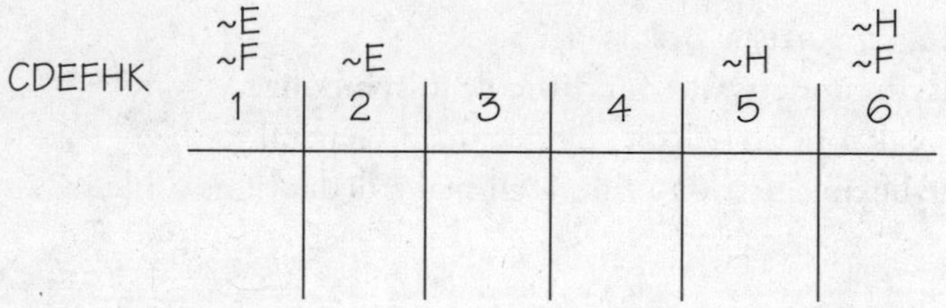

CDEFHK

~E ~F 1	~E 2	3	4	~H 5	~H ~F 6

Question 19 is a Grab-a-Rule so do that one first.

For question 19, use the rules to eliminate answer choices. Rule 1 eliminates choice (E), rule 2 eliminates choice (B), and rule 3 eliminates choices (D) and (C). Because **choice (A) is all that remains, it is the credited response.**

Skip question 20 and move on to your first Specific question, question 21.

Question 21 tells you to place E in slot 6 and determine what must follow. Look at the unusual rules to see if this tells you which scenario must apply. Since E is last, you must use the scenario of rule 2 in which C comes before D and E. Glancing at the answers, you can see that they do not require knowing the exact slot any element is in but rather the relative order. You have just determined that C must come before D and E, so check to see if any answer choices address just that. **Choice (B) correctly states C—D, so it is the credited response.**

The next Specific question is 23, so do that one next.

For question 21, symbolize the condition it requires: D—F. How does this attach to any of the rules? F is in rule 3. Redraw rule 3 with D added.

H
>m
R— f —J

Does this chain tell you anything about which scenario applies from rules 1 and 2? It seems like either scenario from each rule is still workable. The question asks for something that *must be false* (could be true EXCEPT). From the chain you have for this question, you know some things about where H, D, F, and E can and can't go. Scan the answers for anything you can infer from your linked rule 3. The first few choices all seem possible, but choice (B) says that D is in slot 5. D has two things that must come after it: F and E. **Since it is impossible for D to go in slot 5, choice (B) is the credited response.**

Go back to your first General question, question 20.

Question 20 places three of the six elements somewhere and asks which scenario is possible. Use the rules to analyze each one, and, when in doubt, try it out. Choice (D) has F in slot 1, which you deduced is impossible. Eliminate choice (D). Choice (C) has C, H, and D going into slots 2, 3, and 4, respectively. Start with the concrete rule 3, which tells you that two more things have to come after H, so F and E would have to be slots 5 and 6. That leaves K for slot 1. Check rules 1 and 2. K is before H and C. C is before D and E. **All three rules are met so this scenario is possible, and choice (C) is the credited response.**

Go to your next General question, question 22.

Question 22 asks for someone who cannot be first. You deduced that E and F can never be first. **Choice (B) says that E cannot go first, so it is the credited response.**

Go to your last General question, question 24.

Question 24 asks where F can never go. You deduced that F can never be in slot 1 or 6. **Since choice (E) says slot 6, it is the credited response.**

The Princeton Review

Completely darken bubbles with a No. 2 pencil. If you make a mistake, be sure to erase mark completely.

1. YOUR NAME: (Print) Last First M.I.

SIGNATURE: DATE: / /

HOME ADDRESS: (Print) Number

City State Zip Code

PHONE NO.: (Print)

IMPORTANT: Please fill in these boxes exactly as shown on the back cover of your test book.

2. TEST FORM

3. TEST CODE

4. REGISTRATION NUMBER

5. YOUR NAME

First 4 letters of last name | FIRST INIT | MID INIT

6. DATE OF BIRTH

Month: JAN FEB MAR APR MAY JUN JUL AUG SEP OCT NOV DEC

Day | Year

7. SEX

MALE

FEMALE

The Princeton Review

FORM NO. 00001-PR

Test 2

Start with number 1 for each new section.
If a section has fewer questions than answer spaces, leave the extra answer spaces blank.

1.–27. A B C D E

1.–26. A B C D E

1.–25. A B C D E

1.–23. A B C D E

TIMED SECTION I

Time—35 minutes

23 Questions

Directions: Each group of Questions in this section is based on a set of conditions. In answering some of the questions, it may be useful to draw a rough diagram. Choose the response that most accurately and completely answers each question and blacken the corresponding space on your answer sheet.

Questions 1–6

Parker is putting together a schedule for his company's softball team—the Jannettes. The team will play exactly five other teams—Kasmirs, Launcelots, Magnuses, Nicodemuses, and Parkers—During the six weeks of the softball season, they will play exactly one game a week, except for one off-week in which they will not play any game. The schedule is set in accordance with the following:

Jannettes play Magnuses at some point after their off-week.
Jannettes play Launcelots at some time before their off-week.
Jannettes play Nicodemuses at some time before they play Kasmirs.
Jannettes play Parkers either immediately before or immediately after their off-week.

1. Which one of the following could be an acceptable schedule of games and the off-week for the Jannettes in order from the first week to the last week?
   (A) Launcelots, Parkers, off-week, Kasmirs, Magnuses, Nicodemuses
   (B) Launcelots, Nicodemuses, off-week, Parkers, Magnuses, Kasmirs
   (C) Parkers, off-week, Nicodemuses, Kasmirs, Launcelots, Magnuses
   (D) Nicodemuses, Kasmirs, Launcelots, off-week, Magnuses, Parkers
   (E) Nicodemuses, Magnuses, Launcelots, Parkers, off-week, Kasmirs

2. The Jannettes CANNOT play Nicodemuses during which week?
   (A) the second week
   (B) the third week
   (C) the fourth week
   (D) the fifth week
   (E) the sixth week

3. If the Jannettes play Launcelots the week before they play Parkers, then each of the following could be true EXCEPT:
   (A) The Jannettes play Parkers during the fifth week.
   (B) The Jannettes play Kasmirs during the second week.
   (C) The Jannettes play Parkers during the third week.
   (D) The Jannettes play Magnuses during the sixth week.
   (E) The Jannettes play Magnuses during the fourth week.

4. If the Jannettes play Magnuses during the fourth week, then which of the following must be true?
   (A) The Jannettes play Parkers during the second week.
   (B) The Jannettes play Parkers during the third week.
   (C) The Jannettes have an off-week during the second week.
   (D) The Jannettes play Nicodemuses during the fifth week.
   (E) The Jannettes play Kasmirs during the fifth week.

5. Which one of the following could be the order of the Jannettes' games, from earliest to latest?
   (A) Launcelots, Parkers, Kasmirs, Magnuses, Nicodemuses
   (B) Launcelots, Nicodemuses, Magnuses, Parkers, Kasmirs
   (C) Launcelots, Nicodemuses, Kasmirs, Parkers, Magnuses
   (D) Nicodemuses, Parkers, Launcelots, Kasmirs, Magnuses
   (E) Nicodemuses, Kasmirs, Launcelots, Magnuses, Parkers

6. How many of the teams are there, any one of which could play the Jannettes during the first week?
   (A) five
   (B) four
   (C) three
   (D) two
   (E) one

Questions 7–12

A regional playoff, if it occurs at all, will contain teams selected from six local teams: three from the East League—the Cowgirls, the Dreadnaughts and the Eagles—and three from the West League—the Pirates, the Rogues and the Soldiers. Due to a complex tie-breaking system, the playoff teams will be determined by the following restrictions:

If the Cowgirls are not in the playoffs, the Soldiers are in the playoffs.
If the Soldiers are in the playoffs, the Cowgirls are not in the playoffs.
If the Cowgirls are not in the playoffs, the Pirates are also not in the playoffs.
If any team is in the playoffs, the Dreadnaughts are also in the playoffs.

7. Which of the following is a list of all the teams who could be in the playoffs?

(A) The Eagles
(B) The Rogues, The Soldiers
(C) The Dreadnaughts, the Eagles, the Soldiers
(D) The Dreadnaughts, the Eagles, the Pirates
(E) The Cowgirls, the Dreadnaughts, the Pirates, the Soldiers

8. If the Pirates are in the playoffs, which one of the following is a complete and accurate list of the teams who could be not in the playoffs?

(A) The Soldiers
(B) The Cowgirls, the Soldiers
(C) The Eagles, the Soldiers
(D) The Eagles, the Rogues
(E) The Eagles, the Rogues, the Soldiers

9. If there are more teams from the West League than from the East League in the playoffs, exactly how many teams must be in the playoffs?

(A) one
(B) two
(C) three
(D) four
(E) five

10. If there are two teams from the West league in the playoffs, then which of the following must be true?

(A) The Eagles are in the playoffs.
(B) Both the Rogues and the Eagles are in the playoffs.
(C) Neither the Eagles nor the Soldiers are in the playoffs.
(D) All three teams from the East are in the playoffs.
(E) The Rogues are in the playoffs.

11. Which one of the following could be true?

(A) The Eagles are the only team from the East League in the playoffs.
(B) The Rogues are the only team from the West league in the playoffs.
(C) The Pirates and the Soldiers are the only teams from the West in the playoffs.
(D) The Eagles and the Cowgirls are the only teams from the East League in the playoffs.
(E) The Cowgirls are the only team from the East League in the playoffs.

12. What is the minimum number of teams to make the playoffs?

(A) zero
(B) one
(C) two
(D) three
(E) four

Questions 13–17

A contractor is assigning exactly six workers —Joe, Ken, Leo, Max, Ned, and Olga—to three construction sites. Three of the workers are electricians, and three are plumbers. The workers travel together in a company van and get dropped off at their respective sites in the following order: site A, site B, and site C. The workers are assigned in pairs according to the following conditions:

Each pair of workers consists of one electrician and one plumber.
Max, who is a plumber, gets dropped off at an earlier site than Olga, who is an electrician.
Leo is dropped off at site B.
Ken is not dropped off at a site before Ned is dropped off at a site.

13. Which of the following could be a complete and accurate list of the electricians and plumbers, listed in the order in which they are dropped off?

(A) electricians: Ken, Leo, Olga
plumbers: Max, Joe, Ned
(B) electricians: Ned, Max, Olga
plumbers: Joe, Leo, Ken
(C) electricians: Joe, Ken, Olga
plumbers: Max, Ned, Leo
(D) electricians: Ken, Leo, Olga
plumbers: Ned, Max, Joe
(E) electricians: Olga, Leo, Ken
plumbers: Ned, Max, Joe

14. Which of the following is a complete list of the workers who could be a plumber assigned to site A?

(A) Joe, Ken
(B) Max, Ned
(C) Joe, Max, Ned
(D) Ken, Max, Ned, Olga
(E) Joe, Ken, Max, Ned

15. If Max is dropped off at site B, then which of the following could be the pair of workers dropped off at site A?

(A) Joe and Olga
(B) Ken and Olga
(C) Ned and Olga
(D) Joe and Ned
(E) Leo and Ned

16. If Ned is dropped off at site C, then which one of the following must be true?

(A) Leo is a plumber.
(B) Leo is an electrician.
(C) Ned is an electrician.
(D) Ken is a plumber.
(E) Joe is a plumber.

17. If Max is dropped off at site B, then which of the following could be the plumber dropped off at the site immediately before the site at which Ken is dropped off?

(A) Joe
(B) Leo
(C) Max
(D) Ned
(E) Olga

Questions 18–23

After ending a long relationship, Agnes is back on the dating scene. She organizes a series of dates with different people, choosing from people she met through friends, at her gym, at the library, online, or in the workplace. The series of dates that she goes on must conform to the following conditions:

Any time Agnes goes on eight dates in a row, she must include at least one date from each of the different ways she meets people.

If a date with a person Agnes met through friends is preceded or followed by a date with a person Agnes met in the workplace, any date that precedes and any date that follows that pair of dates must be with a person she met at the gym.

No date with someone Agnes met online can precede or follow a date with someone Agnes met at the gym.

Agnes cannot go on consecutive dates with two people whom she met in the same way unless she met those two people at the library.

18. If Agnes goes on exactly eight dates, which one of the following is an acceptable order for the way she met those eight dates?

(A) at the gym, online, at the gym, in the workplace, through friends, at the library, in the workplace, at the library
(B) through friends, at the workplace, at the gym, at the library, at the library, online, in the workplace, online
(C) at the gym, in the workplace, through friends, at the gym, at the library, at the gym, at the library, at the library
(D) at the library, at the gym, through friends, in the workplace, at the gym, online, at the library, through friends
(E) online, in the workplace, at the gym, at the gym, in the workplace, through friends, at the gym, at the library

19. If Agnes goes on eight dates and the second, third, fourth, sixth and seventh dates are with people she met at the gym, at the library, in the workplace, through friends, and at the gym, respectively, then which one of the following must be true?

(A) The fifth date is with someone she met at the library.
(B) The first date is with someone she met through friends.
(C) The eighth date is with someone she met online.
(D) The fifth date is with someone she met online.
(E) The eighth date is with someone she met in the workplace.

20. If Agnes goes on six dates and the first and second dates are with people she met through friends and in the workplace, respectively, then the fifth and sixth dates, respectively, CANNOT be with people she met

(A) online and in the workplace
(B) through friends and online
(C) in the workplace and through friends
(D) at the library and online
(E) online and at the library

21. If the fourth date is with someone she met online, which one of the following could describe how she met her second and third dates, respectively?

(A) at the library, online
(B) in the workplace, through friends
(C) at the library, at the gym
(D) through friends, through friends
(E) in the workplace, at the library

22. If Agnes goes on nine dates, and the first and fourth dates are with people she met through friends while the second and fifth dates are with people she met in the workplace, then which one of the following could be true?

(A) The ninth date is with someone she met in the workplace.
(B) The eighth date is with someone she met at the gym.
(C) The seventh date is with someone she met online.
(D) The eighth date is with someone she met at the library.
(E) The ninth date is with someone she met at the gym.

23. If Agnes goes on eight dates, and the first, second, third, and fourth dates are with people she met at the gym, in the workplace, at the library, and at the gym, respectively, then the fifth and sixth dates, respectively, CANNOT be with people she met

(A) through friends and in the workplace
(B) through friends and online
(C) in the workplace and online
(D) at the library and through friends
(E) at the library and online

ANSWER KEY

1. B
2. E
3. A
4. D
5. C
6. D
7. C
8. E
9. C
10. E
11. B
12. C
13. D
14. E
15. D
16. A
17. C
18. B
19. D
20. C
21. E
22. A
23. A

EXPLANATIONS FOR TIMED SECTION 1 QUESTIONS 1–6

Prepare

Ingredient Scan

Task: Order game; determine the order of five teams and one off-week in a six week schedule.

Inventory: Use a symbol "X" for the off-week, so you have 6 elements (K, L, M, N, P, and X) / 6 slots.

Rules: Because the rules refer to position before or after the off-week, you definitely need a symbol to represent the off-week.

Questions: 6 Questions: 1 Grab-a-Rule, 2 Specific, and 3 General

Red Flags: Other than needing to create a symbol for the off-week, nothing here is too challenging.

Rank: 1

Diagram and Inventory

Create a straightforward ordering diagram with the core labeled 1 to 6.

Symbolize the Rules and Double-Check

Rule 1: X—M

Rule 2: L—X

Rule 3: N—K

Rule 4: [PX] or [XP]

Don't forget to double-check your rules!

Deductions

Links: X is a recurring theme in three of the four rules. Chain together rules 1, 2, and 4 to get L—XP/PX—M.
Spatial restrictions: 4 of the 6 elements are in the composite clue, the other two are linked to each other, N—K. That means only L or N can go first. Add L/N to slot 1 in your diagram. Only M or K could go last. Add M/K to slot 6. Look at the extremities of the big composite clues. What's the latest that L could go? L has three things that must come after it, so the latest L could go is slot 3. Conversely, the earliest M could go is slot 4.
Most restricted: Everything in the composite clue is limited to three different slots.
Least restricted: N and K are only bound by each other. N can't be last; K can't be first. Otherwise, they could each go in five different slots.

Here is your diagram:

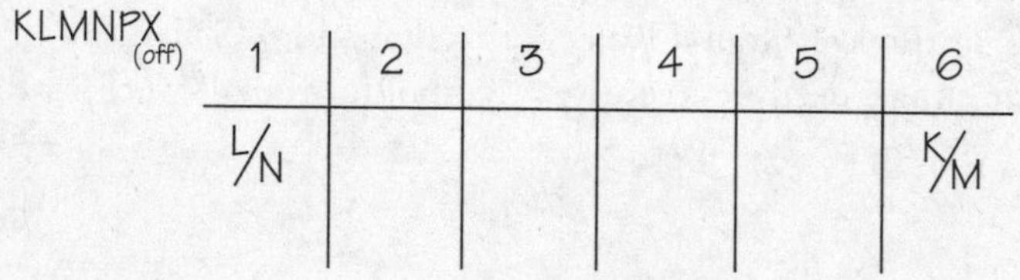

KLMNPX (off)

1	2	3	4	5	6
L/N					K/M

Assess, Act, Answer

Question 1 is a Grab-a-Rule so do that one first. Rule 1 eliminates choice (E). Rule 2 eliminates choice (C). Rule 3 eliminates choice (A). Rule 4 eliminates choice (D). **Choice (B) is the only one left, so it is the credited response.**

Question 3 is the first Specific. question. You need a scenario in which L comes immediately before P. Since X always comes right before or after P, you will have LPX consecutively. In how many different slots can you place LPX? 4/5/6 is impossible because X can't be last (it comes before M). Write a row for other possible scenarios to verify if they are valid. If LPX is 1/2/3, then there is still some flexibility for N, K, and M. Write down limitations you know for sure. K can't go in slot 4 because N has to come first, so slot 4 is N/M. N can't go last because K comes after it, so slot 6 has to be K/M. If LPX is 2/3/4, then what could/must go in slot 1? It must be N. Slots 5 and 6 are interchangeably K and M so write in K/M and M/K. If LPX is 3/4/5, then what could/must go 6? It must be M. That leaves N and K for slots 1 and 2 and they require a certain order, so N must be in slot 1 and K must be in slot 2. The question asks what could be true EXCEPT which means you are looking for something that must be false. **Choice (A) says something impossible about P, so it is the credited response.**

	1	2	3	4	5	6
3.	L	P	X	N/M		K/M
	N	L	P	X	K/M	M/K
	N	K	L	P	X	M

Question 4 is the next Specific question. Place M in slot 4 and see what must be true. Looking at the composite clue, M has three things that must come before it: L, X, and P. L must be first and X and P are interchangeably slots 2 and 3. That means N and K are left for slots 5 and 6 and N must come before K, so N is 5 and K is 6. Since the question asks what must be true, the answer will likely deal with L, N, or K since their positions are set in stone. Scan the answers for those elements. **Choice (D) describes your diagram, so it is the credited response.**

	1	2	3	4	5	6
4.	L	X/P	P/X	M	N	K

Question 2 is the first General question. It asks where N cannot go. N can go in any slot but last since K must still come after N. Look for slot 6 in the answer choices. **This is choice (E), the credited response.**

Question 5 is the next General question. It is almost a Grab-a-Rule question, although it only shows 5 of the 6 elements. Usc the two order chains, L—P—M and N—K, to eliminate answer choices. Choice (A) is wrong because K can't come before N. Choice (B) is wrong because M can't come before P. **Choice (C) looks fine, so it is the credited response.**

Question 6 is all that's left. The question asks how many options there are for slot 1. From your Deductions, only L and N can go in slot 1, so there are two options. **Choice (D) is correct.**

EXPLANATIONS FOR TIMED SECTION 1, QUESTIONS 7–12

Prepare

Ingredient Scan

Task: 2-D In-Out; assign 0–6 teams from two leagues to be in the playoffs or not in the playoffs.
Inventory: 6 elements, 2 columns (In and Out)
Rules: Like most In-Out games, you see mostly conditional rules
Questions: 6 Questions: 1 Grab-a-Rule, 3 Specific, 2 General
Red Flags: It's unusual for an In-Out game to offer the possibility of having nothing In, but this game's setup does just that
Rank: 2

Diagram and Inventory

The elements are C, D, E, P, R, and S, in groups East or West

Symbolize the Rules and Double-Check

Rule 1: ~C → S
~S → C

Rule 2: S → ~C
C → ~S

Rule 3: ~C → ~P
P → C

Rule 4: anyone → D
~D → anyone

Don't forget to double-check your rules!

Deductions

Spatial restrictions: Rule 1 creates a placeholder because having C Out means that S is In. Having S Out means that C is In. It's impossible for S and C to both be Out, so at least one of them must be In. Hence, you put an S/C placeholder in the In column. Rule 2 by the same token tells you that it's impossible for both S and C to be In, since either one being In forces the other one Out. At least one of them must be Out, so you put a C/S placeholder in the Out column. Both placeholders relate to the same two elements. Because of that, one will always be In and one will always be Out, so you can write their placeholders as reciprocals, S/C and C/S. Because one of them is always In, you know by rule 4 that D always must be In. Write D into your master diagram

Links: Rules 1 and 3 will link up with each other in the game.
Most restricted: D
Least restricted: E and R are free agents

Here is your diagram:

East: C,D,E
West: P,R,S

IN	OUT
D C/S	S/C
E	

Assess, Act, Answer

Question 7 is a Grab-a-Rule, so do that one first. Like all In-Out games, the Grab-a-Rule only shows you one of the columns (normally the In column). If it helps you to analyze the rules, you can make your own Out column next to the answer choices; for each answer choice, write all the remaining elements in the Out column. Otherwise, practice visualizing that everything you don't see in an answer choice is in the Out column. Rule 1 eliminates choice (A). Rule 2 eliminates choices (E). Rule 3 eliminates choice (D). Rule 4 eliminates choice (B). **Because only choice (C) remains, it is the credited response.**

Question 8 is a Specific question, so do that one next. It tells you P is In. Look up your conditional rules to see if anything applies to P. It says that C must be In and S must be Out. As always, D is also In. That just leaves E and R, the free agents. They could go anywhere. The question asks for a complete list of which elements could go last. Look for S, E, and R. **Choice (E) is correct.**

	IN	OUT
8.	P C D	S
	N E E	W

Question 9 is also a Specific question, so do that one next. It tells you that there must be more West teams In than East teams In and wants to know how many elements must be In. Since you know that D is always In, you have a minimum of one East team. That means you either have two West teams and one East team or three West teams and one East team, if you want more West teams than East teams In. Check both scenarios. If you're only going to use two East teams, it needs to be R and S since P would bring C, another East team, In. If you're using all three West teams, S forces C to be Out while P forces C to be In. That means that scenario is broken. Cross it out so you don't use it for anything later. Only the first scenario works, so there must be a quantity of 3 teams In. **Choice (C) is correct.**

	IN	OUT
9.	R S D	
	W W E	

Question 10 is also a Specific question, so it should come next. It says there will be exactly two West teams In and asks for something that must be true. You already have a scenario from Question 2 that has two West teams In, so you can use it to eliminate answers. Choices (A) and (B) can be eliminated because they both say that E must be In; your work for question 2 proves otherwise. Choice (C) can be eliminated because it says that S must be Out; your work for question 2 proves otherwise. Choice (D) can be eliminated because it says that all three East teams must be in; your work for question 2 proves otherwise. **Because choice (E) is all that remains, it is the credited response.**

All of the Specific Questions are done, so do your first General question, question 11. It asks for something possible, so if an answer choice describes anything you've seen to be possible from previous work, that's your answer. Choice (A) is impossible because you will always have D representing the East no matter what. Eliminate it. Choice (B) seems plausible since R is a free agent. Naturally, D would also be In, but D is not a West team so this answer choice is still true. Make a quick check to verify that forcing everything else (P, S, C, and E) Out would cause no problems. **Choice (B) doesn't break any rules, so it is the credited response.**

Question 12 is a General question that asks for the minimum number of elements In. From the setup, you see that D and C/S will always be In, so there is a minimum of 2 elements In. **Choice (C) is correct.**

EXPLANATIONS FOR TIMED SECTION 1 QUESTIONS 13–17

Prepare

Ingredient Scan

Task: 2-D Order game, combining order and groups; assign one electrician and one plumber to each of three sites
Inventory: 6 elements, 6 slots, 1:1 ratio
Rules: A couple of range rules, one of which appears challenging to symbolize
Questions: 5 total: 1 Grab-a-Rule, 3 Specific, 1 General
Red Flags: You aren't told which individual elements belong to which groups.
Rank: 3

Diagram and Inventory

The setup describes a two-tiered Order game in which you must determine the order in which 6 workers—j, k, l, m, n, and o—are dropped off at three sites—A, B, and C. Two workers are assigned per site.

Symbolize the Rules and Double-Check

Rule 1: Create two rows in your diagram, one for electricians and one for plumbers.

Rule 2: m_P—o_E

Rule 3: l=B (Put this in your diagram.)

Rule 4: n—k; [n over k] or [k over n]

For rule 4, be careful; there are actually two possibilities here. Either n must be dropped off before k, or both workers could be dropped off at the same time. Be sure to include both when symbolizing the rule. Also, the block must be written both ways, as you don't know anything about n or k with respect to group (electrician or plumber).

Don't forget to double-check your rules!

Deductions

Links: Where k and n go will depend on where m and o end up from rule 2. If either m or o is paired with l at site B, this restricts the options for k and n.
Spatial restrictions: From rule 2, you know that o cannot be at site A and that m cannot be at site C. You also know that m cannot be in the electrician row and o cannot be in the plumber row. From rule 3, you know that l cannot be at either site A or site C.
Most restricted: l must be at site B, but figuring out whether it is an electrician or a plumber depends on which other element is paired with it.
Least restricted: j is not mentioned in any rule, so it can go anywhere.

Here is your diagram:

jklmno

	~l ~o A	(l) B	~l ~m C
~m E	__	__	__
~o P	__	__	__

Assess, Act, Answer

Question 13 is a Grab-a-Rule, so begin there.

For question 13, use the rules to eliminate answer choices. Rule 2 eliminates choice (B) and choice (E). Rule 3 eliminates choice (C) and rule 4 eliminates choice (A). **The only choice left, and therefore the credited response, is choice (D).**

Move on to the Specific questions next. The first Specific question is question 15.

For question 15, place m in the plumber slot for site B. This means that l must be the electrician at site B (rule 3) and o must be the electrician for site C (rule 2). Since the only slots now open are at sites A and C, from rule 4 you know that either k and n are dropped off together at site A, or n is at site A while k is at site C.

Here is your diagram:

		~l ~o A	(l) B	~l ~m C
15.	~m E	k/n	l	o
	~o P	n/k	m	j
		j/n	l	o
		n/j	m	k

The question asks for a pair of workers who could be dropped off together at site A. The only choice that matches what you have in your diagram is choice (D). **Choice (D) is the credited response.**

The next Specific question is question 16.

For question 16, if n is at site C, then k will also have to be at site C (rule 4). You don't know which one is the plumber and which the electrician, so note that accordingly. Since site C is full, this means m must be at site A and o at site B (rule 2). This means l is the plumber at site B (rule 2 combined with rule 3). Since the only remaining open slot is for the electrician at site A, j must be assigned to site A.

Here is your diagram:

		~l ~o A	(l) B	~l ~m C
16.	~m E	j	o	n/k
	~o P	m	l	k/n

The question asks for what must be true; the only choice that must be true based on your diagram is choice (A). **Choice (A) is the credited response.**

The final Specific question is question 17.

For question 17, place m in the plumber slot at site B (rule 2). This means l is the electrician at site B (rule 3) and o is the electrician at site C (rule 2). Since the only slots now open are at sites A and C, from rule 4 you know that either k and n are dropped off together at site A, or n is at site A while k is at site C. j will occupy the remaining slot in either case.

Here is your diagram:

		~l ~o A	(l) B	~l ~m C
17.	~m E	k/n	l	o
	~o P	n/k	m	j
		n/j	l	o
		j/n	m	k

The question asks for which worker could be the plumber dropped off at the site immediately before k is dropped off. In the second scenario in your diagram, m is the plumber dropped off at site B while k is dropped off at site C. **Choice (C) is the credited response.**

Move on to the General question, question 14.

Question 14 asks for a list of all workers who could be the plumber at site A. Based on your work from questions 15 and 16, you know that j, k, m, and n are all possibilities, so they must be included in your answer. The only choice that contains all four elements is choice (E). **Choice (E) is the credited response.**

EXPLANATIONS FOR TIMED SECTION 1 QUESTIONS 18–23

Prepare

Ingredient Scan

Task: Order game
Inventory: 5 elements that can be repeated or left out
Rules: Conditional statements and block clues
Questions: 6 total: 1 Grab-a-Rule, 5 Specific
Red Flags: Not a 1:1 game, don't know how many slots for diagram
Rank: 4

Diagram and Inventory

The setup describes an Order game in which you can use up to five elements—F, G, L, O, and W. Create a diagram with eight columns numbered 1-8 as the core, but keep in mind that you may need to adjust your diagram based on what the questions tell you. You don't know how many dates there are, and elements can be repeated or left out entirely.

Symbolize the Rules and Double-Check

Rule 1: any 8 in a row→all elements used; all elements NOT used→can't be 8 in a row

Rule 2: [WF] or G [WF] G

Rule 3: [G̸O] [O̸G]

Rule 4: [O̸O] [F̸F] [G̸G] [W̸W]

Rule 2 is especially tricky because it does not say that G always has to be before and after FW/WF; it's only true if there are any dates before or after WF/FW. That means that WF (or FW) can be the first two dates or the last two dates with a G only on one end of them. Rule 4 is also tricky. You may be tempted to try to symbolize this as a conditional, but it is better represented by antiblocks for all the elements except L. It just means that L is the only element that can appear twice in a row.

Don't forget to double-check your rules!

Deductions

Links: The best you can do here is link rules 2 and 3, so *if* rule 2 applies, you know that O cannot be next to any G.
Spatial restrictions: None that stick. If WF or FW is used, then you have to have at least three dates.
Most restricted: Since G is in rules 2 and 3, it is the most restricted element—but only if it is used.
Least restricted: L is not limited by any of the rules.

Here is your diagram:

FGLOW	1	2	3	4	5	6	7	8

Assess, Act, Answer

Question 18 is a Grab-a-Rule, so start there.

For question 18, use the rules to eliminate answer choices. Rule 1 eliminates choice (C), rule 2 eliminates choice (A), rule 3 eliminates choice (D), and rule 4 eliminates choice (E). **The only choice left, and therefore the credited response, is choice (B).**

Question 19 is a Specific question, so answer that one next.

For question 19, place G, L, and W in slots 2, 3, and 4, and F and G in slots 6 and 7. From rules 3 and 4 you know that slots 1 and 8 cannot be G or O. You have eight dates, so according to rule 1, you must use O. The only place it could go is slot 5.

Here is your diagram:

	1	2	3	4	5	6	7	8
19.	~O ~G	G	L	W	O	F	G	~O ~G

The question asks for something that *must* be true. The only answer that must be true is that O must be the fifth date. **Choice (D) is the credited response.**

Move on to question 20, the next Specific question.

For question 20, you have only six slots to fill, so put F and W in the first two slots and block out slots 7 and 8. Rule 2 dictates that slot 3 must be G, and rules 3 and 4 mean that slot 4 cannot be G or O.

Here is your diagram:

	1	2	3	4	5	6
20.	F	W	G	~G ~O		

The question asks for something that cannot be in 5 and 6. From your earlier analysis of rule 2, you know that you cannot have FW or WF if G cannot precede them. That matches with choice (C). **Therefore, choice (C) is the credited response.**

Question 21 is the next Specific question.

Question 21 doesn't tell you know how many dates there are, but it does state that O is in slot 4. Put O in slot 4. You know from rules 3 and 4 that neither G nor O can be the third date.

Here is your diagram:

	1	2	3	4
21.			~D ~G	O

You are looking for what could be in slots 2 and 3. From this you can cross off choices (A) and (C). Since there is no G in slot 4, then according to rule 2 WF/FW cannot be in slots 2 and 3. Eliminate choice (B). Choice (D) cannot work because it violates rule 4. **That leaves choice (E), which is the credited response.**

Move on to question 22, another Specific question.

Question 22 stipulates nine slots in the diagram. Draw an extra slot, then fill in the given information. F goes in slots 1 and 4, and W goes in slots 2 and 5. From rule 2, G must be in slots 3 and 6, so slot 7 cannot be G or O. From rule 1, you need to include at least one L and one O. Because O cannot be in slot 7, it must be in slot 8, which means that L must be in slot 7. Slot 9 can now be anything except O or G.

Here is your diagram:

	1	2	3	4	5	6	7	8	9
22.	F	W	G	F	W	G	L	O	~G ~O

Since you are looking for something that *could be true*, you can cross off everything but choice (A) because the other choices all violate the diagram. **Choice (A) is the credited response.**

Move on to question 23, the final Specific question.

Question 23 tells you there are again eight slots. Fill in G, W, L, and G for the first four slots. You know that slot 5 cannot be G or O (rules 3 and 4). Because you have eight slots, rule 1 is in effect, so you still need to include F and O.

Here is your diagram:

	1	2	3	4	5	6	7	8
23.	G	W	L	G	~G ~O			

The question asks which elements cannot be in slots 5 and 6. Start with choice (A). If you put F and W in slots 5 and 6, then slot 7 has to be G, as per rule 2. Now slot 8 cannot be O because of rule 3, and this violates rule 1. Since you know that this cannot work, there is no need to check the remaining answer choices. **Choice (A) is the credited response.**

TIMED SECTION 2

Time—35 minutes

23 Questions

Directions: Each group of questions in this section is based on a set of conditions. In answering some of the questions, it may be useful to draw a rough diagram. Choose the response that most accurately and completely answers each question and blacken the corresponding space on your answer sheet.

Questions 1–6

There are exactly seven scenes in a play, and Delia appears in all of them. In each scene, she will wear one of five different blue dresses: azure, baby blue, cobalt, denim, or electric blue. The following restrictions determine the order in which she wears the dresses:

Delia wears the azure dress exactly three times, and wears the other colored dresses exactly once.

Delia does not wear the baby blue dress in the first scene or the final scene.

Delia wears the electric blue dress in the scene immediately before the scene in which she wears the denim dress.

Delia does not wear the azure dress in consecutive scenes.

1. Which one of the following could be a complete and accurate list of dress changes Delia makes during the play?

(A) baby blue, azure, cobalt, azure, electric blue, denim, azure
(B) azure, cobalt, azure, baby blue, azure, electric blue, denim
(C) azure, baby blue, electric blue, denim, baby blue, cobalt, baby blue
(D) cobalt, denim, electric blue, azure, baby blue, azure, azure
(E) azure, electric blue, denim, azure, cobalt, azure, baby blue

2. If Delia wears the electric blue dress in the first scene, then Delia could wear the cobalt dress during the

(A) second scene
(B) third scene
(C) fourth scene
(D) fifth scene
(E) sixth scene

3. If Delia wears the cobalt dress in the scene immediately following the scene in which she wears the denim dress, then each of the following could be false EXCEPT:

(A) Delia wears the azure dress in the first scene.
(B) Delia wears the electric blue dress in the second scene.
(C) Delia wears the azure dress in the third scene.
(D) Delia wears the azure dress in the fifth scene.
(E) Delia wears the cobalt dress in the sixth scene.

4. If Delia wears the cobalt dress during the final scene, then each of the following must be false EXCEPT:

(A) Delia wears the denim dress in the second scene.
(B) Delia wears the baby blue dress in the fifth scene.
(C) Delia wears the baby blue dress in the third scene.
(D) Delia wears the denim dress in the fourth scene.
(E) Delia wears the denim dress in the sixth scene.

5. If Delia wears the baby blue dress immediately after she wears the cobalt dress, then which one of the following dresses must Delia wear during the fourth scene?

(A) the baby blue dress
(B) the cobalt dress
(C) the denim dress
(D) the electric blue dress
(E) the azure dress

6. If Delia wears the azure dress in the second scene, then which one of the following is a complete and accurate list of dresses, any one of which could be the dress Delia wears in the fourth scene?

(A) azure, denim, cobalt
(B) baby blue, cobalt, electric blue
(C) azure, denim
(D) baby blue, denim
(E) cobalt, electric blue

GO ON TO THE NEXT PAGE.

Questions 7–12

A tourist is traveling around the city on a double-decker tour bus. The tourist must choose exactly one of four types of snapshots—close-up, individual, group, and panorama—to take at each of the six consecutive stops the bus makes. The snapshots can only fall in one of these four categories, and they must align with the following restrictions:

At the fifth stop, the tourist takes a group or panorama snapshot.

If the tourist takes either a close-up or individual snapshot at a stop, he does not take a group snapshot at the next stop.

The tourist takes the same type of snapshot at the first stop as he does at the sixth stop.

The tourist takes the same type of snapshot at the second stop as he does at the fourth stop.

The tourist does not take the same type of snapshot at consecutive stops.

7. Which one of the following could be an accurate list of snapshots the tourist takes at each stop?

(A) panorama, individual, close-up, individual, group
(B) close-up, individual, individual, close-up, panorama, close-up
(C) individual, panorama, group, panorama, group, individual
(D) individual, close-up, panorama, individual, panorama, individual
(E) individual, group, panorama, group, panorama, individual

8. If the tourist takes a panorama snapshot at stop 2, which one of the following could be the photos he takes at the final two stops, in order?

(A) panorama, close-up
(B) group, close-up
(C) individual, group
(D) panorama, group
(E) group, panorama

9. If the tourist takes a panorama shot at stop 5, and the only snapshots he takes during the tour are individual, group, and panorama snapshots, then which photos must he take at the first three stops, respectively?

(A) panorama, individual, and group
(B) group, panorama, and individual
(C) group, individual, and panorama
(D) individual, group, and panorama
(E) individual, panorama, and group

10. Which of the following could be an accurate list of the photos the tourist takes at stops 1, 2, and 3, respectively, if the tourist takes a group snapshot at stop 5 ?

(A) close-up, panorama, group
(B) close-up, individual, group
(C) individual, close-up, panorama
(D) individual, close-up, group
(E) group, panorama, group

11. Each of the following can be an accurate list of the snapshots the tourist takes at stops 1 and 2, respectively, EXCEPT:

(A) panorama, group
(B) individual, panorama
(C) close-up, panorama
(D) individual, close-up
(E) close-up, individual

12. Which of the following, if true, would entirely determine the order in which the tourist's snapshots can be taken?

(A) A group shot is taken fifth.
(B) A panorama shot is taken fifth.
(C) A panorama shot is taken first and an individual shot is taken third.
(D) A panorama is taken first and a panorama shot is taken third.
(E) An individual shot is taken first and a close-up shot is taken third.

GO ON TO THE NEXT PAGE.

Questions 13–17

A designer will create an outfit comprised of two and only two garments—a dress and a vest—for a new line of eco-friendly clothing. One of the garments will be made from a mix of fabrics, and the other garment will be entirely one fabric. The following conditions apply:

Only one fabric will be shared by the dress and the vest.
If the dress is made from a mix of fabrics, then it contains exactly three fabrics.
If the vest is made from a mix of fabrics, then it contains exactly two fabrics.
Organic cotton, hemp, and soy silk are the only fabrics that can be in the dress.
Hemp, soy silk, and wool are the only fabrics that can be in the vest.

13. Which of the following could be a complete and accurate list of the fabrics in the outfit?

(A) dress: organic cotton, hemp; vest: hemp
(B) dress: organic cotton, hemp, soy silk; vest: wool
(C) dress: organic cotton, hemp, wool; vest: wool
(D) dress: organic cotton, hemp, soy silk; vest: soy silk
(E) dress: hemp; vest: hemp

14. If the outfit consists of exactly three fabrics, the vest must be

(A) entirely wool or else soy silk and wool
(B) entirely hemp or else entirely soy silk
(C) entirely hemp or else entirely wool
(D) entirely soy silk or else soy silk and hemp
(E) entirely hemp or else hemp and wool

15. Each of the following could be true EXCEPT:

(A) The outfit consists of both organic cotton and wool.
(B) The outfit consists of both hemp and organic cotton.
(C) The outfit consists of both soy silk and wool.
(D) The outfit consists of both organic cotton and soy silk.
(E) The outfit consists of both hemp and soy silk.

16. If there are exactly two fabrics in the outfit, which of the following must be false?

(A) The vest is made from hemp and wool.
(B) The vest is made from hemp and soy silk.
(C) The vest is made from soy silk and wool.
(D) The dress is at least partially hemp.
(E) The dress is at least partially organic cotton.

17. If at least part of the dress is organic cotton, then which one of the following could be true?

(A) At least part of the vest is soy silk.
(B) At least part of the vest is wool.
(C) The vest is made from a mix of fabrics.
(D) The dress does not contain soy silk.
(E) The dress does not contain hemp.

GO ON TO THE NEXT PAGE.

Questions 18–23

Over the course of five months from January to May, three dogs—an Afghan Hound, a Brittany Spaniel, and a Chihuahua—will each visit the veterinarian exactly once. Each will also visit the groomer exactly once. The following must obtain:

The Brittany Spaniel visits the veterinarian in some month before the month it visits the groomer.

The Afghan Hound visits the groomer in some month before the month it visits the veterinarian.

The Chihuahua visits the veterinarian in some month before the month the Brittany Spaniel visits the groomer and in some month after the month the Brittany Spaniel visits the veterinarian.

The Afghan Hound visits the veterinarian in the same month that the Chihuahua visits the veterinarian.

Any dog that visits the veterinarian in April cannot also see the groomer in April.

18. Which of the following could be an accurate list of when each dog visits the veterinarian?

(A) January: Afghan Hound, Brittany Spaniel, Chihuahua
(B) February: Afghan Hound, Brittany Spaniel; March: Chihuahua
(C) March: Afghan Hound, Chihuahua; April: Brittany Spaniel
(D) January: Brittany Spaniel; March: Afghan Hound, Chihuahua;
(E) April: Afghan hound, Chihuahua; May: Brittany Spaniel

19. If the Brittany Spaniel visits the veterinarian in March, which of the following must be true?

(A) The Chihuahua visits the groomer in May.
(B) The Brittany Spaniel visits the groomer in May.
(C) The Chihuahua visits the veterinarian in March.
(D) The Afghan Hound visits the groomer in March.
(E) The Afghan Hound visits the groomer in February.

20. Which one of the following must be true?

(A) Neither the Chihuahua nor the Brittany Spaniel visits the groomer in February.
(B) Neither the Chihuahua nor the Afghan Hound visits the veterinarian in January.
(C) Neither the Brittany spaniel nor the Afghan Hound visit the groomer in March.
(D) Neither the Brittany Spaniel nor the Chihuahua visits the veterinarian in April.
(E) Neither the Afghan Hound nor the Chihuahua visits the groomer in April.

21. If the Chihuahua visits the veterinarian in some month before it visits the groomer, and it visits the groomer in April, then which of the following could be true?

(A) The Brittany Spaniel visits the groomer in the same month that the Chihuahua visits the groomer.
(B) The Afghan Hound visits the veterinarian in the same month that the Brittany Spaniel visits the groomer.
(C) The Chihuahua visits the groomer in some month before the month in which the Afghan visits the veterinarian.
(D) The Chihuahua visits the groomer in some month before the month in which the Afghan visits the groomer.
(E) The Brittany Spaniel visits the groomer in some month before the month in which the Afghan visits the veterinarian.

22. All of the following could be false EXCEPT:

(A) At least one dog visits the groomer in February.
(B) At least one dog visits the groomer in May.
(C) At least two of the dogs visit the groomer in some month after March.
(D) None of the dogs visits the veterinarian in May.
(E) None of the dogs visits the veterinarian in January.

23. Which of the following could be true?

(A) The Afghan Hound visits the groomer in April.
(B) The Brittany Spaniel visits the groomer in February.
(C) Exactly two dogs visit the groomer in March.
(D) Exactly two dogs visit the veterinarian in January.
(E) Exactly two dogs see the veterinarian in May.

STOP

IF YOU FINISH BEFORE TIME IS CALLED, YOU MAY CHECK YOUR WORK ON THIS SECTION ONLY. DO NOT WORK ON ANY OTHER SECTION IN THE TEST.

ANSWER KEY

1. B
2. C
3. A
4. B
5. E
6. C
7. C
8. B
9. C
10. A
11. A
12. E
13. D
14. B
15. A
16. E
17. A
18. D
19. B
20. B
21. A
22. D
23. C

EXPLANATIONS FOR TIMED SECTION 2 QUESTIONS 1–6

Prepare

Ingredient Scan

Task: 1–D Order; assign 5 dresses to each of 7 scenes in a play
Inventory: 5 dresses total for 7 slots
Rules: Pretty straightforward, one rule fixes the lack of 1:1 correspondence
Questions: 6 total: 1 Grab-a-Rule, 5 Specific
Red Flags: Not a 1:1 setup, but since one element is used three times it operates like a 1:1 game
Rank: 2

Diagram and Inventory

The setup describes an Order game in which five dresses in different shades of blue—a, b, c, d, and e—must be chosen for seven different scenes in a play. One dress is chosen per scene.

Symbolize the Rules and Double-Check

Rule 1: a, a, a, b, c, d, e

Rule 2: b≠1, 7 Put directly into your diagram.

Rule 3: ed

Rule 4: 

Don't forget to double-check your rules!

Deductions

Links: All three a's must be separated but you still need to leave room for the block; this will limit the placement of the a's in any scenario.
Spatial restrictions: From rule 3 you know that d cannot be in slot 1 and e cannot be in slot 7.
Most restricted: Because there are three of them and they can't be adjacent, the a's appear to be the most restricted aspect of the game.
Least restricted: c is never mentioned in any of the rules, so it can be placed anywhere.

Here is your diagram:

aaabcde

~d ~b 1	2	3	4	5	6	~e ~b 7

Assess, Act, Answer

Question 1 is a Grab-a-Rule question, so begin there.

For question 1, use the rules to eliminate answer choices. Rule 1 eliminates choice (C), rule 2 eliminates choice (A) and choice (E), and rule 4 eliminates choice (D). **The only choice left, and therefore the credited response, is choice (B).**

Move on to the Specific questions. The first Specific question is question 2.

For question 2, place e in slot 1. This means that d must go in slot 2 (rule 3). You now have to split up the a's (rule 4) in the remaining spaces. They must be placed in slots 3, 5, and 7. This leaves either b or c for each of slots 4 and 6, though it's not certain which element is in which slot.

Here is your diagram:

	~d ~b 1	2	3	4	5	6	~e ~b 7
2.	e	d	a	b/c	a	c/b	a

The question asks about where c could be placed in the diagram. The only choice that matches either of the possibilities in your diagram is choice (C). **Choice (C) is the credited response.**

The next Specific question is question 3.

Question 3 tells you that you now have a block of three elements to fit, since c must come directly after the block containing e and d (rule 3). Again, start by figuring out where the a's must go in order to leave enough room for the block. There are two possibilities: either the a's can be placed in slots 1, 5, and 7, with the block in slots 2, 3, and 4, or they can be placed in slots 1, 3, and 7, with the block in slots 4, 5, and 6. The remaining slot in either case is filled by b.

Here is your diagram:

	~d ~b 1	2	3	4	5	6	~e ~b 7
3.	a	e	d	c	a	b	a
	a	b	a	e	d	c	a

The question asks for what must be true. Only choice (A) is true in both scenarios in your diagram. **Choice (A) is the credited response.**

The next Specific question is question 4.

For question 4, place c in slot 7. This limits the placement of the three a's (rules 1 and 4), as you must leave room for the block (rule 3). There are only two possible scenarios that work: the a's can go in either slots 1, 4, and 6 or slots 1, 3, and 6. The block can then be placed accordingly.

Here is your diagram:

	~d ~b 1	2	3	4	5	6	~e ~b 7
aaabcde							
4.	a	e	d	a	b	a	c
	a	b	a	e	d	a	c

The question asks for something that could be true. The only choice not contradicted by the diagram is choice (B), which occurs in the first scenario. **Choice (B) is the credited response.**

The next Specific question is question 5.

Question 5 tells you that you now have two blocks to work with, the one involving e and d (rule 3) plus one involving c and b. In order to make them fit and keep all the a's separated (rule 4), one block must go in slots 2 and 3 while the other goes in slots 5 and 6. The a's must be placed in slots 1, 4, and 7.

Here is your diagram:

	~d ~b 1	2	3	4	5	6	~e ~b 7
5.	a	e	d	a	c	b	a
		c	b		e	d	

The question asks which dress must go in slot 4. From your diagram, you know that one of the a's must be in fourth. **Choice (E) is the credited response.**

The final Specific question is question 6.

For question 6, place a in slot 2. You now have to split up the a's (rule 4) and fit the block (rule 3). There are two possible ways to achieve this. Either the a's are in slots 2, 5, and 7, with the block in slots 3 and 4, or they go in slots 2, 4, and 7, with the block in slots 5 and 6. Slot 1 is open in both instances; since b cannot be placed there (rule 2), c must go there, and b will fill the remaining slot, either slot 6 or slot 3, in each case.

Here is your diagram:

	~d ~b 1	2	3	4	5	6	~e ~b 7
6.	c	a	e	d	a	b	a
	c	a	b	a	e	d	a

The question asks which elements could go in slot 4; from your diagram, you know that both a and d are possible. **Therefore, choice (C) is the credited response.**

EXPLANATIONS FOR TIMED SECTION 2 QUESTIONS 7–12

Prepare

Ingredient Scan

Task: 1–D Order; assign 1 of 4 snapshots to be taken at 6 stops
Inventory: 4 snapshots, 6 slots
Rules: Mainly block clues with one conditional clue
Questions: 6 total: 1 Grab-a-Rule, 3 Specific, 2 General
Red Flags: Elements are repeated and can be left out.
Rank: 1

Diagram and Inventory

The setup is a straightforward Order setup with slots 1–6 as the core of the diagram. The inventory consists of C, I, G, and P.

Symbolize the Rules and Double-Check

Rule 1: Put this directly into your diagram.

Rule 2: C or I→~CG and ~IG. This translates into antiblocks:

~~CG~~ ~~IG~~

Rule 3: 1=6

Rule 4: 2=4

Rule 5: ~~CC~~ ~~II~~ ~~GG~~ ~~PP~~

Don't forget to double-check your rules!

Deductions

Links: Rules 1 and 5 will lead to deductions once you know what element is in slot 5.
Spatial restrictions: Rule 5 will limit what can be used, but overall, there are no restrictions you can put in your diagram.
Most restricted: Slot 5 is the most restricted, and rules 3 and 4 will also be very restricting.

Here is your diagram:

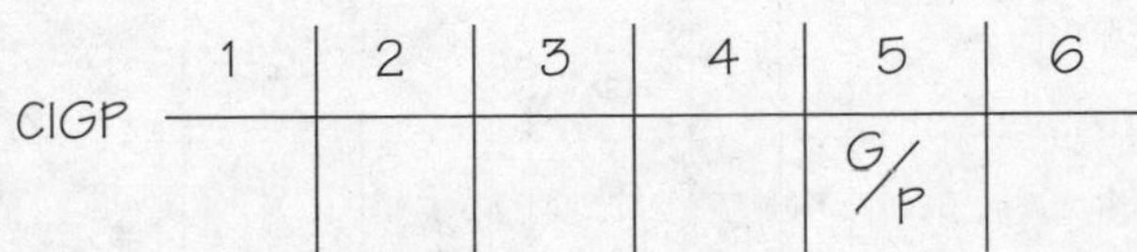

Assess, Act, Answer

Question 7 is a Grab-a-Rule question, so start there

For question 7, use the rules to eliminate answer choices. Rule 2 eliminates choice (E), rule 4 eliminates choice (D), rule 5 eliminates choice (B). There are not six elements in choice (A), so eliminate that as well. **The only choice left, and therefore the credited response, is choice (C).**

Question 8 is a Specific question, so answer that one next.

For question 8, place P in slot 2. From this, P is also in 4 (rule 4) and G has to be in slot 5 (rules 1 and 5.) Neither G nor P can be in slots 1 or 6 (rules 3 and 5.)

Here is your diagram:

	1	2	3	4	5	6
8.	I/C	P	~P	P	G	I/C

Look for something that *could be true* for slots 5 and 6. Because G must be in slot 5, eliminate choices (A), (C), and (D). Choice (E) has a P in slot 6, but if P is in slot 6 P must also be in slot 1 (rule 3), and P can't be in slot 1 because there is a P in slot 2 (rule 5.) **Therefore, the credited response is choice (B).**

Move on to question 9, the next Specific question.

For question 9, place P in slot 5. P cannot be in slots 4 or 6 (rule 5) and from that, P cannot be in slots 1 or 2 (rules 3 and 4.) The question asks for what must be in the first three slots. There are only three elements to choose from for this question: I, G, and P. Let's try I in slot 1. You can deduce that I cannot be in slot 2 (rule 5) and, because P cannot be in slot 2, that leaves G. But this violates rule 2, so I cannot be in slot 1. If it's not I, and it's not P, then G must be in slot 1. Since G cannot now be in slot 2 (rule 5) that leaves only I for slot 2. From this we know that slot 3 cannot be I (rule 5) nor G (rule 2) so it must be P.

Here is your diagram:

	1	2	3	4	5	6
9.	G	I	P	~P	P	~P

The only choice that matches the diagram is choice (C). **Choice (C) is the credited response.**

The final Specific question is question 10.

Question 10 stipulates that G goes in slot 5. G cannot be in slots 4 or 6 (rule 5) and G cannot be in slots 1 or 2. From rule 2, slot 4 cannot be C or I, and from rule 4, slot 2 cannot be C or I either. That leaves only P for slots 2 and 4.

Here is your diagram:

	1	2	3	4	5	6
10.	I/C	P	~P	P	G	I/C

Eliminate choices (B), (C), and (D) because they do not have P in slot 2. Choice (E) has G in slot 1, but you already deduced that G cannot be there, so eliminate this choice. **That leaves choice (A), the credited response.**

Now that the Specific questions are complete, attack the General questions, starting with question 11.

Question 11 asks for what cannot be in slots 1 and 2. Since you saw the combinations in choices (B) and (C) as valid possibilities in question 10, eliminate those, and try the rest. Choice (A) places P in slot 1 and G in slot 2. Rule 3 means P also goes in slot 6, and rule 4 dictates that G go in slot 4.

Here is your diagram:

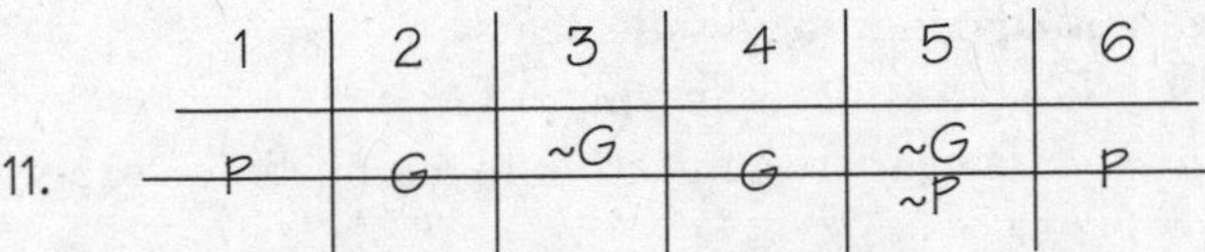

The problem here is that you are supposed to have either P or G in slot 5, as per rule 1, which now conflicts with rule 5. Make sure to cross out any work in your diagram that is not valid. **Choice (A) does not work, making it the credited response.**

Move on to question 12, the final General question.

Question 12 asks for what information determines the entire order of the elements. Looking at previous work, you know from question 10 that choice (A) does not determine the entire order, and from question 9 that choice (B) does not work either. Try the rest. Choice (C) places P in slot 1 and I in slot 3. From rule 3, P is in slot 6, which puts G in slot 5 (rule 1 and rule 5.) Since G is in slot 5, neither I nor C can be in slot 4 (rule 2), but P cannot be in slot 4 either (rule 4), because P cannot be in slot 2 (rule 5). Choice (C) does not work, so eliminate it. Remember to mark in your diagram that this combination does not work. Choice (D) places P in slot 1 and P in slot 3. Place P in slot 6 (rule 3.) Slots 2 and 4 cannot be P now according to rules 5 and 4. Slots 2 and 4 could be I or G, so choice (D) is not the answer. From process of elimination, the answer must be choice (E).

Here is your diagram:

	1	2	3	4	5	6
12. (C)	P		I	P	G	P
(D)			P		P	C
(E)	I	P	C	P	G	I

If I is in slot 1, it is also in slot 6 (rule 3,) and if C is in slot 3, then P must be in slots 2 and 4 (rules 5 and 4) and that leaves G for slot 5. **Choice (E) is the credited response.**

EXPLANATIONS FOR TIMED SECTION 2 QUESTIONS 13–17

Prepare

Ingredient Scan

Task: Group game with variable assignments; assign 4 fabrics to 2 garments
Inventory: 4 different fabrics, 2 garments
Rules: Some unusual conditional statements
Questions: 6 total: 1 Grab-a-Rule, 4 Specific, 1 General
Red Flags: It's not a garden variety game, so it might ne difficult to set up.
Rank: 4

Diagram and Inventory

Create one column for the Dress and one column for the Vest. The setup also says that one garment must be made of entirely one fabric and the other of a mix of fabrics.

Symbolize the Rules and Double-Check

Rule 1: Symbolize on the diagram and/or write down "Dress & Vest share exactly 1"
Rule 2: Mixed Dress→3 fabrics
Rule 3: Mixed Vest→2 fabrics
Rule 4: List these elements above the Dress column.
Rule 5: List these elements above the Vest column.

Don't forget to double-check your rules!

Deductions

Links: The links in the rules have already been taken care of by how your diagram was set up.
Spatial restrictions: Essentially, there are two basic scenarios—one in which the Dress is mixed and the Vest is entirely one fabric, and another scenario in which the Vest is mixed and the Dress is entirely one fabric. Make a master row for each one of these scenarios to see what else applies. If the Dress is mixed, according to rule 2, it has three fabrics so put three spaces in Dress and one space in Vest (since the Vest must be entirely one color in this scenario). Since the Dress only has three elements that can be placed in it and requires three elements for this scenario, add C, H, and S to Dress. Are there any limitations on what Vest's one element can be? The only rule that relates the two columns to each other is rule 1, which holds that exactly one element must be shared by the two columns. That means that W cannot be the only element in Vest. Thus, put an H/S placeholder in the remaining space of Vest. Move on to the second scenario in which

Dress has only one fabric and Vest is mixed. According to rule 3, when Vest is mixed it has exactly two fabrics. So put one space in Dress and two spaces in Vest. It's harder to fill up Vest as you did with Dress in the first scenario, because there are several ways you could choose two of the three elements that are allowed to go in Vest. However, the same logic applies from rule 1, which is that Dress and Vest have to share exactly one element. That means that C cannot be the solitary element in Dress, because then the two columns would share nothing. Hence, put an H/S placeholder in Dress and a corresponding match in Vest. Before going to the questions, summarize your task for each question: If the Dress is mixed, you need only determine whether the Vest is H or S. If the Vest is mixed, you must figure our whether the Dress and the Vest share H or S, and then either of the remaining two choices for the Vest will take the final space.

Most restricted: The number one question is whether the Dress or Vest is mixed.
Least restricted: H and S are bound to appear in every scenario, but they are nearly interchangeable.

Here is your diagram:

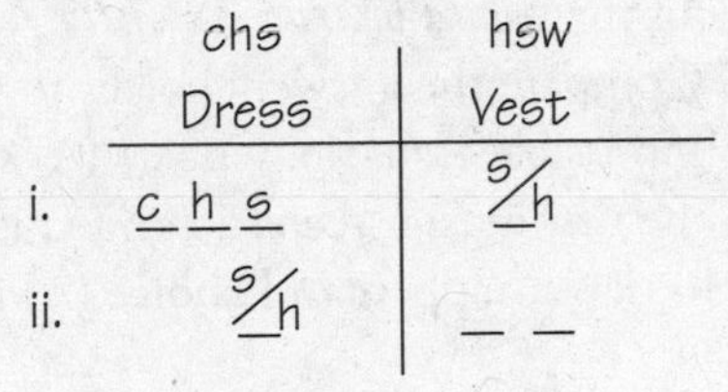

	chs Dress	hsw Vest
i.	c h s	s/h
ii.	s/h	_ _

Assess, Act, Answer

Question 13 is a Grab-a-Rule so do it first.

For question 13, apply each rule, one at a time, to all the answer choices. Rule 1 eliminates choice (B). Rule 2 eliminates choice (A). Rule 3 does nothing. Rule 4 eliminates choice (C). Rule 5 eliminates nothing. Only choices (D) and (E) remain. When all the rules are exhausted and multiple answer choices remain, reread the setup for any limitations the answers might not be meeting. In this case, choice (E) must be eliminated because both the Dress and Vest are entirely one fabric, whereas the setup mandates that one of them be mixed. **Because choice (D) is all that remains, it is the credited response.**

Question 14 is Specific question, so do that one next.

In question 14, three fabrics are being used in a given scenario and the question asks what *must be true* for the Vest. Only the first scenario contains three fabrics. The second scenario, in which the Vest is the mixed garment, will only have two different fabrics. The first scenario tells you that the Vest must be either H or S. **Hence, choice (B) is the credited response is choice (E).**

Question 16 is the next Specific question, so do that one next.

In question 16, only two fabrics are being used, which means you must refer to the second master scenario. It asks for something that *must be false.* Compare the answer choices to the second master scenario and look for something that isn't allowed. You might predict the one impossible thing you know about the second scenario: The Dress can't be C. Choice (E) attempts to confuse by saying the Dress is at least partially cotton, but since you know the Dress only gets to have one element in this scenario, this is impossible. **Therefore, the credited response is (E).**

Question 17 is a Specific question, so go ahead and set it up.

Question 17 says that C is in the Dress. That can only mean your first master scenario. There's no need to write anything out since you already know everything about that scenario except for whether the Vest gets H or S. The question asks for something that *could be true,* so any answer choice that is possible is correct. **Choice (A) is possible and is, therefore, the credited response.**

Finally, go back to your General question, number 15.

Question 15 asks for something that *could be true EXCEPT,* which is the same as asking for something that *must be false.* Compare the answer choices to your two master scenarios and pick any choice that describes an impossible scenario. Choice (A) says both C and W are used in the outfit. W is not an option in the first master scenario and C is not an option in the second master scenario. **Therefore, this could never happen and choice (A) is the credited response.**

EXPLANATIONS FOR TIMED SECTION 2 QUESTIONS 18–23

Prepare

Ingredient Scan

Task: 2-D Order game with five slots in each tier
Inventory: 3 elements per line for 6 total in ten spaces
Rules: All range and block clues with overlapping elements
Questions: 6 total: 1 Grab-a-Rule, 2 Specific, 3 General
Red Flags: Not a 1:1 game
Rank: Rank (1-4): 3

Diagram and Inventory

The setup describes an order game in which you have to keep track of when three dogs visit the groomer and the veterinarian. The five months form the core of the diagram, and one tier is for Vet and one tier is for Groomer. The inventory for symbolizing the clues is best kept track of with subscripts: A_V, B_V, C_V, A_G, B_G, and C_G.

Symbolize the Rules and Double-Check

Rule 1: B_V—B_G

Rule 2: A_G—A_V

Rule 3: B_V—C_V—B_G

Rule 4: 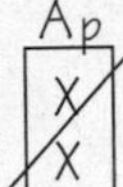

Rule 5: A_p X/X (crossed out)

Deductions

Spatial restrictions: With three elements in five slots per line, there will always be two empty slots per line.

Links: Rules 1 through 4 can be connected into one long chain.

B_V — [C_V / A_V] — B_G
A_G — [C_V / A_V]

As with any range clue, keep track of where elements cannot go so you can narrow down the possibilities of what can go where. Keeping track becomes a counting game. From the linked deduction, there must be at least two months after B_V and after A_G. Also, the C_VA_V block cannot be last and must have at least one month before it. Furthermore, B_G must have at least two months before it, so it must be in March, April or May.

Most restricted: All the elements in the connected rules are very restricted.

Least restricted: C_G has no restrictions on it.

Here is the diagram:

ABC	J	F	Mr	Ap	My
V	~C ~A	~C ~A		~B	~~B ~C ~A~~ (crossed out)
G	~B	~B	~B	~A	~A

Assess, Act, Answer

Question 18 is a Grab-a-Rule question, so start there and use the rules to eliminate answer choices. Rule 1 eliminates choice (E), rule 2 eliminates choice (A), rule 3 eliminates choice (C), and rule 4 eliminates choice (B). **The only choice left, and therefore the credited response, is choice (D).**

Question 19 is a Specific question, so answer that one next.

For question 19, place B in the vet tier under March. From this, C and A visit the vet in April, and B visits the groomer in May.

Here is the diagram:

	J	F	Mr	Ap	My
V			B	CA	X
G			~A	~A	B

Since the question asks for something that *must be true*, look to the diagram for the answer. According to the diagram, the only thing that must be true in this list is that B_G is in May. **Therefore, choice (B) is the credited response.**

Move on to question 21, the final Specific question.

For question 21, place C in the groomer line under April. From this, C_V and A_V are in March (information in question and deductions). You also know that B_G must be in either April or March from your original deductions.

Here is the diagram:

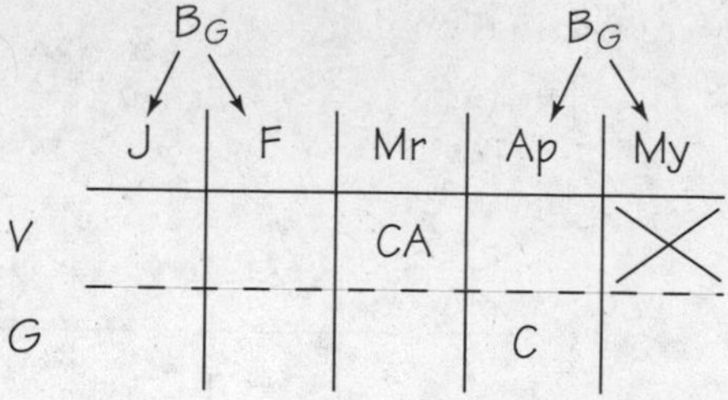

BG
BG
J
F
Mr
Ap
My
V
CA
G
C

Because the question asks for something that *could be true,* find an answer that is in keeping with the diagram. Since B sees the groomer in either April or May, and C sees the groomer in April, then B and C could see the groomer in the same month. **This means that choice (A) is the credited response.**

Now that the Specific questions are complete, attack the General questions, starting with question 20.

Question 20 asks for what *must be true.* Our initial deductions eliminate all the answer choices except for choice (B). **Choice (B) is the credited response.**

Move on to question 22, the next General question.

Question 22 asks for something that *could be false EXCEPT,* which really means you are looking for something that *must be true.* Again, our initial deductions eliminate lead to choice (D). **Choice (D) is the credited response.**

The final General question is question 23.

Question 23 asks for what could be true. Again, you can look to your initial deductions. From these you can eliminate all the answers except that it is possible for exactly two dogs to visit the groomer in March. **Therefore, choice (C) is the credited response.**

TIMED SECTION 3

Time—35 minutes

24 Questions

Directions: Each group of questions in this section is based on a set of conditions. In answering some of the questions, it may be useful to draw a rough diagram. Choose the response that most accurately and completely answers each question and blacken the corresponding space on your answer sheet.

Questions 1–6

A law school applicant is judging the schools to which she was accepted by the percentage of graduates from that school who fail the bar exam. There are six schools she is considering—B, C, G, H, N, and P—none of which have the same fail rate. She will enroll in exactly one school. The following restrictions apply:

The student enrolls in either G or H.
The school she enrolls in has either the second or third lowest fail rate.
H has a lower fail rate than C and a lower fail rate than G.
If C has the fourth lowest fail rate, then C has a lower fail rate than both N and P.
If C does not have the fourth lowest fail rate, then C has a higher fail rate than N and P.
N has the fifth lowest fail rate.

1. Which of the following could be an accurate ranking of law schools from lowest to highest fail rate?

(A) P, G, B, N, C, H
(B) H, N, P, G, B, C
(C) P, H, G, B, N, C
(D) H, C, G, B, N, P
(E) H, G, N, C, B, P

2. Which one of the following schools CANNOT have the second lowest fail rate?

(A) G
(B) H
(C) C
(D) P
(E) B

3. If the student enrolls in H, then which one of the following CANNOT be true?

(A) P has the lowest fail rate.
(B) C has the highest fail rate.
(C) G has the fourth lowest fail rate.
(D) H has the third lowest fail rate.
(E) B has the highest fail rate.

4. Which of the following must be true?

(A) C has a higher fail rate than G.
(B) C has a higher fail rate than N.
(C) G has a higher fail rate than N.
(D) P has a higher fail rate than B.
(E) P has a higher fail rate than G.

5. Which one of the following schools CANNOT have the fourth lowest fail rate?

(A) G
(B) C
(C) H
(D) P
(E) B

6. If H has the lowest fail rate, then all of the following could be true EXCEPT:

(A) C has the highest fail rate.
(B) B has the second lowest fail rate.
(C) G has the third lowest fail rate.
(D) G has the fourth lowest fail rate.
(E) G has the second lowest fail rate.

GO ON TO THE NEXT PAGE.

Questions 7–12

A pond contains eight singing frogs—Ellen, Floyd, Galal, Hertha, Questa, Roman, Sean, and Tasneem. Each frog sings exactly once, and no two frogs sing at the same time. The order in which they sing conforms to the following:

Tasneem sings at some time before Roman.
Both Floyd and Questa sing at some time before Galal.
Both Sean and Ellen sing at some time before Hertha.
Hertha sings at some time before Roman but after Questa.

7. If Galal sings third, then which one of the following CANNOT be false?

(A) Hertha sings seventh.
(B) Roman sings eighth.
(C) Floyd sings second.
(D) Questa sings first.
(E) Tasneem sings fourth.

8. Each of the following could be the fifth song to sing EXCEPT:

(A) Sean
(B) Ellen
(C) Galal
(D) Tasneem
(E) Roman

9. If Questa sings fifth, then which one of the following could be true?

(A) Hertha sings at some time before Tasneem.
(B) Galal sings at some time before Tasneem.
(C) Galal sings at some time before Ellen.
(D) Roman sings at some time before Galal.
(E) Roman sings at some time before Floyd.

10. If Floyd sings sixth, then which one of the following must be true?

(A) Hertha sings at some time before Galal.
(B) Galal sings at some time before Roman.
(C) Ellen sings at some time before Tasneem.
(D) Tasneem sings at some time before Hertha.
(E) Floyd sings at some time before Hertha.

11. Which of the following could be true?

(A) Ellen sings seventh.
(B) Tasneem sings eighth.
(C) Roman sings sixth.
(D) Galal sings first.
(E) Hertha sings second.

12. If Roman sings seventh, then which of the following CANNOT be the fifth song to sing?:

(A) Sean
(B) Hertha
(C) Floyd
(D) Questa
(E) Galal

GO ON TO THE NEXT PAGE.

Questions 13–18

Over the summer, five vacationers—Sandy, Thames, Uma, Valerie, and Wan—each vacation in one or more of exactly three vacation spots: Acapulco, Boca, and Cabo. They do not go anywhere else for vacation. The following conditions must apply:

Valerie goes to more vacation spots than Thames and Uma do.

Sandy does not vacation in any vacation spots where Uma and Valerie do.

There are exactly two vacationers who travel to the same vacation spot or spots as each other.

Thames and Wan both go to Boca.

13. If Sandy does not vacation in Boca, then which of the following must be true?

(A) Valerie vacations in Acapulco.
(B) Wan vacations in Cabo.
(C) Valerie vacations in Boca.
(D) Sandy vacations in Acapulco.
(E) Uma vacations in Cabo.

14. Which one of the following could be true?

(A) Valerie travels to three vacation spots.
(B) Valerie travels to only one vacation spot.
(C) Wan travels to two vacation spots.
(D) Sandy travels to two vacation spots.
(E) Thames travels to three vacation spots.

15. If exactly three of the students vacation in Cabo, then which one of the following could be true?

(A) Uma vacations in Boca.
(B) Wan vacations in Acapulco.
(C) Wan does not vacation in Cabo.
(D) Sandy vacations in Cabo.
(E) Valerie does not vacation in Cabo.

16. Which one of the following could be a complete and accurate list of the vacationers who vacation only in Acapulco?

(A) Wan
(B) Uma
(C) Sandy, Uma
(D) Thames, Wan
(E) Uma, Valerie

17. Which one of the following could be a complete and accurate list of the students who vacation in Boca?

(A) Thames, Wan
(B) Sandy, Thames
(C) Uma, Valerie, Wan
(D) Thames, Uma, Wan
(E) Thames, Valerie, Wan

18. Which one of the following must be true?

(A) Uma vacations in fewer of the vacation spots than Sandy does.
(B) Sandy vacations in fewer of the vacation spots than Valerie does.
(C) Wan vacations in fewer of the vacation spots than Valerie does.
(D) Sandy vacations in fewer of the vacation spots than Wan does.
(E) Thames vacations in fewer of the vacation spots than Wan does.

GO ON TO THE NEXT PAGE.

Questions 19–24

At a circus, six daredevils—Aloysius, Bartholomew, Cornelius, Dave, Faxon, and Harlan—will be fired out of three cannons—X, Y, and Z. They will be fired one at a time, and each daredevil will be fired only once. The order in which they are fired conforms to the following conditions:

Cannon Z can fire out only Aloysius, Bartholomew, and Dave.

Cannon Y cannot fire out Aloysius, Faxon, and Harlan.

Cannon X cannot fire out Aloysius, Bartholomew, and Cornelius.

The cannon that fires first cannot be the same as the cannon that fires last.

Bartholomew must be fired out sometime before Harlan but later than Aloysius.

Faxon must be fired out sometime before Aloysius and before Cornelius.

19. Which one of the following is an acceptable order for the cannon firings, from first to last?

(A) Faxon, Aloysius, Bartholomew, Dave, Cornelius, Harlan
(B) Dave, Faxon, Harlan, Cornelius, Aloysius, Bartholomew
(C) Faxon, Dave, Aloysius, Bartholomew, Harlan, Cornelius
(D) Dave, Cornelius, Faxon, Aloysius, Bartholomew, Harlan
(E) Faxon, Bartholomew, Aloysius, Harlan, Cornelius, Dave

20. Which one of the following is a complete and accurate list of the daredevils, any one of which could be the daredevil fired out of the last cannon?

(A) Aloysius, Cornelius, Dave
(B) Aloysius, Bartholomew, Harlan
(C) Dave, Bartholomew, Harlan
(D) Cornelius, Bartholomew, Harlan
(E) Cornelius, Dave, Harlan

21. If the first cannon fires out Dave, which one of the following CANNOT be false?

(A) Faxon is fired out of the second cannon.
(B) Faxon is fired out of the third cannon.
(C) Bartholomew is fired out of the fourth cannon.
(D) Dave is fired out of cannon X.
(E) Dave is fired out of cannon Y.

22. Each of the following could be false EXCEPT:

(A) Dave is fired out of cannon X.
(B) Bartholomew is fired out of cannon Z.
(C) Dave is fired out of cannon Z.
(D) Cornelius is fired out of cannon Y.
(E) Aloysius is fired out of cannon Y.

23. Which of the following CANNOT be the order in which daredevils are fired out of the cannons, from first to last?

(A) Dave, Faxon, Aloysius, Bartholomew, Harlan, Cornelius
(B) Dave, Faxon, Aloysius, Cornelius, Bartholomew, Harlan
(C) Faxon, Cornelius, Aloysius, Bartholomew, Dave, Harlan
(D) Faxon, Dave, Aloysius, Bartholomew, Harlan, Cornelius
(E) Faxon, Aloysius, Bartholomew, Cornelius, Harlan, Dave

24. If Faxon is the first daredevil fired, which of the following could be the next three daredevils fired, consecutively?

(A) Dave, Bartholomew and Harlan
(B) Dave, Aloysius and Bartholomew
(C) Dave, Cornelius and Aloysius
(D) Cornelius, Harlan and Aloysius
(E) Cornelius, Dave and Aloysius

STOP

IF YOU FINISH BEFORE TIME IS CALLED, YOU MAY CHECK YOUR WORK ON THIS SECTION ONLY. DO NOT WORK ON ANY OTHER SECTION IN THE TEST.

ANSWER KEY

1. C
2. C
3. E
4. A
5. C
6. D
7. B
8. E
9. D
10. A
11. C
12. E
13. C
14. C
15. B
16. B
17. E
18. B
19. C
20. E
21. A
22. D
23. C
24. B

EXPLANATIONS FOR TIMED SECTION 3, QUESTIONS 1–6

Prepare

Ingredient Scan

Task: 1–D Order; place six law schools in order and identify one of them as the enrolled school
Inventory: 6 law schools, 6 slots, 1:1 ratio
Rules: Not very straightforward, conditional rules, rules about a special element.
Questions: 6 total: 1 Grab-a-Rule, 2 Specific, 3 General
Red Flags: Unfamiliar aspect of identifying one element each time as distinct from the others, lots of General questions
Rank: 4

Diagram and Inventory

There are six elements, B, C, G, H, N, and P. Draw six columns and use numbers 1–6 as the core of your diagram. The Grab-a-Rule answer choices to question 1 suggest that the diagram should go from lowest (on the left) to highest (on the right). Place those labels on your diagram above the 1 and the 6. The other wrinkle of this game is that you need to identify which element is the school enrolled in each time, so invent some convention for identifying it (circling it, underlining it, or using an asterisk are all possible ways to signify that one item is special).

Symbolize the Rules and Double-Check

Rule 1: Use a circle to symbolize the enrolled status. List G and H as the two choices.
◯ = enroll
Ⓖ or Ⓗ 2/3

Rule 2: Draw this on your diagram and add the slot limitations to your info about the enrolled element.

Rule 3: $H < \begin{matrix} C \\ G \end{matrix}$

Rule 4: $C_4 \rightarrow C < \begin{matrix} N \\ P \end{matrix}$

Rule 5: $\sim C_4 \rightarrow \begin{matrix} N \\ P \end{matrix} > C$

Rule 6: Write into slot 5 on your diagram.

Don't forget to double-check your rules!

Deductions

Links: There are elements that appear in multiple rules, but it's hard to symbolize any links because the links are only hypothetical. Still, take note of how the rules might connect down the line.
Spatial restrictions: Because rule 4 begins "if C is 4" and rule 5 begins "if C is not 4," invest some time and thought to see what the consequences are of having C in or out of slot 4. Draw two rows and start with the scenario in which C is fourth. Rule 4 says that N and P will have to come after C. N and P would be interchangeable in spots 5 and 6 except that there's rule 6 tells you that N is the only option. So N is fifth and P is sixth. H, G, and B remain for slots 1–3. The enrolled school must be second or third (rule 2) and H must come before G (rule 3). There are several ways that H, G, and B could fit in the first three slots, but the possibilities for the first and third slots are limited by H—G. G can't go first, so put H/B in slot 1. H can't go third, so put G/B in slot 3. Any of the three could go second, so either leave it blank or fill in H/G/B.
Move on to the next scenario, the one in which C does not go fourth. Rule 5 says that N and P must come before C. That means C has to be in slot 6, because N is always in slot 5 (rule 6). There are no other limitations on this diagram that allow you to know anything for certain.
Most restricted: C is the most restricted element; the placement of C will be the driving force of the game.
Least restricted: B is not addressed by any of the rules.

Here is your diagram:

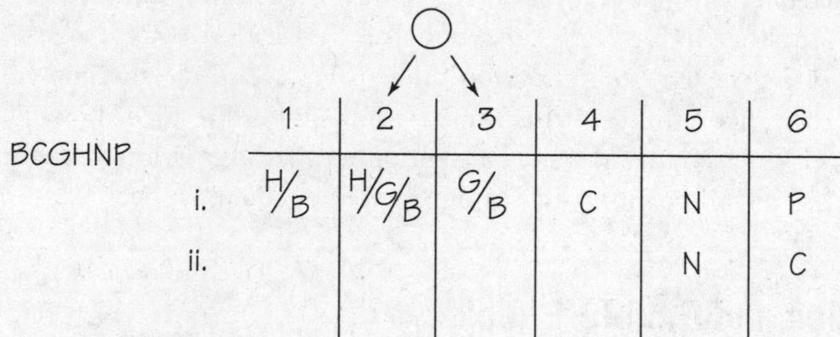

Assess, Act, Answer

Question 1 is a Grab-a-Rule question, so do it first.

For question 1, use the rules to help you eliminate answer choices. Rule 1 by itself is impossible to look for because these answer choices don't identify which school is enrolled in. However, combining rules 1 and 2, you can look to make sure either H or G is always second or third. This eliminates choice (B). Rule 3 eliminates choice (A). Rule 4 eliminates choice (E). Rule 5 eliminates choice (D). **Since choice (C) is all that remains, it is the credited response.**

Question 3 is your first Specific question, so do that one next.

Question 3 says that H will be the enrolled student. That means that H will have to go either in slot 2 or slot 3. Draw a row for each scenario to examine the implications. If H is in slot 2, C could still be in either slot 4 or slot 6. If H is in slot 3, only the second master scenario would be applicable, because H still has to be lower than C and G. Place C in slot 6 and G in slot 4. B and P will split slots 1 and 2. The question asks for something that *must be false,* which eliminates choices (A), (B), (C), and (D). **Choice (E) is the only choice left, and therefore the credited response.**

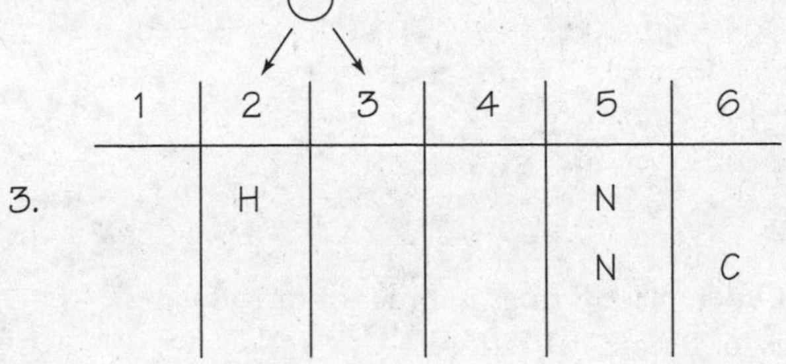

	1	2	3	4	5	6
3.		H			N	
					N	C

Question 6 is the next Specific question, so do that one next.

Question 6 is a *could be true EXCEPT* question, which means you're looking for something that *must be false.* The question says to place H in slot 1. Because that is compatible with either C being in slot 4 or C not being in slot 4, think about the implications of both scenarios. Nothing else is really determined except for the fact that G must be the enrolled element and be in slot 2 or 3. The question asks for something impossible, so eliminate any answer choice that is possible. Choice (A) is possible in the second master scenario. Eliminate it. Choices (B) and (C) are both possible in either master scenario. Eliminate them. Choice (D) is impossible. With H in slot 1, G must be the enrolled element, so it cannot have the fourth lowest fail rate. **Because choice (D) is impossible, it is the credited response.**

Go back to your first General question, question 2.

Question 2 asks which element can never go in slot 2. From your two scenarios, are there any elements excluded from slot 2? Yes, C and N are not in slot 2 in both scenarios. Scan the answers for C or N. **Choice (C) is the credited response.**

Question 4 is the next General question.

Question 4 asks for something that *must be true,* so your job is to find a possible scenario that contradicts each answer choice. If you can't avoid what the answer choice describes, then it is the credited response. Choice (A) says that C will always be after G. Can that be avoided? Looking at the two master scenarios, C is either fourth (with N and P fifth and sixth, respectively) or C is sixth. Either way, there's no way to get G to be after C. **Since choice (A) is unavoidable, it's the credited response.**

Question 5 is the final General question.

Question 5 asks which element can never go in slot 4. Look again at your two master scenarios. In the first one, C is in slot 4. Eliminate choice (B). In the second one, slot 4 is open, but slots 5 and 6 are already filled by N and C, respectively. Given the remaining rules, which element could not go last among the first four slots? Since H must come before C and before G, H could not be fourth. Look for that as an answer. **Choice (C) is the credited response.**

EXPLANATIONS FOR TIMED SECTION 3 QUESTIONS 7–12

Prepare

Ingredient Scan

Task: 1–D Order, place 8 frogs in order from 1–8
Inventory: 8 frogs for 8 slots, 1:1 ratio
Rules: All the rules are range rules, which suggests you might be able to link them all together
Questions: 6 total: 4 Specific, 2 General
Red Flags: None of the range rules specify exactly how many spaces there are between elements
Rank: 1

Diagram and Inventory

The setup describes an Order game in which 8 singing frogs—e, f, g, h, q, r, s, and t—must be assigned to sing one at a time. No frog sings at the same time as another frog.

Symbolize the Rules and Double-Check

Rule 1: t—r
Rule 2: f—g; q—g
Rule 3: s—h; e—h
Rule 4: q—h—r

Don't forget to double-check your rules!

Deductions

Links: You can combine the rules into a larger branched picture to get a clearer idea of which elements must come before others.
Spatial restrictions: From rule 1, t cannot be last and r cannot be first. From rule 2, neither f nor q may be last, and g cannot be first or second, because it's preceded by two elements. Rule 3 tells you that neither s nor e may be last, while h cannot be first or second. Rule 4 tells you that in addition to what you know about q, h, and r from the first three rules, q cannot be seventh, h cannot be last, and r cannot be second. Put all these restrictions into your diagram.

e t
s h r
q
g

Most restricted: Slot 8 is limited to either g or r, since these are the only two elements not followed by any others.
Least restricted: All elements are involved in at least one rule, but t and f each have only one restriction apiece (rule 1 and rule 2, respectively).

Here is your diagram:

efghqrst

	1	2	3	4	5	6	7	8
	~h ~g ~r	~r ~h ~g					~q	~q ~s ~f ~e ~t ~h
								r/g

Assess, Act, Answer

Since there isn't a Grab-a-Rule question, begin with the Specific questions. The first Specific question is question 7.

For question 7, place g in slot 3. If g is third, you know that r must be last from your earlier deductions. You also know from rule 2 that both f and q must sing before g, so they must occupy slots 1 and 2, though you don't know which one is in which space.

Here is your diagram:

	1	2	3	4	5	6	7	8
	~h ~g ~r	~r ~h ~g					~q	~q ~s ~f ~e ~t ~h
7.	f/q	q/f	g					r

The question asks for something that *must be true,* so while you don't have every slot in your diagram filled in, you should have enough information to answer the question. The only choice that you know to be true based on your work is choice (B); all the rest could be true, but don't have to be true. **Choice (B) is the credited response.**

The next Specific question is question 9.

For question 9, place q in slot 5. From rule 2 you know that g must follow q and from rule 4 you know that both h and r must follow q. So for slots 6 through 8, you will have to place g, h, and r. You already know that slot 8 is restricted to g and r. Since h must come before r (rule 4), r cannot go in slot 6, which leaves only h and g for that space. Slot 7 can be g, h, or r.

Here is your diagram:

	~h ~g ~r	~r ~h ~g					~q	~q ~s ~f ~e ~t ~h
	1	2	3	4	5	6	7	8
9.					q	h/g	g/h/r	g/r

The question asks for what could be true. The only choice not contradicted by the diagram is choice (D). **Choice (D) is the credited response.**

The next Specific question is question 10.

For question 10, place f in slot 6. From rule 2 you know that f must come before g, so g must be in either slot 7 or 8. If g is in slot 7, then r would have to be in slot 8, as per your previous deductions. But if g is in slot 8, the only frog available for slot 7 would be r based on the branched picture you have. So slots 7 and 8 must either be g or r, in whatever order.

Here is your diagram:

	~h ~g ~r	~r ~h ~g					~q	~q ~s ~f ~e ~t ~h
	1	2	3	4	5	6	7	8
10.						f	g/r	r/g

The question asks for something that *must be true*. Since there are no open slots after f and since g must sing after f, h must sing some time before g. Therefore choice (A) must be true. **Choice (A) is the credited response.**

The final Specific question is question 12.

For question 12, place r in slot 7. From your earlier deductions, this means g must occupy slot 8. There's not much more that's certain other than that.

Here is your diagram:

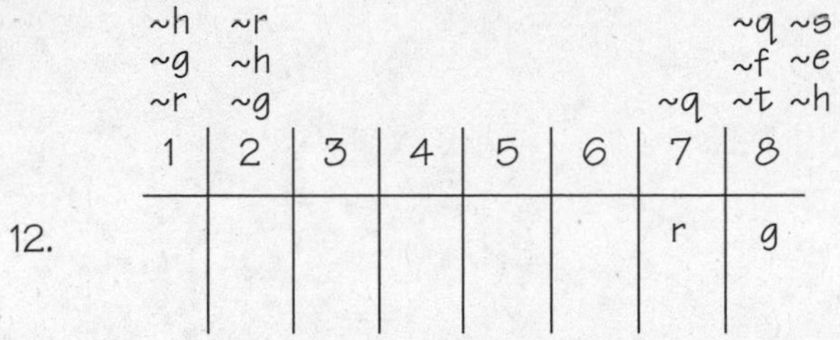

	1	2	3	4	5	6	7	8
	~h ~g ~r	~r ~h ~g					~q	~q ~s ~f ~e ~t ~h
12.							r	g

The question asks which frog cannot sing fifth. Since you know for certain that g must be in slot 8, g can definitely not sing fifth. **Choice (E) is the credited response.**

Move on to the General questions. The first General question is question 8.

Question 8 asks who cannot be in slot 5—be careful, as the work you just did in question 12 is applicable only for that particular scenario. It could still be possible for g to sing fifth under different circumstances. Use your branched picture to help determine the answer. If a frog must have at least five others sing before it, it cannot be in slot 5. Are there any frogs to which this applies? Looking at your picture, you see that r must be preceded by s, e, q, h, and t. This means that r cannot sing fifth. **Choice (E) is the credited response.**

The final General question is question 11.

Question 11 asks for what could be true. Use your deductions and past work to eliminate answer choices. From the deductions on your diagram, you can eliminate choice (B), choice (D), and choice (E). Combining rules 3 and 4 allows you to eliminate choice (A); e must be followed by h, which in turn must be followed by r. Therefore e cannot be seventh, leaving choice (C) as the only remaining possibility. **Choice (C) is the credited response.**

EXPLANATIONS FOR TIMED SECTION 3 QUESTIONS 13–18

Prepare

Ingredient Scan

Task: Group game with variable assignments; select at least 1 but up to 3 vacation spots for each of 5 vacationers.
Inventory: 3 vacations
Rules: A numerical rule that suggests distribution deductions and one rule that doesn't readily lend itself to symbolization
Questions: 6 total: 2 Specific, 4 General
Red Flags: The number of spaces in each group isn't fixed
Rank: 3

Diagram and Inventory

The setup describes a Group game in which three vacation spots—a, b, and c—are visited by five different vacationers—S, T, U, V, and W. Each vacationer goes to at least one spot, but the number of spots visited by each person is not specified.

Symbolize the Rules and Double-Check

Rule 1: T, U<V
Rule 2: U, V≠S (element, not number)
Rule 3: Exactly two groups must have exactly the same elements as each other.
Rule 4: b=T,W

Rule 3 is one of those tricky rules that doesn't allow for easy symbolization. You can either put a star next to it on the page to draw your attention back to it or rewrite it near your other rules so that you don't forget it.

Don't forget to double-check your rules!

Deductions

Links: Because the distribution of spaces isn't fixed in the setup, you need to take the time to work with the rules to figure it out. Rule 1 tells you that group V must have either two or three slots; rule 2 tells you that group V can only have two spaces since it can't share an element with group S and every group must have at least one element (as per the setup). This also means that group S must have only one space. If group V has two spaces, then both group T and group U each have only one space. Put these spaces into your diagram.
Spatial restrictions: From the deduction process above, you know that group T has only one space and that it is taken up by b (rule 4). Therefore, neither a nor c can go in group T.
Most restricted: The interplay between groups U, V, and S (rule 2) will limit which elements go in which groups on a given question.
Least restricted: Though group W contains b, it can have anywhere from one to all three elements, making it the least restricted aspect of the game.

Here is your diagram:

	S	T (~a, ~c)	U	V	W
abc	__	b	__	__ __	b

Assess, Act, Answer

Since there is no Grab-a-Rule question, begin with the Specific questions. The first Specific question is question 13.

Question 13 tells you that b is not in group S; this means either a or c is in that group instead. From your earlier deductions, you know that group V has two spaces; since group S does not contain b, group V must have both b and one of either a or c, depending on which goes in group S (rule 2). Rule 2 also tells you that the space in group U will be taken by either a or c, depending on which goes in group S.

Here is your diagram:

	S	T (~a, ~c)	U	V	W
13.	a/c	b	c/a	b c/a	b

The question asks for something that *must be true*. Based on your diagram, only choice (C) must be true. **Choice (C) is the credited response.**

Move on to the next Specific question, which is question 15.

For question 15, you must place three c's into your diagram. From your earlier deductions about group T and because of rule 2, you can only do this by placing c in spaces U, V, and W. This means the other space in group V will be either b or a, and that the space in group S will be taken by either a or b, depending on which one goes in group V.

Here is your diagram:

	S	T (~a, ~c)	U	V	W
15.	a/b	b	c	c b/a	bc

The question asks for something that *could be true*. The only choice not contradicted by your diagram is choice (B). **Choice (B) is the credited response.**

Move on to the General questions. The first General question is question 14.

Question 14 asks for something that could be true. Use the rules and your deductions to eliminate choices that definitely cannot be true. You already know from your deductions that group V has exactly 2 spaces, so eliminate choice (A) and choice (B). You also know that both group S and group T each have exactly one space, so eliminate choice (D) and choice (E). **The only choice left, and therefore the credited response, is choice (C).**

The next General question is question 16.

Question 16 asks you to identify which groups could contain only a. Use the rules as well as your deductions to eliminate choices. Rule 1 and your deductions allow you to eliminate choice (E). Rule 2 eliminates choice (C). Rule 4 eliminates choice (A) and choice (D). **The only choice remaining, and therefore the credited response, is choice (B).**

The next General question is question 17.

Question 17 asks you to identify which groups could all contain b at the same time. Use the rules and your deductions to eliminate choices. From rule 4, you know that both group T and group W always contain b, so eliminate choice (B) and choice (C). Now try the remaining choices, beginning with choice (B). From your deductions, you know that group V must have two elements in it. If b is limited to only groups T and W, then group V must contain a and c; however, this creates a conflict with rule 2, as group S would also need to contain one of a and c. Eliminate choice (A) and move on to choice (D). Choice (D) presents a similar problem; if only groups T, U, and W contain b, group V would have to have a and c, creating a conflict with rule 2 and group S. Eliminate choice (D). This leaves choice (E) as the only remaining possibility. Choice (E) fixes the problem above by putting b in group V, alleviating the conflict caused by rule 2.

Here is your diagram:

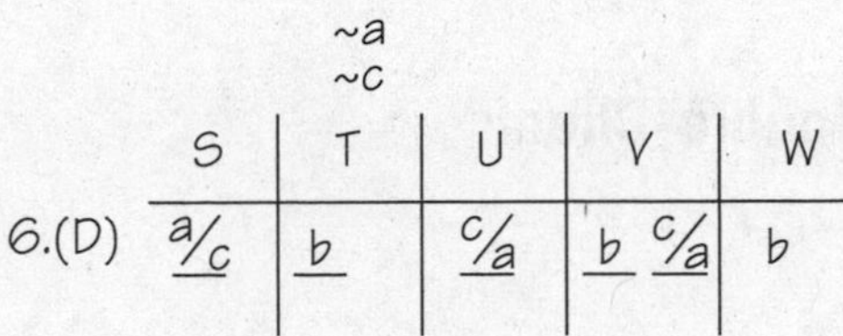

Choice (E) is the credited response.

The final General question is question 18.

Question 18 asks for something that must be true. Use your deductions to help you eliminate choices. Choice (A) is out because group S and group U each have exactly one space. Choice (B) is true—from your deductions, you know that group V has two spaces while group S has only one. Since this choice must be true, there is no need to check the other choices. **Choice (B) is the credited response.**

EXPLANATIONS FOR TIMED SECTION 3 QUESTIONS 19–24

Prepare

Ingredient Scan

Task: 2-D Order; combining order and groups, arrange the order of 6 daredevils and their corresponding cannons.
Inventory: 6 daredevils, 6 slots, 1:1 ratio
Rules: Rules are straightforward and easy to symbolize.
Questions: 6 total: 1 Grab-a-Rule, 2 Specific, and 3 General
Red Flags: None
Rank: 2

Diagram and Inventory

There are six elements to put in order so you need columns numbered 1–6. as the core of the diagram. There is a group aspect of the game to keep track of so you need two tiers, one for elements A, B, C, D, F, and H, and one for cannons X, Y, and Z. Each element must be used once and only once. The setup doesn't say whether or how many times each cannon must be used.

Symbolize the Rules and Double-Check

Rule 1: Z=A, B, D only

Rule 2: Y=B, C, D only

Rule 3: X=D, F, H only

Rule 4: Cannon 1≠Cannon 6. Add to the diagram.

Rule 5: A—B—H

Rule 6:
```
   A
F<
   C
```

Don't forget to double-check your rules!

The first rule narrows down cannon Z's possibilities to three elements. The second and third rule rule out three possibilities each for cannons X and Y, which is more helpful to see as a positive list: Instead of cannon Y≠A, F, H, write it as shown above. The same goes for rule 3 and cannon X.

Deductions

Links: A overlaps in both rules 5 and 6, so link them together.

```
        B—H
   A—
F<
   C
```

Spatial restrictions: You have chained together five of the six elements. C, however, is almost a free agent. It could go anywhere other than first. Whenever you have a chain that involves most or all the elements, concern yourself with what could go first and what could go last. In this case, the only elements that can go first are F and D. Write an F/D placeholder in slot 1. Only H, C, or D can go last, so write an H/C/D placeholder in slot 6. Pay attention to the limitations of each cannon group. F, A, and H all have only one option. B has two, and D has all three options. You may want to write out each element's two-row game piece so that the group information is consolidated.

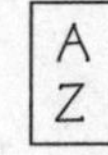

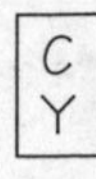

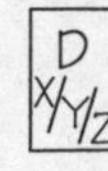

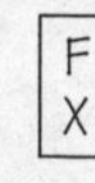

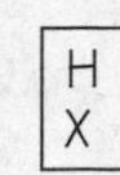

Most restricted: The chain of four is always going to appear in that order.
Least restricted: D could go in any of the six slots, and with any cannon.

Here is your diagram:

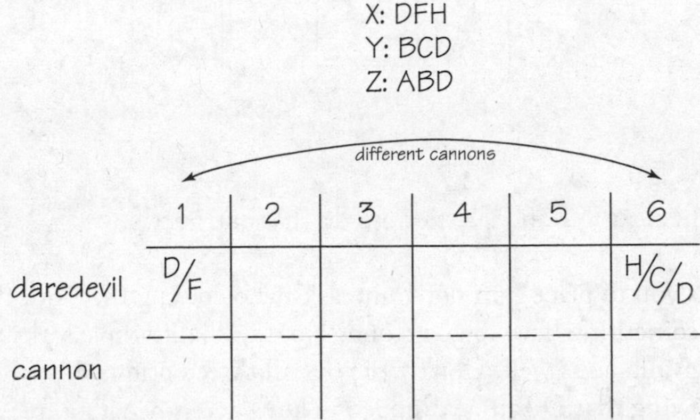

Assess, Act, Answer

Question 19 is a Grab-a-Rule question, so do that one first.

In question 19, use the rules to eliminate answer choices. The first three rules are not very conducive to checking the answer choices, since the answer choices don't directly show the cannons. Start from the bottom instead. Rule 6 eliminates choice (D). Rule 5 eliminates choices (B) and (E). Only choices (A) and (C) remain. In order to tell which one is wrong, you'll have to use your knowledge of which elements can go with which cannons along with rule 4, which says that the first and last elements can't have a matching cannon. Look at choice (A). Do F and H have to be a matching cannon? Yes, they can each only be cannon X. Choice (A) breaks rule 4. **Because choice (C) is all that remains, it is the credited response.**

Question 21 is the first Specific question, so do that one next.

Question 21 asks you to place D in slot 1 and asks what *must* follow. If D is in slot 1, which element will go second? The other five elements are chained together, and the first one in the chain is F, so F must go second. Does something have to go third? Not necessarily. It could be either A or C. **This is all that must be true, which makes choice (A) the credited response.**

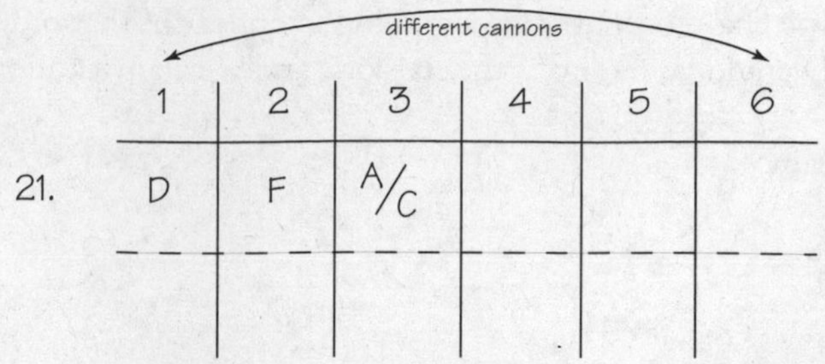

different cannons (1 ↔ 6)

	1	2	3	4	5	6
21.	D	F	A/C			

Question 24 is the next Specific question, so do that one next.

Question 24 tells you to place F in slot 1 and asks who could go second, third, and fourth. With F in slot 1, does something have to go second? No, the chain of five forks off into A or C, and the free agent, D, is available as well. Don't write out all three options. Use the chain of five to analyze the answers, knowing that D can be dropped in anywhere since it's a free agent. The question asks for something that *could be true*. If the answer choice seems possible, test it. If it's impossible, eliminate it. Choice (A) is impossible because it skips over A in the chain of five. Eliminate it. Choice (B) seems fine, so test it. The fifth and sixth slots would have to be filled by C and H, although their order is interchangeable. All the ordering rules are obeyed. Check to make sure rule 4 is also safe. Are the first and last members of the list eligible for distinct cannons? Yes, because F is first (an X), and C could be last (a Y). **Because choice (B) is possible, it is the credited response.**

different cannons (1 ↔ 6)

	1	2	3	4	5	6
24(B).	F	D	A	B	H	C
	x					y

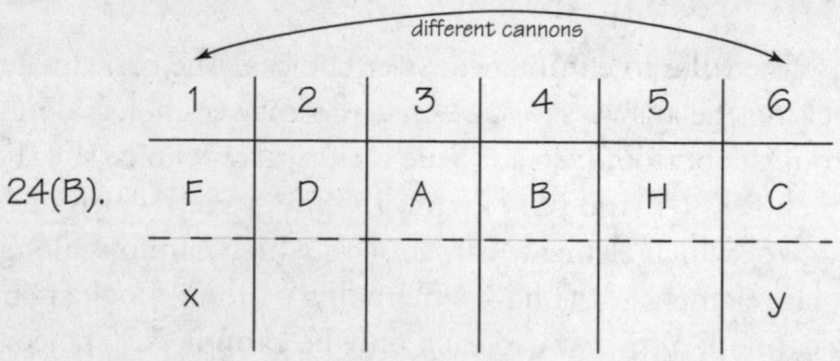

There are no more Specific questions, so go back to your first General question, question 20.

Question 20 asks for a complete list of elements that could go last. From your diagram, you have an H/C/D placeholder. Look for those three as an answer. **Choice (E) is the credited response.**

The next general question is question 22.

Question 22 asks for something that *must be true*. Eliminate answer choices that could be made to be false. Choice (A) is avoidable since D can be cannon X, Y, or Z. Choice (B) is avoidable since B can be cannon Y or Z. Choice (C) is avoidable for the same reason choice (A) was. Choice (D) is unavoidable. C only has Y as an option and must be used once. **Because choice (D) is unavoidable, it is the credited response.**

The final General question is question 23.

Question 23 asks for something that *could be true EXCEPT,* which means something that *must be false.* Because all six elements are shown in each answer choice, this question seems like a Grab-a-Rule, only you're looking for one broken scenario instead of the typical task of finding the one valid scenario. Start with the chain of five since it's the easiest to scan for visually. Makesure every answer choice honors the F—A—B—H order. They all do. Make sure they all honor the F—C order. They do. The rule being broken must be rule 4 again, the idea that the first and last elements can't have the same cannon. You already know that D could be any of the three cannons, so it will never break that rule. That makes choices (A), (B), and (E) seem unlikely since they have D first or last. Choice (C) has F first and H last. They both must come from cannon X, so this choice breaks rule 4. **Because choice (C) breaks the rule and must be false, it is the credited response.**

TIMED SECTION 4

Time—35 minutes

24 Questions

Directions: Each group of questions in this section is based on a set of conditions. In answering some of the questions, it may be useful to draw a rough diagram. Choose the response that most accurately and completely answers each question and blacken the corresponding space on your answer sheet.

Questions 1–6

A department store has six floors, and each floor contains only one of six departments—Accessories, Housewares, Kids, Men, Shoes and Women. There is no elevator, and you can only get from one floor to another by using the escalator. The store is laid out according to the following conditions:

The escalator only goes to the level directly above or directly below a floor.

The Accessories department is directly below the Housewares department.

There is no escalator connecting the Men's department to the Shoes department.

The Kids department is above the Housewares department but below the Shoes department.

1. Which of the following could be a complete and accurate list of the departments, from the first floor to the sixth floor?

   (A) Accessories, Housewares, Kids, Shoes, Women, Men
   (B) Housewares, Accessories, Men, Women, Kids, Shoes
   (C) Men, Accessories, Housewares, Women, Shoes, Kids
   (D) Accessories, Housewares, Kids, Shoes, Men, Women
   (E) Men, Kids, Accessories, Housewares, Shoes, Women

2. If the Housewares department is on the third floor, then which of the following is a complete and accurate list of the floors that the Men's department could be on?

   (A) one
   (B) four
   (C) one, four
   (D) one, two
   (E) two, four

3. If the Shoes department is not the top floor, then which one of the following is a complete and accurate list of the floors that could be the Women's department?

   (A) 5, 6
   (B) 2, 5, 6
   (C) 3, 4, 5, 6
   (D) 2, 3, 4, 5, 6
   (E) 1, 2, 3, 4, 5, 6

4. Which one of the following could be an accurate list of the first and second floor, respectively?

   (A) Accessories department, Men's department
   (B) Housewares department, Men's department
   (C) Men's department, Shoes department
   (D) Women's department, Men's department
   (E) Men's department, Housewares department

5. If the Shoes department is not immediately above the Kids department, then which one of the following could be true?

   (A) The Men's department is the top floor.
   (B) The Men's department is the second floor.
   (C) The Men's department is immediately below the Housewares department.
   (D) The Men's department is immediately above the Kids department.
   (E) The Men's department is immediately above the Women's department.

6. If the Accessories department is the third floor, then which of the following could be true?

   (A) The Women's department is the fifth floor.
   (B) The Women's department is immediately above the Men's department.
   (C) The Men's department is above the Houseware department.
   (D) The Kids department is not immediately above the Housewares department.
   (E) The Shoes department is not the top floor.

GO ON TO THE NEXT PAGE.

Questions 7–12

A landscaper has been hired to plant groupings of shrubbery at up to five locations around town—the fire station, hospital, library, police station, and recycling center—visited in that order. The landscaper uses exactly three types of shrubbery—azaleas, boxwood, and cedar—and plants exactly three groupings of each type. The following must obtain:

Each grouping is comprised of only one type of shrubbery.

No two groupings of the same type are planted at the same location.

There is at least one grouping planted at the recycling center.

The second grouping of boxwood is planted at the hospital.

The third grouping of azaleas is planted at the same location as the second grouping of cedar.

7. Which of the following is a complete and accurate list of the groupings planted at each site?

(A) azaleas: fire station, hospital, library
boxwood: fire station, hospital, police station
cedar: hospital, library, police station
(B) azaleas: fire station, hospital, library
boxwood: fire station, hospital, police station
cedar: hospital, police station, recycling center
(C) azaleas: fire station, library, police station
boxwood: fire station, hospital, library
cedar: hospital, library, recycling center
(D) azaleas: fire station, library, police station
boxwood: fire station, hospital, recycling center
cedar: hospital, police station, recycling center
(E) azaleas: fire station, hospital, library
boxwood: hospital, library, police station
cedar: hospital, library, recycling center

8. If the first grouping of one type of shrubbery is planted at the same location as the third grouping of another type, then which of the following must be true?

(A) Exactly one grouping is planted at the hospital.
(B) Exactly two groupings are planted at the library.
(C) Exactly two groupings are planted at the police station.
(D) Exactly one location gets all three groupings.
(E) Exactly one location gets only one grouping.

9. If the third grouping of azaleas is planted at the library, for how many locations can it be determined that at most two groupings could be planted?

(A) one
(B) two
(C) three
(D) four
(E) five

10. If exactly one grouping is planted at the fire station, then which of the following must be false?

(A) The third grouping of boxwood is planted at the recycling center.
(B) The second grouping of azaleas is planted at the library.
(C) The second grouping of cedar is planted at the police station.
(D) The first grouping of azaleas is planted at the fire station.
(E) The first grouping of cedar is planted at the library.

11. If no groupings are planted at the police station, then all of the following could be false EXCEPT:

(A) At least two groupings are planted at the recycling center.
(B) At least two groupings are planted at the hospital.
(C) At most one grouping is planted at the recycling center.
(D) Exactly three groupings are planted at the fire station.
(E) Exactly three groupings are planted at the library.

12. If the second grouping of cedar is planted at the police station, then which of the following could be true?

(A) The second grouping of azaleas is planted at the hospital.
(B) The second groupings of two different types of shrubbery are planted at the library.
(C) The second groupings of two different types of shrubbery are planted at the police station.
(D) The second groupings of all three types of shrubbery are planted at the police station.
(E) The third groupings of all three types of shrubbery are planted at the recycling center.

GO ON TO THE NEXT PAGE.

Questions 13–19

For a reality television show, a famous jazz mogul is putting together an improvisational jazz band from seven contestants, numbered 1 through 7. The jazz factor is defined as the number of contestants selected to be in the band. The decisions will be made according to the following conditions:

If either contestant 3 or 5 is in the band, then contestant 1 is not in the band.
If contestant 4 is in the band, then neither contestant 2 nor contestant 4 is in the band..
The contestant whose number corresponds to the jazz factor of the band is in the band.

13. Which of the following is an acceptable list of the contestants that could be in the band?

(A) contestant 1, contestant 3, contestant 4
(B) contestant 2, contestant 5, contestant 6
(C) contestant 1, contestant 5
(D) contestant 3, contestant 6, contestant 7
(E) contestant 2, contestant 3, contestant 4, contestant 7

14. If exactly two of the contestants are in the band, then which one of the following contestants must be not in the band?

(A) contestant 3
(B) contestant 4
(C) contestant 5
(D) contestant 6
(E) contestant 7

15. What is the jazz factor's maximum number?

(A) three
(B) four
(C) five
(D) six
(E) seven

16. If contestant 1 and contestant 3 are not in the band, then which one of the following could be two contestants who are in the band?

(A) contestants 2 and 7
(B) contestants 4 and 7
(C) contestants 6 and 7
(D) contestants 4 and 6
(E) contestants 5 and 6

17. If contestants 5 and 6 are both in the band, then which one of the following contestants must be in the band?

(A) contestant 1
(B) contestant 2
(C) contestant 3
(D) contestant 4
(E) contestant 7

18. If both contestant 6 and contestant 7 are not in the band, then what is the maximum jazz factor of the band?

(A) one
(B) two
(C) three
(D) four
(E) five

GO ON TO THE NEXT PAGE.

Questions 19–24

A row of vendors sets up along a path at a State Fair in booths 1 through 6, from the beginning of the path to the end of the path. Along the path, six vendors—Adelfried, Beriszl, Calvine, Dobrila, Edeva, and Farika—each set up in exactly one of the booths. The following restrictions apply:

Beriszl sets up closer to the beginning of the path than Dobrila.

Calvine sets up closer to the end of the path than both Edeva and Farika.

Both Adelfried and Edeva set up closer to the end of the path than Dobrila.

19. Which one of the following CANNOT be true?

(A) Calvine sets up closer to the beginning than Dobrila
(B) Adelfried sets up closer to the beginning than Edeva.
(C) Edeva sets up closer to the beginning than Adelfried.
(D) Dobrila sets up closer to the beginning than Farika.
(E) Farika sets up closer to the beginning than Beriszl.

20. If Adelfried sets up in booth 3, then each of the following could be true EXCEPT:

(A) Calvine sets up immediately behind Edeva.
(B) Calvine sets up immediately behind Farika.
(C) Edeva sets up immediately behind Adelfried.
(D) Dobrila sets up immediately behind Farika.
(E) Farika sets up immediately behind Edeva.

21. Farika could occupy exactly how many booths at the fair?

(A) two
(B) three
(C) four
(D) five
(E) six

22. If Edeva sets up in booth 5, then which one of the following must be true?

(A) Dobrila sets up in booth 2.
(B) Adelfried sets up in booth 4.
(C) Calvine sets up in booth 6.
(D) Beriszl sets up in booth 1.
(E) Farika sets up in booth 3.

23. Which of the following could be an accurate pairing of booths to vendors?

(A) booth 1: Beriszl; booth 5: Edeva; booth 6: Adelfried
(B) booth 3: Dobrilla; booth 4: Edeva; booth 5: Farika
(C) booth 1: Beriszl; booth 3: Edeva; booth 6: Adelfried
(D) booth 3: Adelfried; booth 4: Edeva; booth 5: Calvine
(E) booth 6: Farika; booth 3: Edeva ; booth 6: Calvine

24. Suppose a restriction that Dobrila sets up closer to the beginning of the path than Beriszl replaces the restriction that Beriszl sets up closer to the beginning of the path than Dobrila. If no other restrictions are changed, then which of the following CANNOT be an accurate matching of vendors to booths:

(A) Dobrila: booth 1; Edeva: booth 3; Calvine: booth 5
(B) Dobrila: booth 3; Adelfried: seat 4; Edeva: booth 5
(C) Edeva: booth 4; Beriszl: booth 5; Calvine: booth 6
(D) Edeva: booth 3; Beriszl: booth 4; Adelfried: booth 5
(E) Dobrila: booth 1; Farika: booth 2; Beriszl: booth 6

STOP

IF YOU FINISH BEFORE TIME IS CALLED, YOU MAY CHECK YOUR WORK ON THIS SECTION ONLY.
DO NOT WORK ON ANY OTHER SECTION IN THE TEST.

ANSWER KEY

1. A
2. C
3. A
4. D
5. D
6. B
7. D
8. C
9. B
10. D
11. B
12. A
13. D
14. B
15. C
16. A
17. C
18. C
19. A
20. D
21. D
22. C
23. C
24. B

EXPLANATIONS FOR TIMED SECTION 4 QUESTIONS 1–6

Prepare

Ingredient Scan

Task: 1–D Order; place 6 departments in order
Inventory: 6 departments, 6 slots, a 1:1 ratio
Rules: Straightforward ordering rules
Questions: 6 total: 1 Grab-a-Rule, 4 Specific, 1 General
Red Flags: The vertical aspect makes this game a bit harder to visualize
Rank: 2

Diagram and Inventory

Your six elements are A, H, K, M, S, and W. Create 6 columns, numbered 1–6, as the core of your diagram.

Symbolize the Rules and Double-Check

Rule 1:

Rule 2: [AH]

Rule 3: : ~~[SM]~~ (reversible)

Rule 4: H—K—S

Don't forget to double-check your rules!

Deductions

Links: H appears in both rules 2 and 4, so link those together to get:

[AH]—K—S

Spatial restrictions: Four of your six elements are all contained in your linked chain, so most of this game is locked in place. M and W are not included in the chain. What are your remaining concerns with each of them? M can go anywhere as long as it isn't touching S. When most of your elements are locked in a chain, it is normally not worth the time to note everywhere each of them can't go. All you'll need to do the questions is your chain of four and your awareness that M can never be directly adjacent to S.

Most restricted: S has three things below it so it can only go as low as slot 4. A has three things above it so it can only go as high as slot 3. Part of the chain is an AH block, so that should be one of the first things you ask yourself about each scenario you work on.

Least restricted: W is your free agent.

Here is your diagram:

A,H,K,M,S,W	1	2	3	4	5	6

Assess, Act, Answer

Question 1 is a Grab-a-Rule, so do that one first.

For question 1, use the rules to eliminate answer choices. Rule 2 eliminates choice (B). Rule 3 eliminates choice (D). Rule 4 eliminates choices (C) and (E). **Since choice (A) is all that remains, it is the credited response.**

Question 2 is a Specific question, so do that one next.

Question 2 tells you to place H in slot 3 and asks you to determine how many options remain for M. Because H is part of a chain, placing H in slot 3 places A in slot 2. Look at your chain. What could still come below AH in slot 1? It must be W or M. Make two rows, one with W in slot 1 and one with M in slot 1. For the scenario in which W is slot 1, what are your options for slots 4, 5, and 6 with S, K, and M remaining? S and M can never touch, so it will have to be M in slot 4, K in slot 5, and S in slot 6.

	1	2	3	4	5	6
2.	W	A	H	M	K	S
	M	A	H			

Because the question only asks about M's options, figuring out the rest of the scenario in which M goes first is pointless. You have two different scenarios for M: slot 1 or slot 4. **Therefore, choice (C) is the credited response.**

Question 3 is a Specific question, so do it next.

Question 3 tells you that S cannot be the top floor and wants to know how many options there are for W. If S can't be in 6, what other options does it have? S can only go as low as slot 4, so S must be in slot 4 or 5. Draw a scenario with S in slot 4 and a scenario with S in slot 5. For each one, look at your chain and ask yourself where M and W can or must go. If S is in slot 5, what could go in slot 6? Only W could, since M and S can't touch. Since the question is only concerned with W's options, move on to the next scenario. For the scenario in which S is slot 4, what can go in slots 5 and 6? The only free elements are W and M. M can't touch S, so W would have to go in slot 5 and M would have to go in slot 6. The question asks how many options W has. You have two different scenarios for W: slots 6 and 5. **Choice (A) is the credited response.**

	1	2	3	4	5	6
3.					S	W
				S	W	M

Question 5 is the next Specific question, so do that one next.

Question 5 says that S cannot be immediately above K. Looking at your chain, what does that tell you? Something must come directly below S to keep it from touching K. It can't be M because M and S can't touch. It must be W. Redraw the chain next to question 2 and add that W is directly underneath S.

[AH]—K—[WS]

Because M could potentially fit in several different spots in the chain, it's easier just to use the chain in order to gauge which answer choice could be true. Choice (A) is impossible because putting M on top would have it touching S. Choice (B) is impossible because M can either go in slot 1, below the AH block, or in slot 3, above the AH block. Choice (C) is impossible because rule 2 forces A to always be immediately below H. Choice (D) is possible because M could go above K and below the WS block. **Because choice (D) is possible, it is the credited response.**

Question 6 is a Specific question, so do that one next.

For question 6, place A in slot 3 and figure out what must follow. A is part of a block, so placing A in slot 3 places H in slot 4. Looking at your chain of four, there are only two more spots above H to put K and S. So K must go in slot 5 and S must go in slot 6. W and M remain for slots 1 and 2, and they would be interchangeable there, so put in a W/M and M/W placeholder into slots 1 and 2. Since the question asks for what could be true, it will normally avoid any fixed elements. Scan the answers for W or M in slots 1 or 2. Choice (B) is possible because W could be in slot 2 and M could be in slot 1, **so choice (B) is the credited response.**

Question 4, a general question, is all that remains.

Question 4 asks for a possible pairing of slots 1 and 2. Start by thinking of elements that can never go in slot 1 or 2 so that you can eliminate any answer containing them. S and K could never be in slot 1 or 2 since they have at least two things that must come below them. That eliminates choice (C). Consider the remaining choices. If any is shown to be possible in previous work, it is the answer. Otherwise, consider if the scenario seems feasible. Choice (A) has A in slot 1 and M in slot 2. A is part of a block, so if it goes in slot 1, then H would go in slot 2. Eliminate choice (A). Choice (B) has H in slot 1. Because H must have A come directly below it, H could never go in slot 1. Eliminate choice (B). Choice (D) has W in slot 1 and M in slot 2. Your work for question 6 shows that as a possibility. **Therefore, choice (D) is the credited response.**

EXPLANATIONS TO TIMED SECTION 4 QUESTIONS 7–12

Prepare

Ingredient Scan

Task: 2-D Order, combining order and groups; assign exactly 3 types of shrubberey exactly 3 times to 5 different locations.

Inventory: 3 types of shrubbery, each used 3 times. When you're initially noting your inventory and learn that you must have three A's, three B's, and three C's, you may wonder whether you should bother putting subscripts on each one to identify if it's the first, second, or third of its type. Since the rules refer to elements by this aspect, e.g. "the second grouping of boxwood," "the third grouping of azaleas," it is definitely necessary to differentiate among the first, second, and third of each element.

Rules: Rules are not bad overall

Questions: 6 total: 1 Grab-a-Rule, 5 Specific

Red Flags: The lack of a 1:1 ratio increases the difficulty of an order game.

Rank: 4

Diagram and Inventory

Because the locations, F, H, L, P, and R, are described as having to come "in that order," use them as the core of the diagram. The elements are A, B, and C, which each need to be used three times. Use subscripts to identify more specifically which A, B, or C you're dealing with; you may want to list them that way in your **Inventory:** A_1, A_2, A_3, B_1, B_2, B_3, C_1, C_2, and C_3.

Symbolize the Rules and Double-Check

Rule 1: This rule simply says that a grouping is not allowed to be a blend of A, B, and C. An A is an A, a B is a B, etc.

Rule 2: This rule prevents something like A_1 and A_2 being in the same location. Diagramming this may be more confusing than it's worth. You could use a generic letter, X, to represent that you never want to see two of the same element in the same slot.

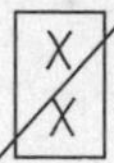

However, as long as you internalize what this means, you're likely to not need it written down.

Rule 3: Put one space in slot R with a plus sign to signify "at least".

Rule 4: Place B_2 in slot H.

Rule 5: A_3 / C_2 (in one box)

Don't forget to double-check your rules!

Deductions

Links: The first three rules tell you very little. Rule 4 puts B_2 in slot H. What does that mean for B_1 or B_3? B_1 must go in slot F since that is the only slot open before B_2. B_3 could go in any of the remaining three slots. Rule 5 is the C_2 A_3 block. Where could this block go? Think about each part of the block separately. What's the earliest that the third A could appear? The third slot. What's the latest that the second C could appear? The fourth slot. Because of that, you can put on your diagram that the C_2 A_3 block must land in either slot L or P. You could potentially work out two master scenarios, one with the C_2 A_3 block in slot L and one with the C_2 A_3 block in slot P. However, the only deductions that would follow relate to the first and second A's or the third C. Consider which elements are eligible to be in slot R, since there must be at least one element there. Because R is the last slot, it could only be the third of any element. Since the third A is stuck in a block going in either slot L or P, the only third elements that remain for slot R are B_3 and C_3. Put a placeholder in slot R to represent this.
Spatial restrictions: The first, second, and third instance of each element will often force elements to fall into place (just as B_1 did based on rule 4).
Most restricted: Like almost all games that have a block, minding that block should always be the first order of business. The block in this game only has two options for where it can be placed.
Least restricted: B_3 is free to be in any of the final three spots.

Here is your diagram:

A_3 / C_2 (block → L or P)

A_1 A_2 A_3
B_1 B_2 B_3
C_1 C_2 C_3

F	H	L	P	R
B_1	B_2	___	___	B_3/C_3

Assess, Act, Answer

Question 7 is a Grab-a-Rule question, so do that one first.

For question 7, use the rules to eliminate answer choices. The first two rules are unlikely to be as useful as the later rules, so it may be better to start from the bottom. Rule 5 eliminates choices (B) and (C). Rule 4 eliminates choices (A) and (E). **Since only choice (D) remains, it is the credited response.**

All the other questions are Specific questions, so do them in order, beginning with question 8.

Question 8 says that the third occurrence of one element is in the same slot as the first occurrence of another element. First of all, does that leave you with any flexibility as to where this third/first block could go? Not really, because the earliest a third can go is the third slot, and the latest that a first can go is the third slot. So this will occupy the third slot no matter what. Try to rule out any 3's or 1's you can't use. B_1 is stuck in slot F. A_1 can't go in the third slot because A_3 has to go in the third or fourth slot. So, the only element you can use is C_1. Can C_1 go with B_3 or A_3? It could only go with B_3 since A_3 must go in a block with C_2. Place a C_1B_3 block in slot L. That forces C_2 to be in slot P (the C_2A_3 block) and C_3 to be in slot R. The only elements remaining are A_1 and A_2. There's still some flexibility because they could be in slots F, H, or L. Since the question asks what *must be true,* don't worry about those A's. Look at the answers for something that is unavoidable, and eliminate answers that could be false. Choice (A) could be false because A_1 or A_2 could go in slot H. Choice (B) could be false because A_2 could be added to slot L. Choice (C) must be true because there are currently two elements in slot P, and there are no more elements you could potentially add to slot P. **Because it must be true, choice (C) is the credited response.**

A_3 / C_2 (block → L or P)

	F	H	L	P	R
8.	B_1	B_2	C_1	A_3	C_3
			B_3	C_2	

The next Specific question is question 9.

Question 9 asks you to place A_3 in slot L, which means placing the C_2A_3 block in slot L. The third A in the third slot means that the first two A's must go in the first two slots. That leaves C_1, C_3, and B_3. Copy down your original deduction that at least one of C_3, and B_3 has to go in slot R. C_1 can go in either of the first two slots. The question asks how many slots top out at a maximum of two elements. So, consider which slots could potentially have three elements. If the first C goes in F, that slot will have three elements. If the first C goes in slot H, that slot will have three elements. If the third B goes in slot L, that slot will have three elements. Slots P and R, however, have no shot at getting three elements. **Because slots P and R could never have more than two groupings, choice (B) is the credited response.**

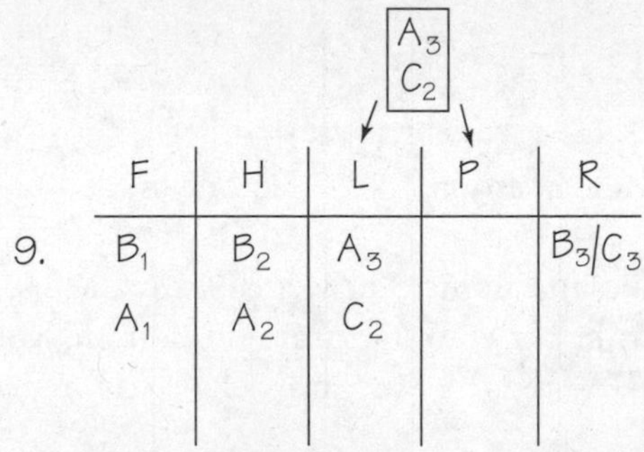

The next Specific question is question 10.

Question 10 posits only one element in slot F. B_1 is already locked in there, so nothing else can go in slot F. The firt A and first C can only come as early as slot H. How does that affect the C_2 A_3 block? It could not go in the third slot, because A_3 would not have enough slots to its left for A_1 and A_2. Therefore, place the C_2 A_3 block in slot P. That forces C_3 to be in the last slot, and it forces A_1 and A_2 into slots H and L, respectively. Still remaining to be placed are C_1 and B_3. There is flexibility here so move to the answer choices; you can write the remaining elements off to the side of the row to remind yourself what is left to be placed. The question asks for something impossible (*must be false*). Eliminate anything that is possible (could be true). Choice (A) asks if B_3 can go in slot R. Sure. Eliminate it. Choice (B) asks if A_2 can go in slot L. It must. Eliminate it. Choice (C) asks if C_2 can go in slot P. It must. Eliminate it. Choice (D) asks if A_1 can go in L. Nope. It must be in slot H. **Because choice (D) is impossible, it is the credited response.**

A_3 / C_2 (block → L or P)

	F	H	L	P	R
10.	B_1	B_2	A_2	A_3	C_3
		A_1		C_2	

The next Specific question is question 11.

Question 11 says that nothing will go in slot P, so make a row for question 11 and scratch out slot P. That means the C_2 A_3 block must go in slot L. Because A_3 is in the third spot, A_1 and A_2 will have to go in the first two slots. Because C_2 is in slot L and nothing can go in slot P, then C_3 must go in slot R. That leaves C_1 and B_3, both of which have a few options. The question is *could be false EXCEPT* which means the answer *must be true.* Scan the answers for something set in stone. Choice (B) must be true because you already have two elements in slot H. **Choice (B) it is the credited response.**

A_3 / C_2 (block → L or P)

	F	H	L	P	R
11.	B_1	B_2	A_3	X	C_3
	A_1	A_2	C_2		

The next Specific question is question 12.

Question 12 tells you to place the C_2 A_3 block into slot P. That forces C_3 into slot R. That's about all it does. Make a note of everything left: C_1, A_1 , A_2, and B_3. The question asks for something possible, so consider each answer choice by determining whether it is feasible given the elements still left to place. Choice (A) says that A_2 would be in slot H. This certainly seems possible given the scenario you have. If you're unsure whether it is, sketch out the rest of any possible scenario in which A_2 is in slot H. **Because it's possible, choice (A) is the credited response.**

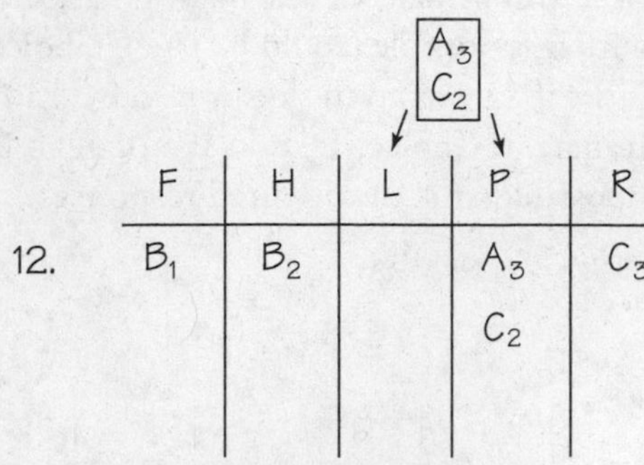

EXPLANATIONS FOR TIMED SECTION 4 QUESTIONS 13–18

Prepare

Ingredient Scan

Task: In-Out; select contestants to join a band
Inventory: 7 contestants
Rules: Two conditionals and one that's hard to symbolize
Questions: 6 total: 1 Grab-a-Rule, 4 Specific, 1 General
Red Flags: The way that the number of spaces is determined is an added complication; strange rule about "the jazz factor"
Rank: 3

Diagram and Inventory

The setup describes an In-Out game in which you must select contestants—1, 2, 3, 4, 5, 6, and 7—for a band (In). The number of contestants selected will vary according to the jazz factor, which dictates how many contestants may be selected; the jazz factor is not a fixed number.

Symbolize the Rules and Double-Check

Rule 1: 3 or 5→~1; 1→~3 and ~5
Rule 2: 4→~2 and ~5; 2 or 5→~4
Rule 3: The band must have a contestant whose number is the same as the jazz factor number.

This last rule is difficult to symbolize without simply rewriting it. One way to make it easier to digest is to consider what it actually means and note this with the rest of your rules. Here, if the jazz factor of the band is 2, that means contestant 2 must be included in the band; if the jazz factor is 3, then contestant 3 must be included, and so on.

Don't forget to double-check your rules!

Deductions

Links: Since contestant 5 is in both rules 1 and 2, combining them means that if contestant 5 is chosen, neither contestants 1 nor 4 may be selected. This means that if the jazz factor is 5, the contestants chosen must be 2, 3, 5, 6, and 7.
Spatial restrictions: There are no spatial restrictions for this game.
Most restricted: Both contestants 1 and 4 have conflicts with two other contestants each.
Least restricted: Contestants 6 and 7 are never mentioned in the rules.

Here is your diagram:

	In	Out
1234567		

Assess, Act, Answer

Question 13 is a Grab-a-Rule question, so begin there.

For question 13, use the rules to eliminate answer choices. Rule 1 eliminates choice (A) and choice (C), rule 2 eliminates choice (E), and rule 3 eliminates choice (B). **The only choice left, and therefore the credited response, is choice (D).**

Go to the Specific questions next. Question 14 is a Specific question.

For question 14, put two spaces in the In column and five spaces in the Out column. Because there are only two contestants, the jazz factor must be 2; from rule 3, you know that contestant 2 must therefore be selected. If contestant 2 is In, then contestant 4 is Out (rule 2).

Here is your diagram:

	In	Out
14.	2_	4____

The question asks for who cannot be in the band, and the only contestant whom you know must be Out is contestant 4. **Choice (B) is the credited response.**

The next Specific question is question 16.

For question 16, place contestants 1 and 3 in the Out column. Doing this doesn't give you much additional insight as to who could be In, however, so you'll have to go to the answer choices to find something that could work. Try choice (A). If you put contestants 2 and 7 into the In column, then the jazz factor could potentially be 2, which fits with rule 3.

Here is your diagram:

	In	Out
16.		1 3

Because choice (A) contains two contestants who could be in the band when contestants 1 and 3 are not, you know that this choice is correct. No need to go through all the others. **Choice (A) is the credited response.**

The next Specific question is question 17.

For question 17, place contestants 5 and 6 in the In column. If contestant 5 is In, then contestants 1 and 4 are both Out (rules 1 and 2). You now have limited choices as to what the jazz factor can be—there are not enough contestants for it to be 6 or 7, and it cannot be 2 because you already have contestants 5 and 6 included. This leaves two possible jazz factor options: a jazz factor of 3, which means you'll have contestants 3, 5, and 6 in the band, or a jazz factor of 5, which means you'll have contestants 2, 3, 5, 6, and 7 in the band.

Here is your diagram:

	In	Out
17.	563	14
	56327	14

The question asks who must be in the band, meaning in either jazz factor scenario. The only additional contestant that appears in both cases is contestant 3. **Choice (C) is the credited response.**

The next Specific question is question 18.

For question 18, put contestants 6 and 7 in the Out column. From rule 3, you know that the jazz factor definitely cannot be either 6 or 7. Try working down from there. If the jazz factor is 5, you know from your earlier deductions that both contestants 6 and 7 would be necessary. Eliminate choice (E). Try 4 as the jazz factor. If contestant 4 is included, both contestants 2 and 5 must be out; this knocks your jazz factor down to three. Eliminate choice (D) and try 3 as the jazz factor. If contestant 3 in included, contestant 1 must be out (rule 1). This leaves contestants 2, 4, and 5 to fill the remaining two spots. From rule 2, you know that contestant 4 cannot be chosen with either contestants 2 or 5, so in order to achieve a jazz factor of 3 here, 4 must be out and contestants 2 and 5 must be selected.

Here is your diagram:

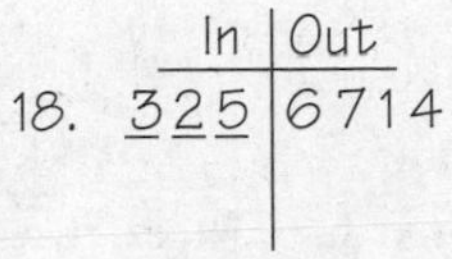

	In	Out
18.	325	6714

The question asks for the maximum jazz factor given these conditions. You've seen that it cannot be greater than 3. **Choice (C) is the credited response.**

The remaining question in the game is a General question, question 15.

Question 15 asks for the maximum possible jazz factor. From your work in question 17, you know it is possible to have a jazz factor of 5, so eliminate choice (A) and choice (B). The jazz factor cannot be 7; from rule 1 it is not possible to have all seven contestants selected, so eliminate choice (E). The jazz factor cannot be 6 either; if you try to select six contestants, rules 1 and 2 taken together do not make it possible to have six people in the band. Choice (D) is out. This leaves 5 as the maximum possible jazz factor. **Choice (C) is the credited response.**

EXPLANATIONS FOR TIMED SECTION 4 QUESTIONS 19–24

Prepare

Ingredient Scan

Task: 1–D Order; place six vendors in order
Inventory: 6 vendors, 6 slots, a 1:1 ratio
Rules: Straightforward ordering rules
Questions: 6 total: 2 Specific, 3 General, 1 Complex
Red Flags: Using *front* and *back* instead of *before* and *after* makes the rules harder to visualize.
Rank: 1

Diagram and Inventory

The diagram is six columns, numbered 1–6. Make sure to label *front* by slot 1 and *back* by six 6. The six elements are A, B, C, D, E, and F.

Symbolize the Rules and Double-Check

Rule 1: B—D

Rule 2: E—C and F—C (E and F > C)

Rule 3: D—A and D—E (D < A and E)

Don't forget to double-check your rules!

Deductions

Links: Combine the overlapping elements. Rules 1 and 3 combine to make B—D—A/E

B — D < A / E

Rule 2 deals with E so you can attach rule 2 to the cluster.

B — D < A / E; E and F > C

Spatial restrictions: When you can link all or even most of the rules together to form a composite rule, don't spend time writing in each element's excluded slots. Unless you have trouble using one, a composite rule that combines all the elements will be your handy road map for every question. Try to narrow down what can be first and what can be last. The only things that can be first are the elements that have no connections to their left: B and F. Put a B/F placeholder in slot 1. The only elements that can be last are those that have no connections to their right. Put an A/C placeholder in slot 6.

Most restricted: With four things following it, B can only be in slot 1 or 2. With four things coming before it, C can only be slot 5 or 6.

Least restricted: F only needs to come before C, so F could be any slot 1 to 5.

Here is your diagram

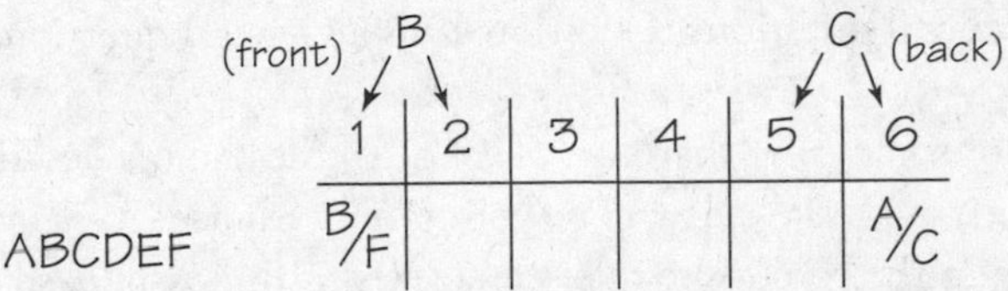

Assess, Act, Answer

Question 19 is a General question. Move on to Question 20, the first Specific question.

For question 20, place A in slot 3 and check your composite rule. Two elements, B and D, must come before A, so that means B must be in slot 1 and D must be in slot 2. Check the last three slots. E and F must come before C, so C must be in slot 6. E and F can be in slots 4 and 5 in either order, so represent those possibilities with E/F and F/E. The question asks for something that *could be true EXCEPT*, which means your answer choice *must be false.* If an answer choice is possible, eliminate it. Choices (A) and (B) are possible according to slots 5 and 6 of your diagram. Eliminate them. Choice (C) is possible for slots 3 and 4 so eliminate it. Choice (D) says D and F are adjacent to each other, which your diagram shows is impossible. **Because it must be false, choice (D) is the credited response.**

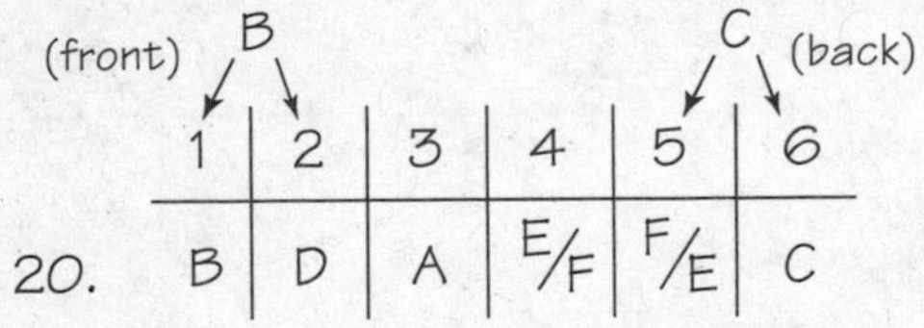

(front) B → 1, 2 C → 5, 6 (back)

	1	2	3	4	5	6
20.	B	D	A	E/F	F/E	C

Question 22 is also a Specific question.

For question 22, place E in slot 5 and check your composite rule. Does anything have to come after E? C does, so C must be in slot 6. Since this question asks for something that *must be true*, check the answers for one pertaining to C in slot 6 to see if you've already done enough. **Choice (C) describes this, so it is the credited response.**

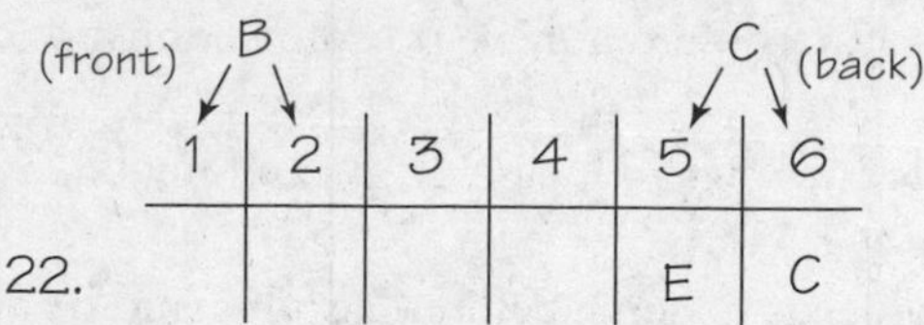

Move on to the General questions. Question 19 is a General question.

Question 19 asks for something that *must be false*. All the choices describe general before/after relationships, so the composite rule will be your guide. Choice (A) is impossible because D must come before C according to the composite rule. **Choice (A) is impossible, so it is the credited response.**

The next General question is question 21.

Question 21 asks how many options there are for F. The only slot F cannot go in is slot 6, so there must be five possible slots for F. **Choice (D) is the credited response.**

The next General question is question 23.

Question 23 asks which scenario is possible. Use your composite rule to gauge the feasibility of each answer. Choice (A) places B in slot 1, which is fine. E and A are in slots 5 and 6. That leaves no room for C to come after E so this scenario is impossible. Eliminate it. Choice (B) has D in slot 3. What two things could go before D? B and F are the only choices, so they would be used in slots 1 and 2. However, this choice says F appears again later in slot 5. Eliminate it. Choice (C) has B in slot 1, which is fine. E is in slot 3, which also is fine as long as D is in slot 2. A in slot 6 is fine since nothing has to come after A. **Because this scenario works, choice (C) is the credited response.**

(front) B (1, 2) — C (5, 6) (back)

	1	2	3	4	5	6
23.	B	F	D	A/E	A/E/C	C/A

The final question is a Complex question, question 24.

Question 24 forces you to reverse rule 1 and make D—B rather than B—D. This will change your composite rule, so redraw the new one starting with D—B. Add on the clusters from rules 2 and 3 and examine your new composite rule.

What could be first and what could be last now? Only D or F could be first. A, B, or C could be last.

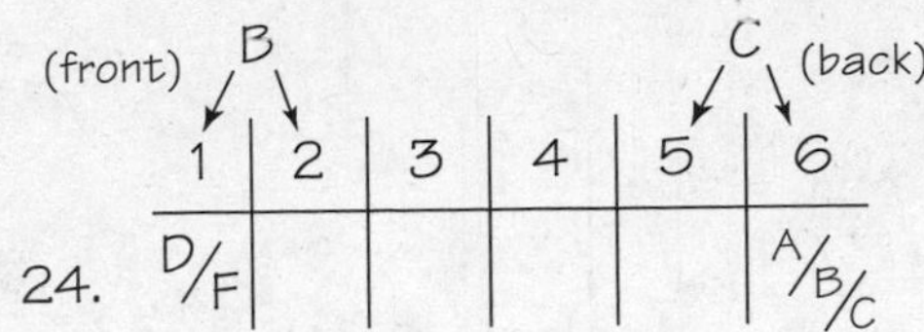

The question asks for choices that *could be true EXCEPT*, so you're looking for an impossible scenario. Choice (A) puts D first, which is fine. E is slot 3, which is fine as long as A, B, or F is slot 2. C is slot 5, which is fine because A or B could still come in slot 6. This choice seems fine, so eliminate it. Choice (B) has D in slot 3. What two things could come before D? Only F can come before D, so this choice is impossible. **Because choice (B) is impossible, it is the credited response.**

Conditional Statements

Arrows and Negation

We use arrows to symbolize the meaning of a conditional statement, to remind us that these statements only point in one direction. The symbol A → B tells us that when we know A is true, we can conclude that B is also true. At times, we may need to negate statements on either side of the arrow; in these cases, we use a tilde sign (~) to indicate the word not. Keep in mind that there may be many ways to trigger a negated statement. The statement "the sun is not setting" may be true under several different circumstances—when the sun is rising, when the sun is in the sky at midday, when the sun is down, or at midnight. Take this statement:

~the sun is setting → ~the dog is barking

Anytime the sun is not setting, we know that the dog is not barking. At dawn, midday, or midnight, we could infer equally well from this statement that the dog is not barking. If the sun were setting, we wouldn't know anything for certain. This is what we mean when we say that conditional statements only point in one direction. If the sun is setting, we can't infer anything; the dog might be barking, or the dog might not be barking.

The Contrapositive

Every conditional diagram A → B can be written in an alternative way, as a second conditional. Consider the conditional statement we used above. What if we hear the dog barking? In this case, there is something else we know. While the sun isn't setting, we know for certain that the dog won't be barking. Any time the dog is barking, we can be sure the sun is setting. Otherwise, the dog would be violating the conditional rule. This gives us another conditional statement:

the dog is barking → the sun is setting

This statement is called the contrapositive of our first one. It's another way of writing the conditional. The way we generate the contrapositive from our initial diagram is to flip and negate: that is, reverse the order of the statements around the arrow and negate both of them. In this case, because our statements were negative to start with, negating them again gives us positive statements. A double negative, in other words, becomes a positive statement.

There's one other possibility we haven't considered. What if the dog is not barking? If we look at our initial statement and its contrapositive, we see that the statement "~dog is barking" doesn't appear in front of either arrow. This means we can't make an inference from either statement; the sun might or might not be setting. When you think about our initial discussion of the statement, this makes sense. We said that when the sun is setting, we can't be sure whether the dog will be barking. When the sun is not setting, the dog will not be barking. Anytime the dog isn't barking, it could be because the sun isn't setting, but it also could be because the sun really is setting, but the dog has decided not to bark for whatever reason.

If, If...then, All, Every, Whenever

Statements involving any of these key words can be translated into conditional diagrams in very similar ways. Consider this set of equivalent statements:

All cows are mammals.
Every cow is a mammal.
If an animal is a cow, then it is also a mammal.
An animal is a mammal if it is a cow.
Whenever you see a cow, you're seeing a mammal.
The diagram for each of these statements is the same:

cow → mammal

To get its contrapositive, we simply flip and negate:

~mammal → ~cow

Only, Only if

Statements involving these key words can also be translated into conditional diagrams. However, the method used with these is not exactly the same as the one used with if and if… then. Some prefer to think of the arrow on these statements as pointing backwards. An easy way to translate these is to cross through the word only with an arrow pointing to the right. Whatever is immediately to the right of the only or the only if goes to the right of the arrow, and the other statement goes to the left of the arrow. Take this trio of equivalent statements:

> Only the well-dressed are permitted to attend.
> You will be permitted to attend only if you are well dressed.
> Only if you are well dressed will you be permitted to attend.

The diagram for each of these is the same:

permitted to attend → well dressed

Once we have the diagram, we no longer have to worry about the original phrasing of the conditional statement. We simply flip and negate to arrive at the diagram of the contrapositive:

~well dressed → ~permitted to attend

Note that being well dressed is necessary to being permitted to attend. You only have a chance of attending if you're well dressed, but being well dressed doesn't guarantee that you will be permitted to attend.

Unless

Unless can also be used to describe necessary conditions, but because the grammar of these sentences is a little different from those involving only if, we need a slightly different diagramming method. If we rewrite the only statements above as an unless statement, here's what we wind up with:

You will not be permitted to attend unless you are well dressed.

Notice that we had to insert a not in the statement of the condition to arrive at a sentence with the same meaning. In order to get from here to the diagram we need, we'll have to negate again. Some people like to diagram unless statements by crossing through the word unless and writing if not. The statement you get might not be particularly grammatical, but it can be translated as if it were an ordinary if… then statement. Here's what happens when we replace unless with if not in the statement we wrote above:

You will not be permitted to attend if not you are well dressed.

This sounds kind of nonsensical, but we can see that this fits the pattern B if A that we saw above. Starting with the if part and preserving all the negatives, we get this diagram:

~well dressed → ~permitted to attend

Once we have the diagram, we simply flip and negate to get the contrapositive:

permitted to attend → well dressed

These are the same diagrams we came up with for the equivalent only if statements. In the end, symbolizing an unless statement is simple: Take the two statements, put one on each side of the arrow, and negate the one in front of the arrow. Take this one, for example:

I will not play baseball unless I do not play soccer.

We take each statement (~baseball and ~soccer), put one on either side of the arrow, and then negate the one in front, leading to this symbolization:

baseball → ~soccer

We could just as easily have chosen to put the soccer statement in front and the baseball statement on the other side. Again, we must remember to negate the one in front. Had we symbolized the statement this way, we would have gotten:

soccer → ~baseball

This is the contrapositive of our first symbol and is also what we would have gotten by doing the if not substitution. Whatever method we use to translate the unless statement, once we have a diagram, we can work with it without referring to the original statement. The diagram is a complete and accurate representation of the information in the original. By the same token, a diagram can be translated back into language that uses any of the connectives we've seen so far. Initially, we got this diagram from the statement "I will not play baseball unless I do not play soccer." Going from the diagram, we see that this statement could also have been represented:

If I play baseball, I will not play soccer.
Only if I do not play soccer will I play baseball.

The meaning of the statements is equivalent.

No, None

These statements point out two characteristics that are never seen together or two groups that have no members in common. They can also be represented with conditional diagrams. Take a look at this pair of equivalent statements:

No Jets are Sharks.
None of the Jets are also Sharks.

If we interpret these statements for ourselves, we should wind up with something like this: If a person is a member of the Jets, then that person is definitely not a member of the Sharks. Interestingly, the pair of statements above mean exactly the same thing as this pair of statements:

No Sharks are Jets.
None of the Sharks are also Jets.

In the statements we've seen so far, we can't go around switching the parts willy-nilly. If you try that with an all statement, you'll get yourself in trouble:

All Texans are Americans.
All Americans are Texans.

These are definitely not the same statement. In practice, statements involving no and none can be switched around without changing the meaning of the statement, but you can't do this with all statements. Returning to our Jets and Sharks example, the appropriate diagrams would be:

Jet → ~Shark
Shark → ~Jet

We diagram statements with no or none by putting each part on a different side of the arrow, then negating the one on the arrow's point—its right-hand side. Don't mistake the words no or none for the word not. They mean something different.

And, Or, Nor

As you've seen in Games, these little conjunctions have specific meanings when it comes to conditional statements and the LSAT. A condition involving and requires that both conditions be true in order for the result to be assured:

If I have milk and cookies, I will be satisfied.

Milk by itself, cookies by themselves, or neither milk nor cookies isn't enough to be certain of satisfaction. The diagram is:

milk AND cookies → satisfied

When we know that the consequence of a statement that hinges on an and is true, we can be assured that each of its parts is true separately. Take this statement:

Only if there are clowns and balloons will a birthday party be successful.

We translate it to arrive at this diagram:

successful party → clowns AND balloons

If we are told that a birthday party was successful, then this statement allows us to infer that there were clowns at the party, and it also allows us to infer that there were balloons at the party.

Suppose, alternatively, that the birthday party is missing clowns or balloons or both. Do we know anything else? Because a successful party definitely has both of them, then a party that's missing either will not be successful. This turns out to be the contrapositive of our statement, which we write this way:

~clowns OR ~balloons → ~successful party

An or statement is triggered when one of the statements is true alone, and it is also triggered when both are true. When we have clowns but no balloons, the party is not successful. Similarly, when we have balloons but not clowns, the party is not successful. Finally, when we have neither clowns nor balloons, the party is not successful.

As usual, we've gotten to this contrapositive by flipping and negating. Notice what happened to our and when we negated the statement "clowns AND balloons." We negated each of the individual constituent statements, and we also changed the and into an or to arrive at "~clowns OR ~balloons." When we negate an and statement, we must negate all of its parts, which involves changing the and into an or.

When we know that an or statement is true, we can only infer that at least one of the constituent statements is true, although we can't be sure which one, and it's possible that both are true. Take this statement:

If the weather is good, I will take a walk or clean house.

This leads us to this diagram:

good weather → walk OR clean house

When there's good weather, what can we infer? It's possible that I will take a walk but not clean house. It's possible that I will clean house but won't take a walk. Finally, it's possible that I will both take a walk and clean house. Knowing that an or statement is true doesn't tell us much for certain. In fact, the only possibility it excludes is that I both won't take a walk and won't clean house. That gives us our contrapositive:

~walk AND ~clean house → ~good weather

Negating the or statement involves negating each constituent statement separately, and then changing the or into an and. This matches nicely with what we did when we negated and statements.

There is another way of expressing the statement "I will not take a walk and I will not clean house" that reads a little more nicely. When we want to put two negative statements together, we use the construction neither… nor. We could express this same statement in this way: "I will neither walk nor clean house." Neither… nor is another way of expressing the negative of an or statement, and as we know, when we negate an or statement, we wind up with an and statement. In other words, the conjunction nor is correctly translated as and. You can think of it as a contraction of not-or, if that helps. We should translate the statement…

If the seminar is attended by neither Fred nor Jenny, then it will also not be attended by Joe.

…into this diagram:

~Fred AND ~Jenny → ~Joe

Once we have the diagram, we flip and negate to get the contrapositive, remembering to change the and when we do so:

Joe → Fred OR Jenny

NOTES

NOTES

NOTES

NOTES

NOTES

NOTES

NOTES

NOTES

NOTES